AF444884

Anatomy of a Medically Abusive Childhood

Candace Ahalse

Published by Candace Ahalse, 2024.

While every precaution has been taken in the preparation of this book, the publisher assumes no responsibility for errors or omissions, or for damages resulting from the use of the information contained herein.

ANATOMY OF A MEDICALLY ABUSIVE CHILDHOOD

First edition. March 6, 2024.

Copyright © 2024 Candace Ahalse.

ISBN: 979-8224967438

Written by Candace Ahalse.

Table of Contents

Dedication

For those who have died of medical abuse. We must be your voice.

Acknowledgments

To acknowledge people by name would be to put a target on their backs in many cases. I have not survived alone, worked through trauma alone, or dealt with the heavy emotional burden of writing this book alone. Thank you to those who have been there.

Use of Names

I have written this book under a pen name that has no relation to my given name. Any similarity between my pen name and any actual person's name is pure coincidence. In addition, while I have used the real names of abusers in publicly known cases, I have changed all third-party names in incidents from my own life.

PART I. ABOUT MEDICAL ABUSE

Introduction

You cross paths with very dangerous people more often than you likely know. This book is about an underestimated category of very dangerous people with whom you will likely cross paths at some point in your life. I want you to know what you're dealing with before it's too late.

This book starts by outlining the major threats to society as a whole that medical abusers present. I then provide a pattern chart of well-known cases. This demonstrates a connection to other dangerous behaviors and crimes not always associated with medical abuse in popular culture's understanding of it. I follow this with a section explaining terminology.

The largest section in this book contains incidents from my own medically abusive childhood. These are arranged by patterns in my abusers' behavior instead of chronologically. While these are useful, some of them can be very difficult to read, and you don't need to make yourself read all of them.

I follow this with a section on spotting cases, a section explaining why smart people often miss the warning signs, and another section outlining types of medical abusers by primary motivation. I then go over the Hare Psychopathy Checklist and discuss whether it is relevant or helpful in these cases.

Following this section, I detail types of legislation that can help make us all safer, as well as what you personally can do. The number one thing you can do is spread the word. This book is about getting out information that will save lives. Please share this book with others in your life. It will make a difference and maybe even save a life.

The Threat to Society

Many of the threats to society this type of abuser poses jump out clearly from the chart following this section. Three categories of threat, in particular, stand to damage society on a much larger scale than the harm to individual victims.

<u>Contagions - The Threat of Epidemic and Pandemic</u>

These abusers are often not medical experts, but they often mess around with contagious things. This includes viruses, bacteria, and fungi. Contagion is one of the few things that hold the potential to wipe out the human race. Throughout human history, it has wiped out civilizations, changed the course of history, collapsed empires, and caused massive death and suffering. Even in less severe cases, epidemics and pandemics cause enormous death tolls and economic losses.

In many cases, abusers have no medical expertise but play around with contagions for their own personal amusement, often guessing at the effects they will have. In other cases, abusers have some medical knowledge but pretend to have more than they do. They know just enough to be even more dangerous. In still other cases, abusers have a lot of medical knowledge but no regard for anyone other than themselves. Medical abusers are often sadists. The potential for a spread from their intended victims is not a deterrent.

<u>Arson - The Threat of Fire Spread and Lost Towns</u>

In recent history, we have seen several tragedies when fires raged out of control. The United States, Portugal, and Australia, just to name a few, have all lost entire towns as fires spread too fast to contain. Even our modern technology and emergency systems cannot always get victims out before it's too late.

You will see the connection between arson and medical abuse in the following chart. This does not list all such cases, just a sample. This pattern has also been documented in academic research on medical abuse. For example, see "Psychopathology of Perpetrators of Fabricated or Induced Illness in Children: Case Series" by Christopher Bass and David Jones (available through the British Journal of Psychiatry).

In today's environment, an arsonist is a threat to society at large. Just as these abusers do not care if an illness they targeted one person with spreads out of control, they also do not care if a fire they targeted one person with spreads out of control. Potential damage or death caused to others is not a deterrent.

<u>Economic Costs - Taxpayer Burden and Insurance Losses</u>

These abusers cost society at large massive amounts of money in several ways.

1. Insurance

Abusers run up insurance costs for everyone else. The medical bills for elaborate and unnecessary medical procedures pile up, especially when an abuser is not caught on his or her first victim. These costs are split amongst all of us on an insurance plan. This is true for medical insurance, as well as malpractice insurance, both of which are likely to face massive expenses as a result of such abusers.

2. Fraud and Theft

Who pays for the losses businesses face from shoplifting, fraud, bad checks, and other forms of theft? You do every time you shop at those businesses. It's factored into the cost of doing business and what they need to charge for products and services in order to stay afloat. In the following chart, you will see that fraud and theft are major patterns for medical abusers.

3. Taxpayers, Social Security Disability, Medicare, and Medicaid

Here, I'm referring to benefit programs in the United States, but you can apply this to any country that has such programs. Such abuse is often intertwined with various types of benefits fraud. If an abuser renders people too sick to work, who pays for food, housing, and medical care for those people? You, the taxpayer, do. Over the course of a chronic illness, this is a massive amount of money, even for just one person. Now consider that there are abusers like this scattered throughout society running up these costs.

4. Lost Productivity and Lost Contribution to Society

Consider the potential of the average child to contribute to society. As this person grows into an adult, they will, at a minimum, get a job, pay taxes, and contribute to the economy by purchasing a home, a vehicle, furniture, and the other necessities of a young person establishing a life. Most will also aspire to contribute something positive to society.

Now consider how much of this will still happen if that child is kept too sick to leave home, think clearly, or perform basic functions. That's if the child even lives into adulthood. Now multiply this by an entire population of victims in every generation.

Pattern Chart

Abuser	Primary Abuse Type	Stealing/Fraud (Other than FDIA) - 14
My Parents	MBP	X
Gregory Mom/ Dad/Grandma (Sickened)	MBP	X
Rajneesh Cult	Poisoning - Other	X
Jim Jones	Poisoning - Other	X
Donald Harvey	Poisoning - Other	X
Beverley Allitt	MBP	
Jolly Jane Toppan	Poisoning - Other	X
Charles Cullen	Poisoning - Other	X
Dee Dee Blanchard	MBP	X
Kristen Gilbert	Poisoning - Other	X
Christoper Duntsch	Med Abuse - Other	X
Hope Ybarra	MBP	X
Lacey Spears	MBP	
Juliet Tuttle	Poisoning - Other	
Teresa Milbrandt	Med Fraud/Money	X
Kelly Renee Turner-Gant	MBP	X
Blanca Montano	MBP	X

Abuser	Primary Abuse Type	Sadism (Enjoys others suffering) - 11
My Parents	MBP	X
Gregory Mom/ Dad/Grandma (Sickened)	MBP	X
Rajneesh Cult	Poisoning - Other	X
Jim Jones	Poisoning - Other	X
Donald Harvey	Poisoning - Other	X
Beverley Allitt	MBP	X
Jolly Jane Toppan	Poisoning - Other	X
Charles Cullen	Poisoning - Other	X
Dee Dee Blanchard	MBP	
Kristen Gilbert	Poisoning - Other	
Christoper Duntsch	Med Abuse - Other	X
Hope Ybarra	MBP	X
Lacey Spears	MBP	
Juliet Tuttle	Poisoning - Other	X
Teresa Milbrandt	Med Fraud/Money	
Kelly Renee Turner-Gant	MBP	
Blanca Montano	MBP	

Abuser	Primary Abuse Type	Murder or Attempted Murder - 10
My Parents	MBP	?
Gregory Mom/ Dad/Grandma (Sickened)	MBP	
Rajneesh Cult	Poisoning - Other	X
Jim Jones	Poisoning - Other	X
Donald Harvey	Poisoning - Other	X
Beverley Allitt	MBP	X
Jolly Jane Toppan	Poisoning - Other	X
Charles Cullen	Poisoning - Other	X
Dee Dee Blanchard	MBP	
Kristen Gilbert	Poisoning - Other	X
Christoper Duntsch	Med Abuse - Other	X
Hope Ybarra	MBP	
Lacey Spears	MBP	X
Juliet Tuttle	Poisoning - Other	
Teresa Milbrandt	Med Fraud/Money	
Kelly Renee Turner-Gant	MBP	X
Blanca Montano	MBP	

Abuser	Primary Abuse Type	Cruelty to Animals - 9
My Parents	MBP	X
Gregory Mom/ Dad/Grandma (Sickened)	MBP	X
Rajneesh Cult	Poisoning - Other	X
Jim Jones	Poisoning - Other	X
Donald Harvey	Poisoning - Other	X
Beverley Allitt	MBP	X
Jolly Jane Toppan	Poisoning - Other	
Charles Cullen	Poisoning - Other	X
Dee Dee Blanchard	MBP	
Kristen Gilbert	Poisoning - Other	
Christoper Duntsch	Med Abuse - Other	X
Hope Ybarra	MBP	
Lacey Spears	MBP	
Juliet Tuttle	Poisoning - Other	X
Teresa Milbrandt	Med Fraud/Money	
Kelly Renee Turner-Gant	MBP	
Blanca Montano	MBP	

Abuser	Primary Abuse Type	Coercive Control - 8
My Parents	MBP	X
Gregory Mom/ Dad/Grandma (Sickened)	MBP	X
Rajneesh Cult	Poisoning - Other	X
Jim Jones	Poisoning - Other	X
Donald Harvey	Poisoning - Other	
Beverley Allitt	MBP	X
Jolly Jane Toppan	Poisoning - Other	X
Charles Cullen	Poisoning - Other	
Dee Dee Blanchard	MBP	X
Kristen Gilbert	Poisoning - Other	
Christoper Duntsch	Med Abuse - Other	
Hope Ybarra	MBP	
Lacey Spears	MBP	
Juliet Tuttle	Poisoning - Other	
Teresa Milbrandt	Med Fraud/Money	X
Kelly Renee Turner-Gant	MBP	
Blanca Montano	MBP	

Abuser	Primary Abuse Type	Non-Medical Sick Stories - 8
My Parents	MBP	X
Gregory Mom/ Dad/Grandma (Sickened)	MBP	X
Rajneesh Cult	Poisoning - Other	
Jim Jones	Poisoning - Other	X
Donald Harvey	Poisoning - Other	
Beverley Allitt	MBP	X
Jolly Jane Toppan	Poisoning - Other	X
Charles Cullen	Poisoning - Other	
Dee Dee Blanchard	MBP	X
Kristen Gilbert	Poisoning - Other	X
Christoper Duntsch	Med Abuse - Other	
Hope Ybarra	MBP	
Lacey Spears	MBP	X
Juliet Tuttle	Poisoning - Other	
Teresa Milbrandt	Med Fraud/Money	
Kelly Renee Turner-Gant	MBP	
Blanca Montano	MBP	

Abuser	Primary Abuse Type	Sexual Abuse - 7
My Parents	MBP	X
Gregory Mom/ Dad/Grandma (Sickened)	MBP	X
Rajneesh Cult	Poisoning - Other	X
Jim Jones	Poisoning - Other	X
Donald Harvey	Poisoning - Other	X
Beverley Allitt	MBP	
Jolly Jane Toppan	Poisoning - Other	X
Charles Cullen	Poisoning - Other	
Dee Dee Blanchard	MBP	X
Kristen Gilbert	Poisoning - Other	
Christoper Duntsch	Med Abuse - Other	
Hope Ybarra	MBP	
Lacey Spears	MBP	
Juliet Tuttle	Poisoning - Other	
Teresa Milbrandt	Med Fraud/Money	
Kelly Renee Turner-Gant	MBP	
Blanca Montano	MBP	

Abuser	Primary Abuse Type	Malnutrition - 7
My Parents	MBP	X
Gregory Mom/ Dad/Grandma (Sickened)	MBP	X
Rajneesh Cult	Poisoning - Other	
Jim Jones	Poisoning - Other	X
Donald Harvey	Poisoning - Other	
Beverley Allitt	MBP	
Jolly Jane Toppan	Poisoning - Other	
Charles Cullen	Poisoning - Other	
Dee Dee Blanchard	MBP	X
Kristen Gilbert	Poisoning - Other	
Christoper Duntsch	Med Abuse - Other	
Hope Ybarra	MBP	X
Lacey Spears	MBP	X
Juliet Tuttle	Poisoning - Other	
Teresa Milbrandt	Med Fraud/Money	
Kelly Renee Turner-Gant	MBP	X
Blanca Montano	MBP	

Abuser	Primary Abuse Type	Stalking/ Harassment - 6
My Parents	MBP	X
Gregory Mom/ Dad/Grandma (Sickened)	MBP	
Rajneesh Cult	Poisoning - Other	X
Jim Jones	Poisoning - Other	
Donald Harvey	Poisoning - Other	
Beverley Allitt	MBP	X
Jolly Jane Toppan	Poisoning - Other	
Charles Cullen	Poisoning - Other	X
Dee Dee Blanchard	MBP	
Kristen Gilbert	Poisoning - Other	X
Christoper Duntsch	Med Abuse - Other	X
Hope Ybarra	MBP	
Lacey Spears	MBP	
Juliet Tuttle	Poisoning - Other	
Teresa Milbrandt	Med Fraud/Money	
Kelly Renee Turner-Gant	MBP	
Blanca Montano	MBP	

Abuser	Primary Abuse Type	Fire Setting - 6
My Parents	MBP	?
Gregory Mom/ Dad/Grandma (Sickened)	MBP	X
Rajneesh Cult	Poisoning - Other	X
Jim Jones	Poisoning - Other	
Donald Harvey	Poisoning - Other	X
Beverley Allitt	MBP	X
Jolly Jane Toppan	Poisoning - Other	X
Charles Cullen	Poisoning - Other	X
Dee Dee Blanchard	MBP	
Kristen Gilbert	Poisoning - Other	
Christoper Duntsch	Med Abuse - Other	
Hope Ybarra	MBP	
Lacey Spears	MBP	
Juliet Tuttle	Poisoning - Other	
Teresa Milbrandt	Med Fraud/Money	
Kelly Renee Turner-Gant	MBP	
Blanca Montano	MBP	

Abuser	Primary Abuse Type	Religion Tied to Abuse - 5
My Parents	MBP	X
Gregory Mom/ Dad/Grandma (Sickened)	MBP	X
Rajneesh Cult	Poisoning - Other	X
Jim Jones	Poisoning - Other	X
Donald Harvey	Poisoning - Other	X
Beverley Allitt	MBP	
Jolly Jane Toppan	Poisoning - Other	
Charles Cullen	Poisoning - Other	
Dee Dee Blanchard	MBP	
Kristen Gilbert	Poisoning - Other	
Christoper Duntsch	Med Abuse - Other	
Hope Ybarra	MBP	
Lacey Spears	MBP	
Juliet Tuttle	Poisoning - Other	
Teresa Milbrandt	Med Fraud/Money	
Kelly Renee Turner-Gant	MBP	
Blanca Montano	MBP	

Abuser	Primary Abuse Type	Voyeurism or Nonconsensual Recording - 5
My Parents	MBP	X
Gregory Mom/ Dad/Grandma (Sickened)	MBP	X
Rajneesh Cult	Poisoning - Other	X
Jim Jones	Poisoning - Other	
Donald Harvey	Poisoning - Other	X
Beverley Allitt	MBP	
Jolly Jane Toppan	Poisoning - Other	
Charles Cullen	Poisoning - Other	
Dee Dee Blanchard	MBP	
Kristen Gilbert	Poisoning - Other	
Christoper Duntsch	Med Abuse - Other	
Hope Ybarra	MBP	
Lacey Spears	MBP	X
Juliet Tuttle	Poisoning - Other	
Teresa Milbrandt	Med Fraud/Money	
Kelly Renee Turner-Gant	MBP	
Blanca Montano	MBP	

Abuser	Primary Abuse Type	Crime Framing - 5
My Parents	MBP	X
Gregory Mom/ Dad/Grandma (Sickened)	MBP	X
Rajneesh Cult	Poisoning - Other	X
Jim Jones	Poisoning - Other	
Donald Harvey	Poisoning - Other	
Beverley Allitt	MBP	X
Jolly Jane Toppan	Poisoning - Other	
Charles Cullen	Poisoning - Other	
Dee Dee Blanchard	MBP	
Kristen Gilbert	Poisoning - Other	X
Christoper Duntsch	Med Abuse - Other	
Hope Ybarra	MBP	
Lacey Spears	MBP	
Juliet Tuttle	Poisoning - Other	
Teresa Milbrandt	Med Fraud/Money	
Kelly Renee Turner-Gant	MBP	
Blanca Montano	MBP	

Abuser	Primary Abuse Type	Terror Threats or Acts - 4
My Parents	MBP	X
Gregory Mom/ Dad/Grandma (Sickened)	MBP	
Rajneesh Cult	Poisoning - Other	X
Jim Jones	Poisoning - Other	X
Donald Harvey	Poisoning - Other	
Beverley Allitt	MBP	
Jolly Jane Toppan	Poisoning - Other	
Charles Cullen	Poisoning - Other	
Dee Dee Blanchard	MBP	
Kristen Gilbert	Poisoning - Other	X
Christoper Duntsch	Med Abuse - Other	
Hope Ybarra	MBP	
Lacey Spears	MBP	
Juliet Tuttle	Poisoning - Other	
Teresa Milbrandt	Med Fraud/Money	
Kelly Renee Turner-Gant	MBP	
Blanca Montano	MBP	

Abuser	Primary Abuse Type	Public Defecation or Exposing Others to Feces-3
My Parents	MBP	X
Gregory Mom/ Dad/Grandma (Sickened)	MBP	
Rajneesh Cult	Poisoning - Other	
Jim Jones	Poisoning - Other	
Donald Harvey	Poisoning - Other	
Beverley Allitt	MBP	X
Jolly Jane Toppan	Poisoning - Other	
Charles Cullen	Poisoning - Other	
Dee Dee Blanchard	MBP	
Kristen Gilbert	Poisoning - Other	
Christoper Duntsch	Med Abuse - Other	
Hope Ybarra	MBP	
Lacey Spears	MBP	
Juliet Tuttle	Poisoning - Other	
Teresa Milbrandt	Med Fraud/Money	
Kelly Renee Turner-Gant	MBP	
Blanca Montano	MBP	X

Abuser	Primary Abuse Type	Distributed CSAM - 2
My Parents	MBP	X
Gregory Mom/ Dad/Grandma (Sickened)	MBP	X
Rajneesh Cult	Poisoning - Other	
Jim Jones	Poisoning - Other	
Donald Harvey	Poisoning - Other	
Beverley Allitt	MBP	
Jolly Jane Toppan	Poisoning - Other	
Charles Cullen	Poisoning - Other	
Dee Dee Blanchard	MBP	
Kristen Gilbert	Poisoning - Other	
Christoper Duntsch	Med Abuse - Other	
Hope Ybarra	MBP	
Lacey Spears	MBP	
Juliet Tuttle	Poisoning - Other	
Teresa Milbrandt	Med Fraud/Money	
Kelly Renee Turner-Gant	MBP	
Blanca Montano	MBP	

Abuser	Primary Abuse Type	Total Boxes Checked
My Parents	MBP	15
Gregory Mom/ Dad/Grandma (Sickened)	MBP	12
Rajneesh Cult	Poisoning - Other	11
Jim Jones	Poisoning - Other	9
Donald Harvey	Poisoning - Other	7
Beverley Allitt	MBP	7
Jolly Jane Toppan	Poisoning - Other	6
Charles Cullen	Poisoning - Other	5
Dee Dee Blanchard	MBP	5
Kristen Gilbert	Poisoning - Other	5
Christoper Duntsch	Med Abuse - Other	4
Hope Ybarra	MBP	3
Lacey Spears	MBP	3
Juliet Tuttle	Poisoning - Other	2
Teresa Milbrandt	Med Fraud/Money	2
Kelly Renee Turner-Gant	MBP	2
Blanca Montano	MBP	2

Pattern Chart Explanation

The preceding section is a chart of some famous MBP, medical abuse, and poisoning cases. This is a book about the medical child abuse in my own childhood, but I have included this short section on other cases because it helps demonstrate larger patterns not specific to my own case.

<u>Cases Covered</u>

This is far from a complete list of cases. It only covers a small selection of famous cases. In addition, I have no inside knowledge of any of these cases - only what has been presented in books, documentaries, and newspapers. It's entirely possible that some of these cases should have more boxes checked than what I show here.

The cases in this chart with the most boxes checked are my case, the case portrayed in "Sickened" by Julie Gregory, and the cases involving cults. This strongly suggests that a certain number of boxes will only be checked if you have first-hand information from someone who lived with these abusers day in and day out. It's also worth noting that medical professionals in the chart consistently have more boxes checked than parents in the chart. This is likely a result of better record-keeping and investigations in hospitals. I do not believe it demonstrates that more medical professionals than parents actually fit these patterns.

<u>Checked Boxes</u>

In some cases, a filled or empty box does not tell the entire story. For example, I checked the sexual abuse box for Dee Dee Blanchard because although she never sexually abused her daughter, she became involved with her daughter's father when she was 24 and he was 17.

I also checked the voyeurism/nonconsensual recording box for Lacey Spears. Many would automatically think of this category as sexual, and sometimes it is, but I haven't found any evidence of that in this case. In this case, Lacy Spears took hundreds of death photos of her son after killing him and shared them on social media.

In other cases, I have not checked the box for sadism, even if victims suffered just as much as the victims of sadists. This simply means that the abuser did not seem to enjoy the suffering itself.

In addition, many abusers committed other types of fraud or theft unrelated to the abuse in addition to medical fraud. Of course, all of these abusers are committing fraud of some sort, but I have not checked the boxes in this column when I could only find medical fraud in service of FDIA.

These are just a few examples of how a chart does not tell the entire story.

<u>Cases Not Covered</u>

A truly comprehensive pattern chart and accompanying details would necessitate its own book. That would absolutely be a worthwhile task, but it is not what this book is. This book is a study of my childhood. This chart is to give you a rough estimate of how likely or not themes you will see in my childhood are to be common amongst the broad range of poisoners and medical abusers out there. I hope you will consider helping to raise public awareness of these patterns, as well as documenting other patterns I may have missed. It will make us all safer. As you will see in this pattern chart and throughout this book, those in danger of such abusers are not just those in their custody, but society at large.

The following is a small sample of cases worth charting that are not yet in the chart. They are not less important to study. A chart including all cases we know about is simply beyond the scope of this book.

<u>Not Included in the Chart (This is not a comprehensive list.)</u>
- Tiffany Alberts
- Tiffany C. Johnson
- Lisa Hayden Johnson
- Niels Hogel
- Elisabeth Hunnicutt
- Rachel Kinsella
- Shauna Dee Taylor
- Wendi Michelle Scott
- Richard Angelo
- Marybeth Tinning
- Laurie Dann
- Nannie Doss
- Lucy Letby

You may also find it useful to compare these cases and the cases in the chart to the Hare Psychopathy Checklist. See my write-up of the checklist at the end of the 'Make it make sense' section.

Terminology

A Note: First, I should mention that this terminology is still evolving as of the writing of this book. You will not always hear consistent usage, even amongst experts. There is still debate going on about how best to label this. In addition, terminology varies from country to country. This section focuses on terminology used in the United States.

Munchausen Syndrome by Proxy: This is the older terminology (established in 1977 by Dr. Roy Meadow) for a mental disorder associated with Munchausen by Proxy abuse. The current terminology in the U.S. is "Factitious Disorder Imposed on Another."

Common abbreviations: MSBP, MSbP, MSP

You will often hear people use this terminology even though it is outdated because it is what they are used to. You may also hear people confuse this with the terms for the abuse itself.

Munchausen by Proxy: Some refer to this as the abuse associated with what used to be called "Munchausen Syndrome by Proxy" and is now called "Factitious Disorder Imposed on Another." Some people use this as an umbrella term to cover both FDIA and Medical Abuse. Some continue to use it simply because it is what's currently most recognizable in terms of public awareness, even if they do not believe it's the best label.

Common abbreviations: MbP, MBP

MBP vs. MSBP

There is still a debate as to whether MSBP should even be considered a diagnosable condition. Should these urges to commit medical abuse be diagnosed as a mental illness, or should they instead be identified as a behavioral tendency associated with other mental illnesses? Some say a person "has MSBP," much as one would say a person has pyromania or kleptomania. Others say this is inaccurate and is akin to saying a person "has serial killing," or "has burglarizing," or "has raping." I tend to think this phrasing as a behavior and not an illness is more accurate. I say that my mother committed MBP abuse against me.

Factitious Disorder Imposed on Another: This is the newer terminology (established in 2013 in the DSM-5) for the mental disorder that used to be called Munchausen Syndrome by Proxy. Some describe this as specifically relating to medical abuse and falsifications. In my experience that has not been the case, although it has included medical abuse and falsifications. You will see examples of this throughout the book. Also, as I mentioned above, I believe that although abusers may have a variety of mental illnesses, it makes more sense to define the abuse rather than defining a mental disorder.

Common abbreviations: FDIA

Medical Abuse: This is a more general term that describes behavior only.

Some prefer to use this terminology, especially if they are not diagnosing an abuser but simply stating the facts. Not everyone who commits medical abuse is diagnosable with FDIA.

Borrowing: This is the terminology some use to describe the behavior of lifting stories of sickness or tragedy to reapply to oneself or one's victims. "Borrowing" may be done from urban legends, movies, books, TV shows, or other people's real-life events. My mother lifted from all of these sources. See the "Imitating or Banning Stories" section for examples. This is one of the easier ways to spot such a person. If you hear a story you aren't sure is true try searching online for a source or asking others if they've ever heard of such a story in pop culture.

Other Common Terms (Not an exhaustive list):
Medical Child Abuse (MCA)
Caregiver-Fabricated Illness in a Child (CFIC)
Abuse by Pediatric Condition Falsification (APCF)
Fabricated or Induced Illness by Carers (FII)

My use of terminology: You will see me use all of these terms. There is really no perfect choice. As you will see throughout this book, this is part of a larger cluster of behaviors, and in my opinion, none of the terminology fully captures what I am describing. For now, what we have is terminology that reflects the fact that there is still a lot to be learned about this subject.

PART II. INCIDENTS IN MY CHILDHOOD

32

About These Incidents

I first tried to write down the abuse I'd lived through 17 years ago. Today, writing about the abuse is still difficult, but not as difficult as it used to be. At times, it even lifts a weight off me. It gets better. The path to better is not always a straight line. Sometimes, it's two feet forward and one foot back, but it still gets better.

Triggers and Patterns

Many of you reading this book have been through your own trauma. I have arranged this memoir into subjects instead of arranging it chronologically. You will get something out of every section but don't pressure yourself to read every section. If you need to skip a section, the rest of the book will still make sense.

In addition to grouping the book by subjects, I have also listed incident tags, or trigger warnings, at the top of most incidents I retell. You can use these to spot patterns in the abuse, to avoid triggers, or both. Of course, many people have triggers that others couldn't possibly guess at. I have only accounted for common triggers I'm aware of.

In the course of this book, you're going to see patterns that are common to MBP, patterns that are common to abuse in general, and patterns that are specific to my family.

Mental Illness

There is a lot about mental illness in this book that is not universal amongst all people who commit MBP abuse. My mother has a substance abuse disorder. She probably also has some sort of a personality disorder. She likely has other diagnosable issues, too. I'm not a psychologist. You will read a lot in this book about her hallucinations. She abused so many chemical substances so consistently that I cannot even begin to guess whether the hallucinations were there before she started. She started well before I was born.

Time and Events Covered

This book covers the time period between my earliest memories at 3 and my move out of my parent's house at 18. I had originally meant to include my entire life up until this point, but it quickly became clear that such a book would be too long and too overwhelming. The rest of my life after 18 is a subject for a different future book. This book also does not contain details of my childhood that are not relevant to the subject, even when those details were significant in my life in other ways.

<u>Setting</u>

The appendix of this book contains a section titled Settings that will paint you a picture of the surroundings for these incidents. Many of them take place in the same few locations. Rather than describe these settings over and over again in each incident, I will describe them all here and reference this section to tell you where an incident took place. I am including this section mostly because many readers find it useful to be able to picture the place where something described happened. Please feel free to skim this section or skip it altogether if you don't feel the need to visualize the setting. You will not miss anything of substance that is not repeated elsewhere.

<u>How To Read This Part of the Book</u>

Although you can read this part of the book from start to finish if you wish, it may make more sense to treat this part as reference material. This part does not follow a chronological narrative. You can choose to skip to a section that interests you within this part if you wish.

<u>Names</u>

All names of innocent third parties in this section have been changed. Any similarity between names used in this section and names of actual people is pure coincidence, with the exception of publicly known cases that I mention in comparison to my own. I have also written this book under a pen name that is in no way related to my family of origin's name.

1. Traditional Munchausen and MBP

About

<u>About "Traditional" Munchausen & MBP</u>

This section is about what is traditionally thought of as Munchausen behavior (playing sick), and MBP behavior (making others sick). That does not necessarily mean that behaviors in other sections aren't traditionally and commonly a part of the MBP spectrum of behaviors. It just means this section contains what has traditionally been identified as MBP behavior.

Doctors are sometimes taught that these abusers want their attention and love. This may in some cases be true, but in many cases such abusers enjoy outwitting doctors, playing with doctors psychologically, and inflicting psychological pain on doctors. Medical professionals should never rule out the possibility of MBP just because the person is difficult and abrasive with them rather than fawning and affectionate.

People often think of MBP as a bid for attention. That may be part of it, but as you observe the behavior it becomes clear that it's also about sadism, power, and control. This is easier to see from the standpoint of the victim than from the standpoint of the doctor. I believe this is why this aspect has traditionally been overlooked.

It's worth noting that there is a parallel here. MBP behaviors not traditionally considered MBP behaviors, such as vehicle "accidents," terror threats, and infrastructure sabotage, just to name a few, are less visible to the medical community. Most literature over the years about MBP has traditionally been written by the medical community. It's good that the medical community pursues an understanding and awareness of this. More people from other parts of society need to start coming forward and speaking out. People from different parts of society who come up against this need to start speaking with each other to formulate a more complete picture of what's going on.

This section contains samples from my childhood but is not a complete list of MBP incidents throughout my childhood. Making such a list would be exhausting and very time-consuming. This section simply gives enough examples for the reader to begin to get a picture of my childhood and the MBP abuse. This is the pattern that most sections of this book follow. In most sections, there are simply too many incidents that would fit into that category to make listing them all practical or useful. I simply describe enough incidents in each section for the reader to get an understanding of each pattern. In addition, it's important to note that there were probably incidents in each pattern that I am still not aware of to this day.

Bike Accident

Incident Tags/Trigger Warnings

Traffic Accidents, Munchausen, MBP, Emergency rooms, ambulances

Incident

It was a sunny, busy day at the beach by our apartment. (See the beach description in Settings if you want a more detailed description.) We were surrounded by the buzz of the crowd. We were by the beach concession stand, which smelled of hot dogs, nachos, and other beach snacks. The concession stand was across a large sidewalk from the beach. People often rode quickly by on bikes. Parents often walked their kids across the sidewalk just to be safe. Occasionally, someone would be hit by a bike.

It had started as a normal day at the beach, but then something changed. My mother insisted on each of us going across alone. She told us each of us would run individually when she told that kid to go. Several times, she told a younger kid with us to go at the worst possible moment when he would certainly have been hit by a bike going very fast. He was very little at the time, just old enough to be able to run. I kept on pulling him back when he was about to be hit. I knew the situation was unsafe, but I didn't realize she was doing it on purpose. It was obvious, but it simply wasn't within the realm of possibility within my mind. I tried explaining to her what she was doing wrong. She refused to acknowledge it, claiming that it would have been safe to go. I couldn't understand why this kept on happening.

Finally, she talked him into ignoring me. I knew there was going to be an accident, and I was trying to figure out how to stop it. I was still arguing, and things were getting tense. I would grab him and stop him, but it was clear I couldn't keep this up. Finally, she insisted that one of us was going to go when she said so. It was clear that the only way to stop him was to go myself instead. I knew it wasn't safe, and I didn't want to, but I knew I didn't have another option. I reluctantly agreed to go in order to prevent him from going. I hoped that I would have a somewhat better chance since I was a bit older and I could run a bit faster. She timed it too well, though. She sent me into the path of a bike.

The next thing I knew, I was lying on the sidewalk, badly hurt. The left side of my face, including my eye socket and nose, had been broken badly by the bike frame. My entire body was badly scraped up, and my knee had been cut deeply by the bike chain. I lay there screaming. There was nothing else I could do. I watched the lifeguards yell angrily at my mother. She was more focused on them. They yelled at her to get back to me on the sidewalk so I wouldn't be hit by another bike.

It felt like it took an eternity for the ambulance to arrive. When it finally did, a nice paramedic attempted to soothe me and calm me by giving me the "job" of holding an ice pack to part of my body. My mother kept on saying things that caused me to freak out again, and the paramedic scolded her and kept trying to soothe me. At one point, my mother asked me what I could see. I could see things that one normally couldn't see all at the same time because they were too far away from each other to be seen at the same time. My left eye was pointing in a direction it shouldn't have been pointing in. They had words with each other over her emphasizing this to me. He was trying to calm me, and she was pointing this out to me in order to get more of a reaction out of me.

When we finally arrived at the emergency room, she became very fascinated with the medical staff and medicine. I remember lying on a table in terrible pain as she chatted with workers and asked about medication. She wanted to know about everything they were using. She didn't show concern but curiosity.

The emergency room eventually sent me home, believing that my parents would take me for the follow-up surgeries and appointments they had said I needed. It probably never occurred to them that a parent wouldn't do that. They did not. People tend to associate FDIA with unnecessary medical procedures, but it often involves withholding necessary medical procedures to cause more problems down the line. For some, this may be about making it last. For others, it may be about sadism. For some, it may be about both.

I was in so much pain I begged to be taken to a doctor. I knew something was very wrong. I was only chewing on one side of my mouth. I could feel bones or cartilage sticking out of the roof of my mouth on the left side. I could no longer pronounce certain sounds like R without touching the broken pieces of my mouth with my tongue, causing terrible pain. My mother told me to chew on the right side of my mouth and not make those sounds. I knew this was not a solution, but I was so young that I had no power to change this.

Eventually, the pieces of my nose, mouth, and eye socket set crooked. After they healed, I could chew on both sides of my mouth again, but I could never say my R's again. The roof of my mouth was too crooked. This suited her well. It made it easier for her to convince people that I was "special needs." I continued to experience terrible sinus congestion with a nose that I couldn't breathe through, and terrible headaches from the left eye socket. This also suited her well. It satisfied her sadism. The fact that I could only breathe through my mouth also made it easier for her to convince people that I was "special needs." It didn't match the symptoms of being what was back then often termed as being "special needs," but it did match stereotypes, and that's all she really needed. Occasionally, a doctor would scold her about not taking me for reconstructive surgery, but she always found a way out of it. Sometimes, this involved doctor switching or doctor shopping. Though my nose was somewhat crooked, the vast majority of the damage was not visible from the outside. This also helped her avoid the medical help that would have cleared up chronic headaches, congestion, and speech impediment.

<u>Points To Make</u>

Do not discount the possibility of FDIA when you see a child missing medical care they should be getting. This can be a long-term strategy to cause longer-term problems.

<u>Legislation</u>

There are already some mandated reporting laws involving the medical profession. This should be expanded where necessary.

The Flu

Incident Tags/Trigger Warnings

Poisoning, vomiting, food deprivation

Incident

I was eight. My mother's adoptive father was dying of lung cancer, and she was struggling. As usual, the flu went around the class in the fall. This time, however, was different. It didn't feel like any flu I'd ever had, and every time I thought I was getting better and could go back to school, I would get sick again.

I remember being bent over on the old nasty brown carpet between the dining table and cabinet, racked with heaving. Above me were the white and black prints of hieroglyphs on the walls. One was of someone drawing a thorned rope through their tongue in a blood sacrifice.

Some days, I would continue to throw up every few minutes for hours on end, even after my stomach was empty of food. It was terribly painful. I would dry heave repeatedly and eventually throw up bile. This went on for more than a month. My hair began to thin out. She liked to dwell on this fact and play with it repeatedly. She continued this behavior for months afterward as if the thinned-out hair was like a souvenir for her.

I was desperately hungry. I would beg for food, but she insisted that we had to "starve a fever." I would ask if I could even have just some water and crackers. I was going to throw up either way, but it hurt less if I had a bit of water and crackers instead of just dry heaving and throwing up bile. She would often not allow this, though.

Eventually, I was sent back to school on about the same timeline needed to avoid the number of absences that would have triggered a call to the authorities. School officials had already been threatening to report the number of absences to authorities, and she had pushed it just as far as she could without getting into trouble. At the time, it did not occur to me that it was too much of a coincidence that I had recovered on just exactly this timeline down to the day. They should have contacted authorities sooner, but I think they were reluctant to get involved in the drama and to lose the tuition. I returned to school emaciated with thinned-out hair. Everyone knew something was wrong, but I was back in school, so they let it go.

<u>Points To Make</u>

This also never resulted in a trip to the doctor. As much as I hated going to the doctor, I begged to see a doctor because I was in so much pain, and I knew that a month-long flu should be a reason to see a doctor. She always refused. She knew that she would be caught if she took me to a doctor at this point. If a child is out sick for a month, skinny and pale, and there has been no trip to a doctor, it is time for a call to authorities.

<u>Legislation</u>

Private schooling loopholes for mandated reporting should never exist under any circumstances.

I Can't Move

Physical abuse, head injuries, doctors, paralysis.

Incident

We were standing at the front desk of the doctor's office, waiting to pay and leave. I was greatly relieved that the appointment was over. I had huge anxiety attacks every time I had to visit the doctor. I was done and going home, and that was a big deal. My mood had changed from intense fear and anxiety to relief. My mother's mood did the inverse. She would often be aggravated or even angry at my happiness, whereas she very much enjoyed people's fear and pain, including my own. My mood had suddenly lifted, and her mood had suddenly soured. I stood by the counter, unable to see what was going on because my head was just at the height of the edge of the counter.

Suddenly, I experienced being elsewhere. I believed I was on a school bus full of rowdy kids from my class. It was like a dream. I came to on the floor, already screaming and crying. The other parents in the waiting room were very angry and yelling. They all claimed that my mother had slammed my head into the counter and knocked me out. She insisted that I had slipped and hit my head on the counter, but the receptionist and other parents kept on claiming that they had seen her slam my head into the counter and knock me out. Her story didn't make any sense. It's not possible to slip and fall while standing still on carpet. It's also not possible to hit a counter with enough force to knock yourself out by simply falling forward from the distance I was from the counter without some extra force behind that strike. Everyone else in the room was insisting they had seen her. The staff had a talk with her and sent me home with her, which made the other parents angry.

When we got home, I sat down at my usual spot by the coffee table in front of the TV. At first, things were going as normal, but then I started to feel strange. I was in pain, but it was a pain I hadn't felt before or since. I still don't have words for it. It was a pain combined with a strange, indescribable feeling. One-half of my body just felt off. I complained, but my mother blew it off no matter how many times I insisted something was wrong and that I needed help. The feeling grew worse and worse. I lay down on the floor and contorted myself into a weird pose, trying to get relief. The top half of my body was under the coffee table. I was on my back. That's when I realized I couldn't move. I wanted to contort my body into a different pose, trying to find some relief, but one-half of my body was paralyzed. I was also experiencing a mental fog. It was terrifying. I called for help, but my mother simply acted aggravated and told me to stop goofing around. I explained that I couldn't move, but she insisted that this wasn't true.

After a few hours, the feeling subsided, and I was able to move myself out from under the coffee table again. My mother never acknowledged what had happened, but her attempts to cover it up gave her away. Every time I tried to tell the doctor what had happened at later appointments, she would talk over me and try to change the story. After several tries, I was finally able to get the point across to the doctor. He got angry with my mother and scolded her. I was describing symptoms he had specifically told her to bring me back in for if I displayed them after the head injury. Instead, he was seeing me at the next scheduled appointment several months later. This still did not trigger a call to the DCFS. My mother was using this doctor for a reason.

<u>Legislation</u>

Mandated reporting needs to be enforced. Unenforced mandated reporting laws will not have the protective effect they're meant to.

<u>Advice for Third Parties</u>

If you witness something like this, you can act. In this situation, I think that the other parents saw the doctor as an authority figure, which changed their behavior. They reacted angrily when the staff didn't file a report with authorities, but they did not go around the staff and do this themselves. If an authority figure is making a bad choice, you don't need to go along with that.

Vitamins

Poisoning, MBP

Incident

Every morning, I sat on the floor at the coffee table in front of the TV as I ate my breakfast. Other family members' breakfasts and mine were pretty similar, except that mine had lots of "vitamins" lined up along the placemat for me to take every morning. At first, I accepted this fact, but as time went on, I began to question it. Why did they not get bunches of vitamins all in a row? Why did I? Her answers were evasive. She couldn't explain why or what they were. I began refusing to take them, and she got angry. One morning, a family member, probably trying to make peace, joined in on, telling me I should just take them. I had no suspicion that they were anything bad. I simply believed that they were unnecessary, and I didn't enjoy taking pills. I countered by suggesting he take them instead. He agreed, probably in an effort to show me it was no big deal. The next morning, I offered them to him again, believing I'd found a solution. I minded taking the pills, and he didn't. He refused, and when I pressed the matter, he told me that they had made him feel bad. He would not elaborate on what that meant. Maybe he didn't have the words to describe it. I didn't have a baseline for feeling well in childhood, so I wasn't quite sure what he was talking about. My mother eventually dropped the tactic but moved on to others.

Cookies for Maintenance

Poisoning

Incident

My mother always loved baking cookies for people. She sometimes gave baked goods even when no one else did. As a kid, I was embarrassed when she would sometimes offer baked goods in situations where the people receiving them and observing the interaction clearly found it odd. I never thought it suspicious, though, because I did not yet suspect what she was up to. She often baked for the maintenance team for the building we lived in until, one day, they stopped accepting her baked goods. "What's in them?" they asked. I didn't understand what they meant. They informed her that they couldn't accept them anymore.

Advice for Victims

If this happens to you, please consider filing a police report. If an entire work team gets sick after eating something from someone who seems off or whom they previously had a conflict with, please don't just shrug it off. Documenting such behavior helps make everyone safer. You don't know how far such behavior will escalate in the future. Documenting such behavior before it escalates can help save lives. FDIA has one of the highest death rates of any form of abuse.

Sleeping Meds

<u>Incident Tags/Trigger Warnings</u>

Munchausen, MBP, drugs

<u>Incident</u>

When I was little, my mother "volunteered" at a local natural history museum. This, in large part, consisted of showing up and giving tours uninvited in areas she wasn't trained for. They knew she was a problem, but I think they weren't quite sure how to handle her. It was a very large public place, and it was difficult to keep someone who was a problem out. I think they also felt bad for her. She was good at making up sob stories to prey on people's sympathy. At the time, I genuinely believed she was a volunteer, just like the rest of the volunteers, because I was too young to know any different.

She particularly liked the earth lodge. This was a structure inside a larger Native American history exhibit that was meant to be a replica of an actual earth lodge. People could go in and sit down to listen to a program given by volunteers. Guests would sit in a circle along the walls of the lodge, and volunteers would stand in the center and give a talk. I had been inside during programs before, sometimes as my mother stood in the middle and attempted to talk over the people who were actually supposed to be giving the talk.

This day was different because of a new behavior I had never seen before. She approached a little boy when his grown-ups were temporarily distracted and offered him a little cup of juice to drink. At the time, I was too young to understand what was going on. I now recognize the juice and cup as over-the-counter sleeping medication and the little cup that comes with it. I also recognize the dose she gave him as unsafe for his age and size.

I couldn't understand why only he and none of the other children got juice. I asked her, and she denied what I had just seen right in front of my eyes. I couldn't understand this either, but I didn't realize the consequence, so I eventually let it go as just another odd adult behavior. When you're very young and have a parent who is very off, there is not always a clear visible line between inexplicable adult behaviors in the world in general and inexplicable adult behaviors in your parent in specific. Looking back as an adult, it's very obvious. As a young child who has never known any other context, it is not, though.

My mother made a point of seating him next to me instead of next to his adults. As the program went on, the child fell asleep and began to drool excessively. His adults probably just thought that he was being a typical child sleeping through a presentation that he found boring. I figured the same. Of course, kids are used to seeing each other fall asleep during educational presentations or presentations geared toward adults.

At one point, my mother stopped in front of us and asked in mock concern if he was ok. I insisted he was because I was too young to understand any different, and I was used to my mother making a very big deal over very small things. She tried a few more times to get me to say something was wrong, but I genuinely didn't think there was. The presentation went on, and guests remained focused on the actual presenters despite her efforts.

His adults became alarmed at the end of the program when it became clear to them that something was wrong. They could tell that something was off about him as if he had been drugged. They began to question the volunteers in alarm. This started an argument as the actual volunteers couldn't understand what was happening and why they were being questioned in such a way. Eventually, the family left, unable to prove what had happened and understandably creeped out about the idea of staying. Everyone else just moved on as if nothing had happened.

Allergies

MBP, Poisoning

Incident

When I began to go through puberty, I developed terrible headaches. I believe that this was due to previous head trauma from throughout my childhood. New sinus cavities begin to open up during puberty, but for me, this was complicated by previous damage to my sinuses that I'd never received proper treatment for. At the time, I had a badly deviated septum, with the bone and cartilage in my nose completely blocking my left nostril.

Many have noted that some medical abuse begins with an actual medical problem, which the abuser then becomes enamored with. In some cases, this can broadly mean medical problems for a victim in general. In other cases, this can be a particular new medical problem in someone who was already a victim. This was what happened here. Rather than getting me treated for the actual problem, my mother piled more complications on. She got me sick with colds and sinus infections as often as possible. She tried to find things to trigger sinus reactions and cover my environment with irritants to trigger congestion.

Soon, I was going for weekly allergy shots that never seemed to change anything at all. It gave my mother an excuse for a weekly medical visit, though. We drove out to an old building near the dividing line between the city and suburbs. The building guard was always on the first floor, where people came in from the parking lot. He and my mother always talked about football, which she never watched. Often, she would drone on for more than an hour with him. He was polite about it and probably just thought she was lonely.

The allergist's office was a few floors up. The nurses were mother and daughter. They often talked about what celebrities they thought were handsome. She would talk to them for a long time but didn't tend to engage in celebrity talk or talk about who was handsome in general. In both cases, she just kind of morphed into someone interested in what they or the guard had to say for long periods of time. It was a social event for her to go there.

After years of this, she discovered that some of the kids at my high school went to a different office for the same doctor downtown. She suddenly decided we would switch to that one. She was always desperately trying to fit in with the crowd at school in ways that didn't really make sense. The new building was a tall building downtown wedged in amongst other buildings. The lobby had high ceilings and elevator banks. The building style was much older and grander than the 70s-era industrial building we usually went to. It was a pre-glass-and-steal era high rise. There was always a uniformed guard stationed in the lobby. We went there for a few months before things fell apart.

One day, I mentioned to my mother that it was time to go to the appointment. She told me we weren't going anymore. At the time, I didn't realize she was making me sick, and I was still hoping that the shots would eventually make me feel better. We went back and forth about it a bit. I couldn't understand why I was finding out on the day of the appointment that my mother had decided we weren't going any more ever. It made no sense to me. She couldn't explain it. Eventually, instead of giving me an explanation or simply making something up, she changed her mind and said we were going.

When we arrived at the building, things were immediately off, just as her reaction had been. The guard, who had always been friendly before, told her that she wasn't allowed in. He didn't explain why, though. I persisted in the naive belief that it was all one big misunderstanding. We made our way upstairs, but they would not see us. The nurses who had always seemed so friendly were very agitated. They told me that I didn't have allergies. With no explanation of what medical abuse was and very little public awareness of it back in the '90s, I couldn't make any sense of what they were saying. I knew what I was experiencing, and their statement made no sense to me. They told me that she was doing something to me. I still didn't understand.

We left quickly afterward. I asked my mother what they were talking about, but she wouldn't explain. I left for college shortly afterward, and what

I still believed were allergies suddenly cleared up. I felt better than I had in years. It would still take me a few more years to put things together and figure out what was going on. Distracted by the changes in college life, I didn't think about why I felt so much better. I just enjoyed it.

<u>Legislation</u>

See mandated reporting.

Older Ladies

Incident Tags/Trigger Warnings
MBP, elder abuse, breathing difficulty, poisoning

Incident

My mother has always found elderly ladies to glom onto. Sometimes, she would meet them through the museum. Other times, they were distant family or random acquaintances. She would always follow the same pattern. She would start out as an acquaintance, move on to friendship, and then move on to a helper role as they got sicker and frailer. I'll give them pseudonyms for the purposes of this section. There was Gretta, and Sally, and Debbie, just to name a few.

Sally was a distant relative through adoption. She seemed to have no interest in Sally at all, but once Sally was older and frail and in a wheelchair, all of a sudden, my mother was interested. She picked her up in a long drive to the suburbs, then took her to the museum, where she pushed her around in a wheelchair for hours. She insisted Sally was very interested in exhibits that Sally was very clear about not being interested in. Sally was ready to go, but she was stuck until my mother decided Sally was done. Sally declined to socialize with her again.

Gretta was a woman she knew through the museum. At first, she got into a routine of going grocery shopping with her. I think Gretta was just socializing, but my mother was casting herself as "helping" her grocery shop as if she needed help with that. Eventually, Gretta refused to have anything to do with her. I'm not sure what happened.

Around the same time as Gretta, there was Debbie. This was the most alarming case that I was aware of. When I first met her, she seemed to be in fine health. As my mother spent more time with her, she had more and more trouble breathing until she was on oxygen.

One day, my mother insisted I come along with her on a trip to see Debbie. She insisted Debbie would love to see me even though I barely knew her. Lately, she had come home quickly after leaving to see Debbie. She had explained that someone else was there. That didn't really make sense. That's not what would happen if they were actually friends or if she was actually supposed to be there.

The day she insisted I come with her started with Debbie's refusal to answer the door. When we didn't leave, she opened it just a crack to talk to us, but not let us in. She treated us with suspicion. "What's in the soup?" she asked several times. My mother never gave a straight answer. For months, she had been bringing Debbie mason jars full of soup. Debbie insisted she knew they weren't safe to eat. At the time, I didn't suspect my mother and didn't know what Debbie was talking about.

Eventually, my mother made her way past Debbie and into the apartment. She began taking stacks of papers and boxes and random crap from Debbie's couch and tables and carrying it into Debbie's bedroom. There, she would stack it on the bed, making the bed unusable. This was a reversal of the story my mother had told me several times before. My mother had claimed that Debbie had stacked the things on her bed and had been forced to sleep on the couch as a result. She had insisted that Debbie had some sort of problem that made her want to do this and that she had helped Debbie move all the stuff off the bed. It wasn't Debbie doing this strange activity. My mother had reversed the story.

As Debbie continued to complain and tell her to stop, she continued, aware that there wasn't anything Debbie could do about it in her physical condition. Debbie insisted that it had taken her actual helpers hours to undo the mess the last time my mother had done this. I stood there confused and unsure what was going on and what to do.

Debbie made a phone call, and some of her relatives showed up. They shooed us out of the apartment. My mother drove us home totally unfazed, never acknowledging that there had been something off about the interaction.

In another incident, my mother decided that one of her older lady friends needed special assistance from the local transit authority. I'm not sure which acquaintance this was, but the saga went on for months. I would have paid closer attention at the time if I had realized what was going on.

It started when my mother decided to apply on this lady's behalf for special rides from the transit authority. They ran a number of trains and buses, but for those with special needs, they had a service that involved shuttle buses with helpers. They had to approve that a person was medically qualified for this service. The woman my mother applied on behalf of did not need this service and was very clear with the transit authority about this. Naturally, the transit authority rejected the request when the subject of the request itself informed them that she wasn't interested in the service, had no need for it, and didn't qualify for it. My mother appealed.

The people who wrote the procedural regulations never anticipated someone like my mother. They had assumed that such a decision would only be appealed if the subject of the matter actually wanted it appealed. They had never taken steps in the writing of the regulations and procedures to prevent a 3rd party from wasting their time. The story my mother told me at the time was that this woman, in fact, needed the help but was too proud to accept it. She alternately claimed that the meetings with the authority had happened to fall on days when the lady was feeling somewhat better, causing the authorities to mistakenly believe that she didn't need the service. The back and forth wasn't a deterrent to my mother. It was an incentive. Even without the service ever being granted, she was getting what she wanted through the drama. She cast herself as the strong advocate of a needy, sick lady and got attention for doing so. Meanwhile, those in the transit authority got to pause the actual important work they were doing for people who actually needed it to deal with her repeatedly. Your tax dollars at work.

<u>Points To Make</u>

There are more cases like this not in this book due to the fact that this book only covers the first 18 years of my life. In addition, there is much more to Debbie's case that took place after my childhood. I suspect that she may have eventually played a role in Debbie's death, though I cannot prove this.

<u>Proposed Legislation</u>

We can avoid wasting time and money by ensuring that statutes, regulations, and official procedures prevent third parties from involving themselves in benefits cases against the wishes of the actual potential recipient of those benefits. If a person tells the government that they do not want or need a benefit, this should be the end of it. I'm sure this is what was always intended, but many times, laws are written without anticipating people like my mother and such behaviors.

Bitter Food

Poisoning, Food deprivation, enabling

<u>Incident</u>

It was a usual weekly meal. It was chicken and rice. Usually, we got buttery rice and chicken with the Lowry's seasoning. It was a very common meal for us. It was different this time, though. I sat down hungry and ready to eat, but as soon as I put the food in my mouth, it was terribly bitter. Everything was, including the chicken and the rice. There wasn't anything on the plate that didn't taste that way. I objected and got told to eat it just like a usual scene with a child at a dinner table. This wasn't a usual scene with a child at a dinner table, though. I knew that there was something very wrong with my food. The argument escalated. I was hungry and wanted something to eat, but I couldn't eat that.

I was made to sit on the extra chair by the south-facing window next to the radiator. I had to sit separately until I finished the plate. I kept on complaining that I was hungry and that something was wrong with the food.

Finally, after they had finished, my father tasted it to make a point. He reacted immediately. He could taste it, too. It was very obvious. He yelled at her. He wasn't confused. He knew what had happened. It wasn't a revelation to him. He simply hadn't known that it had happened this particular time until he tasted the food, but he knew her tendencies. Despite yelling at her, he did not change the punishment he had assigned me. I had to eat it or go hungry. I think he cared about winning the argument with me more than anything else. He didn't want to go back on what he'd said before. It sounds bizarre, and that's because it is. It fit his behavior in general, though. They were together for a reason.

I went hungry that night. I don't know what would have happened to me if I had eaten it.

The Wheel Chair

Incident Tags/Trigger Warnings

MBP, drugs, wheelchairs

Incident

I was a little kid. My mother insisted I needed to see some kind of a specialist. I couldn't understand why. I insisted I was fine. She took me to a doctor who gave me some sleeping medicine and then observed me sleep while I was wearing sensors.

My mother had made a big deal about the fact that we would go to the museum where she 'volunteered' afterward. She told me that they had wheelchairs they let guests borrow in case I was still drowsy from the appointment. She repeated this over and over again as if fixated on it.

When we arrived at the museum after the appointment, she insisted on getting a wheelchair even though I felt fine to walk on my own. Before that moment, it had only been a suggestion, but now it was a requirement. I think she was hoping that I would follow the suggestion and view it as my choice, but that hadn't happened. The sleeping medication had totally worn off, and the specialist had told her that I would be fine on my own, but she insisted on the chair 'for safety's sake.' She ignored the fact that the specialist had told her it was totally unnecessary. She ignored the fact that people don't generally have wheelchairs in case they ever need to take sleeping medication. That would be an inherently silly idea. At a certain point, it became clear that I was going to be in the chair no matter what I said or did, so I gave up and allowed her to push me around the museum in the chair.

At a certain point, we ran into some museum workers she knew, and she pretended that this was by chance. They fussed over me as adults do with small children, and especially with small children who may have special needs. The subject of the chair came up, and I told them that I didn't actually need to be in it. They at first thought that I was just trying to act like an ordinary kid who didn't need a chair. They reassured me that it was ok. I got up and demonstrated that I could easily stand and walk on my own. This was when everyone's demeanor changed. I believe this was the moment when they connected this to other behaviors they'd seen in my mother before. My mother was, to say the least, not thrilled, but I was happy to finally be out of the chair.

<u>Points To Make</u>

A lot of people who observe behavior like this are unsure of what to do. They know that they can call authorities if they see physical or sexual abuse, for example, but they don't know what to do if they see a kid in a wheelchair who doesn't need to be. I was being hurt in lots of ways, as described throughout this book, but they didn't know that. All they knew was that I was in a chair I didn't need to be in against my will. A lot of people are uncertain of how to handle this. They've been taught how to handle other forms of abuse, but not this. It's ok to call the authorities if this type of incident described above is all you know. It's enough of a reason on its own to make a phone call. Don't let anyone tell you otherwise.

Strings

Incident Tags/Trigger Warnings

Munchausen/Factitious Disorder

Incident

My mother would tie strings around her finger to ruin circulation to show her doctor. We were in the kitchen of the Chicago house. I'd seen her do it before, but this was the time we actually had a discussion. Before, she'd always managed to shrug it off. When I was younger, many inexplicable things adults did fell into the category of adults just being weird. At this point, though, I was a teenager. She told me that her doctor had called her weird. I asked her why she did it. She couldn't or wouldn't explain it.

Medical Records

<u>Incident Tags/Trigger Warnings</u>

Dentists, doctors

<u>Incident</u>

I was a little kid. We were checking out and getting ready to leave the pediatric dentist's office. I still had the flavor of the gritty polish in my mouth. We stood in front of the desk between the waiting area and the exam rooms. It was a long, built-in desk area. The files were in rows of shelving lining the area behind them. They had color-coded tabs. This was when most doctors still kept paper records.

One of the things that my mother seemed to enjoy most was chatting with helpers. She would often talk their ears off and have to be told they had other work they had to get back to. This day was no different. They were used to her and thought nothing of it.

She asked the lady behind the desk a question that required her to get up and look at something else. While the lady was doing this, she slipped behind the counter and began to look through the files. She hastily put them back into the wrong places as she kept looking through more. They weren't just our files. They were random files. The lady caught her. Her voice was first pleasant, then stern, as she went from normal customer service to realizing what happened. My mother made an excuse that seemed to smooth things over. The woman calmed a little and explained that if she wanted to see something in our files, she could ask, and they would show it to her. The conversation went back to normal, and the woman went to finish what she had started away from the desk, believing that the matter had been settled. My mother tried it again. The woman caught her again. This time, she was very stern. She talked about what could happen to other patients if their files were screwed up. Other employees also joined the conversation at this point, probably having heard the tone of what was going on. Now, multiple employees were giving her a talking-to.

Eventually, things simmered down again as my mother listened, and the employees talked themselves out. She was allowed to pay and leave with us. Although they considered things to be resolved, they really weren't. This was part of a pattern of behavior that needed to be addressed with more than just a talk.

<u>Points To Make</u>

Between this and the alcohol (see the 'Antibiotics' incident in the 'Exposing Us To Substances' section), it's really not good that they still didn't call child services. I'm sure that's why we went to that dentist. If you become known as the doctor who doesn't report this stuff, you will wind up putting up with more and more of it endlessly. Abusers network and tell each other what doctors to use. This will draw you long-term into a practice with more legal jeopardy. You can be blamed for what they do, blamed for malpractice, or wind up harming a 3rd party if you don't realize your other records were messed with.

This incident is similar to another incident not described here in which my mother switched urine samples that had been left unsecured at the pediatrician's office. This may have been simple maliciousness, or it may have been an attempt to hide something that would show up in my urine. There are only so many incidents I can include without turning this into an encyclopedia-length project, and many of the incidents resemble each other.

Knee Jerk

MBP, Doctors

Incident

I was in a new doctor's office, not the one we usually went to. It was in a larger hospital building. It had the usual sterile look and smell of most doctors' offices. I was a little kid, and still at that age where I was very gullible to stuff my mother would tell me. She had convinced me that I had been doing that knee-jerk test wrong all these years. It was that usual test that doctors do when they hit a knee with a small rubber device to make sure the reflexes are working as they should. She had convinced me that I must not move my body at all in reaction to the test. I had walked in believing that I had been dragged to a specialist because I'd gotten it wrong before. I was convinced that I needed to keep my leg perfectly still so as not to endure more testing and specialists.

The doctor tried the test as usual and then began hitting harder in concern. It hurt after a while, and I said so, but I wouldn't let my knee react because I thought that's what I was supposed to do. When he asked me about it, I explained it to him. He was aggravated with my mother when I explained, but he didn't follow up. This seems like a problem.

Legislation

Mandated reporting needs to be expanded to cover behaviors such as coaching a child to fail a physical. This is a sign of a larger problem that poses significant danger to the child.

It's Not Real

Incident Tags/Trigger Warnings

ER visit

Incident

One day, towards the end of high school, I was at home on the weekend when I heard my father calling for help. He was usually a physically healthy person, but all of a sudden, he could barely stand and walk on his own. I suggested calling an ambulance, but he told me he just wanted help getting to a cab and for me to call the museum to find my mother after I got him in the cab.

I helped him to a cab and went back to his office to make the call. I called the museum and asked around if anyone could locate her. I explained the situation. The woman I got ahold of sounded exasperated. "It's not real," she told me. When I asked what she meant, she said that it never was. There seemed to be a bit of back and forth on the other end of the line as people in the room discussed, but I couldn't make out what they were saying. I asked for clarification. I knew what I had seen. Eventually, the woman got tired of the conversation and simply hung up. I called the main line back and tried a different series in the menu, trying to find someone who could help. Eventually, I got connected to a woman who told me she would pass the message on to my mother.

Eventually, my father was diagnosed with extreme vertigo; I think by process of elimination because they could never come up with another cause. I never questioned this or thought much about this phone call until years later, when I began to piece things together.

Neck Spasms

<u>Incident Tags/Trigger Warnings</u>
pain, immobility, (and death under the points to make section)
<u>Incident</u>
One night, after craning my neck at an odd angle to see the board in my freshman year of high school, I woke up, shifted, and pulled my neck. I was in pain and had difficulty moving. After a few difficult tries, I got myself off of my dirty, old, second-hand mattress and went to go ask my mother for help. She took me out to the living room and put me on the living room floor with a hot washcloth on my neck.

At one point, she was helping me shift positions when she said something, which indicated that she was surprised it was real because she had assumed I was faking until she realized how much help I needed moving. I was incredulous. I said something disparaging of anyone who would do such a thing. I don't remember my exact words, but the words and tone were admittedly judgmental. I didn't expect that to upset her because she was often judgmental and enjoyed making fun of others, and I wasn't on to her Munchausen behavior pattern yet. (See the 'Bad Back' incident under the 'Substance Abuse and MBP' section.)

She immediately became angry and dropped me. Unable to catch myself, I landed in an awkward position on the floor in terrible pain. Her voice was shrill and angry. I was baffled. I couldn't understand what the source of the conflict was. She was defensive but couldn't come out and tell me what she had been doing. We went back and forth for a bit. I pleaded for help, and she yelled about vague nonsense I couldn't understand. Eventually, she picked me back up and placed me into a better position. Pursuing the fight any further was going to get her caught.

<u>Points To Make</u>
Have you ever met anyone who always assumes that others are making up illnesses, no matter how illogical this belief might be in context? This is a red flag. In another incident not detailed in this book, she acted jealous of my 3rd-grade teacher whose daughter had died, assuming she must have been

happy about it. My mother often had difficulty distinguishing between her thought patterns and those of others.

Chinese Food

Incident Tags/Trigger Warnings
Poisoning, cancer, family fights

Incident

I was in elementary school when my mother's adoptive father was dying of lung cancer. We drove eight hours to surprise her parents. My mother made a point of bringing a large selection of Chinese food from the restaurant across the street from our apartment. She insisted they would love it - Chinese food that had been sitting in a car for eight hours.

We stood at the front door as my mother rang the doorbell. I had been prepped for a joyful reunion and happy surprise, which is what I was fully expecting at my young age. I could hear my grandmother behind the door approaching and speculating about who it was. She opened the door and emitted a low scream of terror from the pit of her stomach. She was shocked, breathless, and clearly scared. Her whole body reacted with stress. My mother held up the bags of Chinese food and smiled. My grandmother shouted to my grandfather who it was.

I expected we were going to go in and spend the night. As the conversation between my mother and grandmother went on, we remained standing at the door. They went back and forth for some time, speaking literally and metaphorically above my head about what was going on. My mother foisted the bags of food off on her even though she questioned what was in them and insisted they wouldn't eat them.

Finally, my grandmother shut the door, and my mother informed me that we were getting back in the car and driving home that night. I protested. The last thing I wanted to do was get back in the car. I was tired and hungry. If we couldn't spend the night at our grandparents couldn't we at least spend the night at a motel? There was no arguing. We piled back in the car and made the long way back home that night.

Fast Food

Incident Tags/Trigger Warnings

Parasites, worms, poisoning, fraud

Incident

When I was in elementary school, my mother ordered a microscope from a mail-order catalog. The shipment was delayed, and she got very fussy. I wasn't sure why. It wasn't for my schoolwork, and she had no use for it. She had asked me if I wanted one, and I didn't express any interest. She bought it anyway. It was an odd behavior for someone who often avoided spending money on me. She contacted the company repeatedly as if time was somehow of the essence. Finally, it arrived. She was so excited. She looked at some sample slides that had come with it and had me do so as well. It all seemed anti-climactic to me, but it was a big deal to her.

We would often go to one of the popular burger chains that had a restaurant down the street. We went there, as usual, a bit after the microscope arrived and brought the food back to the apartment. I was a few bites into my food when she claimed to see something on it and made a big production about it. I insisted it was fine and just as normal. She insisted it was not. She was on the other side of the kitchen when she made the claim, and the burger was right in front of me. I insisted she couldn't even see anything from where she was standing when she made the claim. She took the burger and the microscope and began to do an inspection. All the while, she was praising her own foresight in buying the microscope and exclaiming over what a good thing it was that we had one. She claimed that she had found little worms in the burger. That sounded silly to me. I didn't think she was lying, but I didn't believe she was correct either. I kept on trying to correct her because I didn't realize at my age that she had planned this entire 'discovery.'

She contacted my pediatrician and told the story. This eventually resulted in me taking a long course of medication. This wasn't the end of it, though. She also insisted on telling the story around my elementary school, especially focusing on the more gossipy parents and staff. Soon enough, the saga was news all over school.

Points To Make

This is similar to incidents in which my mother purposefully exposed people to ticks and put parasitic wasps on caterpillars to watch what would happen. MBP abusers often behave like parasites. All abusers do to some extent, but MBP abusers often do so much more literally.

This is also similar to other incidents in which my mother made fake product injury claims. Over the years, my mother made similar injury and contamination claims about a can of tuna, a jar of salsa, and a soda. These are just the ones I know about. Those who deal with product injury claims need to be well educated on MBP.

The Chicken Pox

Incident Tags/Trigger Warnings
Pain, Disease, skin picking, open sores

Incident

I got the chicken pox when I was twelve years old. The chickenpox vaccine had just become available in the U.S. a few weeks earlier. We were due for a doctor's appointment, and she couldn't put it off any longer and keep us in school. It was the last possible point at which I could become infected. Most of my friends had chicken pox years earlier because parents in those days exposed their kids early to protect them from serious side effects that tended to happen only in older people with chicken pox. My mother had always made a big deal about not doing this and acted like the rest of the parents were being bad parents.

I was sitting at the dinner table when I absent-mindedly scratched my chest, noticed something odd, looked down, and saw open sores. We already had an appointment for the vaccination, and I couldn't believe my bad luck. The next week and a half were miserable. I had a high fever with sores everywhere, including inside my mouth and on my eyelids. People had always told me the chicken pox itched, but mine did not. They hurt. I'm not sure if this was simply a bad reaction or if my mother had done something to create an unusual case somehow. I supposed it could have been something she put in an ointment, but I don't know for sure.

On a particularly bad day, I was lying on my bedroom floor because I couldn't stand the feeling of my bedding against my skin. My mother came in and inquired about my symptoms in detail. I told her about them, but she kept on pressing. She wanted to know which specific sores hurt the most. One on my side was particularly large and painful, I explained to her. I explained I was trying to be careful not to pop it because they hurt so much worse when they popped. Some would pop if I brushed against something, and the sensation was like knives stabbing me. This was the sensation with the bad ones even before they popped, but when they opened, it was so much worse.

Just after this discussion, she made a show of trying to turn me over. I told her no because I didn't want to disturb any of the sores. She insisted, then I felt terrible pain. The act had been a pretext for an opportunity to scratch open the worst sore. She dug her nail in deep, ripping my flesh raw. She claimed she hadn't, but just like in other incidents in which she denied her behavior, it was obvious. There was a large fingernail scratch right where I had told her to be careful.

<u>Points To Make</u>

Note the long-term planning here. This was something she saved up for years and timed. Although these abusers may at times act impulsively, there's often a great deal of pre-meditation that goes into this type of abuse.

Wisdom Teeth

Incident Tags/Trigger Warnings

dental work, dental surgery, infection

Incident

I was sixteen when I got my wisdom teeth out. I went in for surgery under local anesthesia, and my mother came with me. The procedure was uneventful. I thought everything was settled.

My mother decided that we were going on a road trip out of state to visit Carlsbad Caverns right afterward. I still wasn't done healing, but I figured it was ok as long as I followed post-surgery instructions, and I was excited to go see a new place.

Our first night there, we were in a motel, and I was cleaning my teeth, attempting to follow the doctor's instructions to make sure everything healed properly. My mother, acting as if she was being helpful, asked to have a look in my mouth and make sure everything was ok. I felt her press hard on the wound, and I told her not to do that. She insisted everything was fine. I felt like something was still there, stuck in my wound where she had pressed, but she insisted there was not anything there. I figured I was just feeling the after-effects of her pressing too hard on it because she insisted it was clean, and I still had not figured out her behavior pattern.

The next day, I knew something was wrong. I could tell it was infected. I kept asking her for help, asking to go back home, and asking to go back to the doctor. She insisted I was fine and kept on insisting we proceed with the trip. She dragged me along to hiking trails and cave tours as I felt increasingly sick and depleted. Eventually, she'd had enough. Maybe she decided that she'd waited long enough to let the infection set in sufficiently to cause enough medical problems. Maybe she was just bored and wanted another doctor's visit.

When we got back home, and I got in to see the doctor, he told me I had an infection in my mouth that needed follow-up work. He placed me under local anesthesia again and spent quite a while cutting the wound back open and cleaning and draining it. He informed me that something had, in fact, been stuck where I felt something had been stuck. He had words with my mother. He clearly believed she had done it on purpose and warned her that he would report it if she did it again.

Points To Make

Mandated reporting laws exist for a reason. Throughout this book, you will see several examples of school workers and medical workers disregarding mandated reporting laws. I still believe in these laws. They just need more enforcement.

Throughout my childhood, people told my mother the same thing. They always warned that they would report it if it happened again. It always happened again, but never within their sight. There is a reason why this is not how the law works. We need better enforcement of mandated reporting laws. It will save lives.

Shorts

<u>Incident Tags/Trigger Warnings</u>
Munchausen, MBP, shitting, confrontation, poisoning
<u>Incidents</u>

The following are incidents that would also be in this section if I'd done a full write-up of them. Each one gets a short blurb. Some are so straightforward that they do not need a full write-up. Others are ones I cut from a full write-up for length because they are similar to others I have already done a full write-up of. Others are short because there is no point in putting myself or you, the reader, through all the gory details simply to get the information across.

<u>Her Mother</u>

My mother's adoptive mother also had a Munchausen and MBP side to her personality. When I was little, my mother left us together in an open-air parking garage for a few minutes while she parked. My grandmother kept asking me if I was ok and insisting I was overcome with fumes. I had no idea why she thought that, even though I kept insisting I was fine. When my mother got back, she very dramatically related how we both almost passed out from the fumes.

***

In another incident, there was a family argument when we were over at my grandmother's house over the fact that she had served everyone there tomatoes she grew in her own garden and fertilized with her own shit. She insisted that they were her tomatoes and she could fertilize them however she wanted to. Then she acted like others were being rude and picky for not eating them.

***

My mother seemed to be conflicted about how honest to be about her mother. She had a lot of rage at her mother, but she didn't want to explain what medical abuse was because this would make people more likely to catch her also. She told me repeatedly that she always got sick when she came home from college because she was just so exhausted and could finally let go and collapse. Later, when I mentioned she said this, she was shocked. She just kept saying, "I can't believe I said that." She told me that's not why she got sick, but she wouldn't tell me why she got sick.

<u>Doctor's Offices</u>

There was a doctor's office in the lobby of the building we lived in. Sometimes, my mother would get an appointment there. Other times, she would just sit in the waiting room even though she didn't have an appointment. I would be bored to death, just like any little kid in a waiting room. The difference was we weren't waiting for anything a lot of the time. The front desk workers would keep telling her to go away. Eventually, she stopped the behavior when it was clear it wasn't going to be tolerated anymore.

***

We lived near a large hospital that would eventually be shut down as a result of a Medicaid fraud scandal in which some people died of unnecessary procedures. The hospital and records were left abandoned, and eventually, it was all torn down. What happened to me in that hospital? I have some very old, very cloudy, very bad memories. Were we living near that hospital on purpose?

***

When I was a little kid, my mother took me to a dermatologist's office for my vitiligo. I wasn't going for treatment. I was going for him to take photos for documentation. I didn't want to. My mother insisted we had to go, and I needed to be good and let him take whatever photos he wanted. I was self-conscious. Others had made a big deal of it in the past, and I didn't like being treated like I was different. When we got there, he told her how glad he was that we had agreed to this and that it would be helping him out. He explained that a lot of other people had said no but that this would be perfect for some sort of book or journal article he was working on. I didn't want to be in one of those, but my mother had been very clear that I wasn't allowed to say no or act uncomfortable. He did the right thing by trying to make sure I was comfortable and ok with it, but he didn't know I'd been coached. He had specifically declined to do the same thing with other patients because they had expressed discomfort. He began snapping photos and remarking what a great set of examples it was. As he went on, he began to see my discomfort and unhappiness. He asked me about it, and I explained to him that I knew I wasn't allowed to act like that. He put the camera down, realizing what was going on.

***

There was a large children's hospital downtown that my mother would sometimes drag me to for various reasons. They had a big billing office downstairs with murals painted on the wall. We would spend a lot of time there. My mother would talk their ears off whenever she got the chance. I would suffer in boredom, wondering when we would get to leave. The workers would also suffer in boredom as my mother droned on and on. Finally, one day, one of them had enough. She scolded my mother. There were parents of seriously ill children there who actually needed their help, and she was wasting their time. We spent less time there after that, though we still went back from time to time.

Random

One year, an influencer or talk show got it into my mother's head that it would be fashionable to put all the old Christmas cards from over the years into a basket to display during the holiday season. I was going through them one day when I came across one from my father's mother mentioning me having reconstructive surgery. I asked my mother about it. She confiscated the card and insisted that I not look at any more until she had a chance to go through them all.

***

My mother once told a story about how, on a Christmas before I was born, everyone on my father's side of the family except for her and my father got terribly ill from food poisoning. When I asked his family about it, they suggested that it had been her doing, but they wouldn't get into it.

***

My mother once threw a fit inside the little food market we used to go to because they started carrying just multivitamins instead of all the individual vitamins sold separately. It wasn't a big box store but just a little independent market where people in the neighborhood shopped. They'd checked with all of their customers and realized they could save money by just stocking the multivitamins. The customers would save money that way, too. My mother took all the vitamins that were in the multivitamins separately, which is why they thought it would be ok with her to just take the multivitamin. It was not. The next thing I knew, she was screaming in the aisle, yelling at them for this. She had wanted to take them all individually.

***

My mother would occasionally decide that a random person in her life had terrible allergies. Allergies were kind of a go-to catch-all for her. One year, she made a big to-do about the idea that her sister-in-law was so allergic to cats that her parents would have to lock the cats in the basement so that my aunt wouldn't throw up. In another incident, she claimed that an uncle of hers was so allergic to peanuts that if his wife ate peanut butter ice cream and then kissed him later in the day, he would die. He had no idea what she was talking about when this came up later. In another incident, she claimed that her adoptive father was terribly allergic to metal and could never touch it.

***

My mother would also occasionally decide that a random person in her life had some sort of debilitating mental illness. On a different holiday, she decided that her sister-in-law was locked up in a bedroom, unable to interact with the rest of the family because her depression was so bad. She did this multiple times. When this sister-in-law would show up in some other part of the house totally fine and enjoying the holiday with others, my mother would insist that she had just gotten better, as if this was somehow plausible.

***

When I was in elementary school, I would sometimes stub and jamb my toe. My mother convinced me that the way to fix it so it didn't hurt anymore was to slam it really hard again. Kids on the playground told me she lied because she wanted to hurt me. I didn't believe them. I think it was because I couldn't emotionally.

***

For a long time, I was vegetarian because of the trauma of what she had done to me and what she had done to animals and the connection between that. She was stricter about my vegetarianism than I was and even forbade sharing serving utensils between dishes. I think changing my diet accidentally presented her with an opportunity to keep me sick in a way that would avoid detection. If someone took a serving utensil from dish to dish, she would take it and throw it in with the dirty dishes so they couldn't do that again. She tried to play it off as if she was just obsessive-compulsive or quirky. Looking back on it, though, I now realize that she was avoiding detection. If everyone who shared a serving utensil with me also got sick, we would figure it out.

***

For a time, she was slipping something into our food or drink that would make my pinky finger and the pinky fingers of those who'd shared food with me tremor. When I got away from her, these just went away. I don't know much about medications, as I don't have any medical training, but I think she may have been testing out her own psychiatric meds on us. This may have been a form of Munchausen abuse, or it may have been her paranoid attempt to investigate what medication she was being prescribed, or it may have been both.

***

My mother always made a big deal of not going to buffets because of what people do to them, as she said. Before I realized what she was up to, I never understood why she had a paranoia of what others might be doing to buffets.

***

My mother always made a big deal of not being put on life support. She would always make it very clear that if anything ever happened to her to make her vegetative or completely incapacitated, she didn't want to be kept alive artificially. In other words, she never wanted the tables to be turned.

***

My mother sometimes kept things in old jars in the spice rack that were not spices. She would use emptied-out spice containers to disguise what she was doing. One had one type of beetle in it. Another had another type of beetle. They were well organized. It was not that bugs had gotten into the spices. They were separated out by type into different containers. I don't know what she was doing with them.

***

My mother would sometimes practice opening a candy bar or granola bar just so without tearing the wrapper at all so that she could stick the ends back together and make it look like they'd never been opened. She knew people were avoiding unwrapped food around her, and she was finding a way around that.

***

One day, when I was a little kid, my mother took me for a picnic in the park. I insisted that the food smelled, that there was something wrong with it, and that I didn't want to eat it. She got mad and insisted. I was trying to take little nibbles and avoid eating the whole thing. Some neighbors saw us and stopped by to chat. They heard the argument. They saw something I didn't and were horrified and told me to stop eating. They scolded my mother and told her not to do that, but then they left and never reported it to anyone.

***

One day, when I was little, my mother took me to an amusement park when I was very badly injured. It was one of my so-called "accidents." I was in terrible pain and only wanted to rest at home. She dragged me to an amusement park on a hot day in the middle of the summer. I trailed after her miserably, begging to be allowed to go home. Some other mothers at the park saw what was going on and yelled at her that she needed to take me home and that I was in pain. They could see that I was badly injured. She had wanted to be seen with an injured child, but it had not occurred to her that she would get this reaction. She was aiming for sympathy and fawning attention, but she didn't have enough empathy to correctly predict how others with empathy would react. They scolded her. She became defiant. We separated from those parents, but she continued dragging me around the park. Maybe she was hoping that others would have a different reaction, or maybe she was just still enjoying my misery.

***

When I was a little kid, I used to ask my mother why I'd had hernia surgery. She answered that it was to get rid of my hernias, of course. I said I knew the second hernia surgery was to get rid of the hernias, but asked why I'd had the first hernia surgery to give me the hernias in the first place when I hadn't had them before. She insisted this never happened. I remembered it distinctly. I always insisted that this had happened, and she always insisted that it hadn't. The two surgeries had been in separate states. They both happened when I was very young.

***

When I was a teenager, I got a flu and told my mother I was going to try to sweat it out by napping under a bunch of heavy blankets even though I was already feeling too hot from the fever. She told me not to. I went into my room, closed the door, and did it anyway. It worked. I woke a few hours later, weak, tired, and dehydrated, but feeling much better. I could tell the sickness was gone, and I was so relieved. I was drenched in sweat and had to lean against the wall as I walked, but it was worth it. I sat down in the kitchen and drank a bunch of cold juice. My mother was irritated and just kept saying that I hadn't had permission to do that.

***

When I was a kid, my mother kept files on each person and pet in the household in her computer. We weren't allowed to look at them, not even the ones with our own names on them. Once, when she wasn't looking, I tried taking a peek at mine and the cats'. At the time, it was totally incomprehensible to me. Each was just one big block of text without any paragraphs or punctuation. There were no individual sentences. I saw words I recognized here and there, but I didn't even recognize most of the words. I now realize these were dosages of medications and chemical substances.

***

When I was a little girl, I saw a TV show where someone mentioned cradle cap. I asked my mother what it was. She said it was a disease that little babies get and that she'd always hoped I would get it, but I never did. I asked why she'd hoped I would get it. She couldn't explain.

2. Terror Threats

81

About

<u>About Terror Threats & MBP</u>

What do MBP abusers get out of terror threats that they also get out of MBP abuse?

- They alone know that they are pulling the strings and exerting this power over others.

- A mysterious threat, like a mysterious illness, creates drama and throws others into distress.

- It elicits fear. Some MBP abusers, such as my mother, enjoy other's fear.

- Other MSBP cases involving this pattern: The Kristen Gilbert case is another such example. She called in bomb threats.

Also, although terror and arson are not the same thing, they overlap. It's worth looking at the fire-starting column in the pattern spotting chart if you're studying this section.

High School Bomb Threats

Incident Tags/Trigger Warnings
terror, threats, bombs, drills, evacuations, school lockdowns
Incident

When I was in high school, another student in the class had been in trouble for calling in bomb threats. Unaware of my mother's tendencies, I told my family about this after I learned of it. A few days later, we were evacuated from the school for what I thought was a fire drill at the time. The fire alarm was going off, and we were being ushered out of the building. We all clustered on the sidewalk as usual in a fire drill.

That's when something unusual happened outside of the normal fire drill routine. A few men, from what I thought at first was the fire department, angrily approached the group of students I was standing in. One of them started yelling, but I couldn't understand what he was talking about. At first, I didn't even know I was the one he was yelling at. I was in a group of students clustered together, and I just assumed it had to be directed at one of the other ones since what he was saying made no sense to me. He was yelling at whoever was behind the threat, and I knew that was not me.

A few of the teachers interrupted him to inform them that they were wrong. At first, he was so amped up that he wouldn't listen to them. This was in the days before cell phones, and I did not live near the school. They explained to him that even though the caller had claimed to be me, that could not possibly be true. The call had come from the landline at my house, and they had been able to account for me all day long at that point, making it physically impossible that it had been me. Eventually, they got him to listen. They walked off in a huff. I was still too confused by the whole thing to even be upset. I just couldn't understand what had happened.

My mother was the only one who could have made the call. All other family was at work or school. No one else had access to the house. My mother never faced any consequences. They never contacted DCFS or pursued charges. I think the lack of accountability had to do with money, but it may also have been laziness, fear, or all of the above.

Leaving The Time Bomb

Don't leave a ticking time bomb. They confirmed that there was no bomb at the school but failed to do anything about the metaphorical ticking bomb at the same time. Don't fail to stop a ticking time bomb once you've already cleared the area for a physical bomb.

<u>Legislation</u>

Mandated reporting needs to cover all schools, not just public schools. It also needs to cover all abusive and illegal activity. Schools cannot be allowed to choose to avoid scandal at the expense of the safety of society at large.

<u>Advice for Third Parties and Victims</u>

Do not let it go. If a school has helped brush something like this under the rug in order to handle it internally, you can talk to the press or even just submit an anonymous tip. If you are being pressured to go along with keeping a school safety issue quiet, you can help prevent tragedy by speaking out. You don't even need to identify yourself. A good journalist will be happy to accommodate keeping you anonymous.

The Mall Garage

<u>Incident</u>

When I was a teenager, my mother and I went to the mall one day. This was one of the big popular malls downtown that we had been to many times before. She had previously been asked to leave various stores within the mall as a result of her behavior throughout the years but had not been banned from the mall entirely.

This time, things went differently. We approached the entrance to the underground parking garage with her in the driver's seat and me in the passenger seat as usual. Security guards were stationed at the entrance to the garage, stopping each car. I couldn't tell what they were doing. When we approached, they checked the underside of the car with mirrors. They wouldn't let us in. I couldn't understand why. The conversation between them seemed to suggest that there had been a previous incident between them, but I couldn't catch any details. I still don't entirely know what happened here. I know, given context clues, that it probably belongs in this section.

<u>Legislation</u>

Mandated reporting needs to be extended to private security. When behavior escalates to a certain level, it needs to be on file with law enforcement even if the property owner does not intend to take any further action.

After Childhood

<u>Incident Tags/Trigger Warnings</u>

terror threats

<u>Incident</u>

As stated in other parts of this book, I generally only cover the first eighteen years of my life in this book. I have included this, however, because I think there is some critical stuff to mention here. Throughout my adult life, I've had to wonder if an incident here or there was connected to my mother. Certain types of FDIA behaviors are easier to get away from. After a certain age, you can physically keep someone trying to poison you away from you. After a certain age, you have control of your own medical decisions. This is not, however, the way it works with terror threats. Subsequent books that cover other periods of my life will have more on this. The terror threats section of this book is one of the shortest for two reasons:

1. I believe there is a lot of stuff in this category during my childhood that I'm still unaware of.

2. A lot of the threats my mother made happened after my childhood during periods this book doesn't cover.

I don't want anyone reading this to mistake the shortness of this section for an indication that such behavior is less common among FDIA abusers or less of a problem. Neither of those things is true. Please see the Terror Threats/Terror Acts column in the pattern chart. It is also worth having a look at the Fire Setting column in this context.

3. Infrastructure and Transportation Sabotage

About

<u>About Infrastructure and Transportation Sabotage & MBP</u>
Other MBP cases involving this pattern: Although infrastructure sabotage and arson are not the same thing, they overlap. It's worth looking at the fire-starting column in the pattern spotting chart if you're studying this section.

Throughout this book, you will observe categories in which my mother hurts beings or things other than people as well. This includes pets, plants, and vehicles. This is another such category.

Sometimes, her infrastructure and transportation sabotage involved ways to inconvenience or endanger people. This overlaps with sadism discussed in other sections. Other times, it overlaps with the Hurting to be Right section. Other times, it overlaps with the glomming onto older ladies as a caretaker. Other times, it overlaps with attention-seeking behaviors.

My mother had a lot of motivations for transportation and infrastructure sabotage. Motivation does not unite all these stories. What ties them all together is the fact that she decided to allow herself to do this to others in order to get what she wanted. This is a major theme in this section and also throughout the other sections of this book.

The Transformer

Incident Tags/Trigger Warnings

power outages, fires, explosions

Incident

When I was in junior high, my mother ordered an old-fashioned oil and wick lamp from a mail-order catalog. It seemed to be a big deal to her. She thought it was really cool. Everyone else seemed to think that she'd wasted money on something stupid. She insisted that we would get a lot of use out of it, and no one else agreed.

One day, after I'd gotten home from school, the power went out in our building. It was a high-rise building with a certain percentage of retirees and people in ill health who relied on the elevators. My mother jumped into action. She didn't seem all that surprised. She pulled out the oil lamp for us to do homework by, making a big deal of it. She then went out into the fire escape. The building had two large concrete fire escapes. They were matching internal stairwells with double fire doors and fire hoses on every floor. I remember them generally smelling of dust and paint. The stairs and walls were concrete with no padding.

On this night, the fire escape was crowded with people trying to get out of the building with the elevators out of service. Some of them were having difficulty. My mother took it upon herself to begin "guiding" an older woman downstairs against her wishes.

Many had just gone to the stairwell as a meeting place to gather information from each other, knowing that some would be there evacuating. Some on the landings had no plans of evacuating, knowing that it was safer for them to stay in place rather than to try to manage dozens of flights of stairs. They also knew that they could not possibly get back up that number of stairs in their health and wanted to be sure to be able to stay in their apartments that night.

My mother took hold of the woman despite her objections. The woman had no choice but to continue to step down, knowing a fall could be dangerous if my mother dragged her down the stairs. Others tried to stop her, but by using words instead of physical force. I believe that was because they didn't understand that my mother understood. They believed that if they cleared up the confusion, the behavior would stop. Eventually, the others succeeded in backing her off, but only after she'd taken her down several flights of stairs.

My mother's next stunt was to call into a radio show. One of my sibling's classmates had a father who worked in local radio. They were running a pre-recorded summary of local news included in a loop with their other programming that night. The power outage was included in this. They estimated that about 100 people were affected, a low estimate for a 55-story building, though the estimate didn't much matter, and the rest of the story seemed correct. She seemed pretty upset at the low estimate and kept on repeating that it was more like 1,000 people. She called into the show and left a voicemail, very peeved, correcting the estimate harshly. They found this very amusing and added it to the broadcast along with their commentary, making fun of it. She called back repeatedly, at one point prompting me to back her up on the facts, which I awkwardly complied with.

I had spent the evening doing homework, listening to the radio show on the battery-operated radio, and going into the main halls and stairwells to see what I could learn. I had no suspicion of my mother at the time despite the fuss over the oil lamp, the strange behavior in the stairwell, and the calls into the radio show. I, like a lot of people around my mother, had a blind spot. It simply didn't occur to me that anyone would do such things on purpose. I began wondering what had caused the outage. I began to speculate out loud. My mother explained that the outage had started with an explosion in which a transformer caught on fire. I asked how she knew this, and she provided some kind of an answer which I did not understand. Some people from the building came by at one point to talk to her about it. I couldn't understand why that would happen. Ultimately, I don't believe they could prove anything because otherwise, we would have been kicked out of the building years before we eventually moved.

<u>Points To Make</u>

Note the similarity between this and the story of the person in the wheelchair who needed the elevator in the random section. This incident also has some similarities with the Hurting to be Right section in terms of the fixation on the oil lamp. This incident also has some similarities with the write-up of her fixation on older ladies in the Traditional MBP section.

The Rafts

<u>Incident Tags/Trigger Warnings</u>

Stranding, jungle, poop

<u>Incident</u>

When I was about ten, my mother went on a trip to the jungle to visit Mayan ruins while we stayed with our father in the city. When she came back, she had lots of stories to tell. She told a story of how one night, while they were sleeping, someone had cut all their river rafts loose and let them float down the river far away. This was dangerous because it left them stranded, and they had to hike very far with no other way to get out. Some people had a very tough time with it. I asked why anyone would do this, and she said that's just what some people would do there. I continued to question her, not out of distrust but out of confusion. She claimed that bandits had done it, but this story fell apart because nothing had been stolen. I didn't understand. She talked about everyone's reaction when they woke up the next morning and found out. I asked about her reaction when she found out. She told me she wasn't surprised because she already knew. I didn't understand that either.

Later, I was at a gathering where a group of people who had been on the trip met up. Apparently, on the trip, she had dropped trow and shit only a few feet away from where they were eating in an effort to prove how continental she was. She had cut the rafts in retaliation for a bad reaction to this.

<u>Points To Make</u>

Notice the similarity between this and the shitting incident in the Neighbors section. Also, note the similarity between this and the public defecation column in the pattern chart.

Gas Stoves

93

My mother had a strong dislike for random things. One of these things was gas stoves and appliances. Anywhere we moved, she insisted on electric stoves. This was in the days when electric stoves were the kind with exposed coils instead of flat glass tops. I could never understand why she was so offended by gas stoves. This was in the 1980's. There was no controversy over gas appliances at the time like there is today. At the time, they were not considered to be bad for the environment or the air quality at home, or at least there was no public attention on the matter. I think that her issue with gas appliances was that she couldn't be trusted around them. I believe she knew that she had bad impulses around something that could be used for suicide, murder, poisoning, and explosions.

Elevator Shafts and Stairwells

My mother liked to mess with the elevators and stairwells in our building. I think that part of it had to do with enjoying inconveniencing people, and part of it had to do with attention. There may have been other motives I'm not aware of. She would sometimes press all the buttons in the elevator like little kids would for a prank. She would sometimes push the emergency stop button for no reason in an elevator full of people. Sometimes, she would drop her keys down the elevator shaft so that maintenance would have to stop the elevator and go get a long stick with a magnet on the end to fish them out. This particular behavior started after she witnessed it happen to someone else. Another time, she witnessed maintenance unlock a maintenance access stairwell on the sun deck when someone dropped something down it. After that, she made up a game in which we would send our toy cars racing down there and then call them, pretending that she hadn't encouraged the behavior. They were irritated with her when they figured out what was going on. She didn't seem to care, but she stopped the behavior when she realized they were no longer going to respond to those calls.

The Playground

breaking toys

Incident

When I was a kid, I had a favorite playground downtown and a favorite spring horse at that playground. It was one of those standard bobbing animals on the end of a spring with handlebars that kids could pretend to ride. If my mother was going downtown for some reason, she would sometimes take us there.

One day, I asked if we could go there again, and she told me that the playground was closed down because someone had vandalized it and torn it apart. In fact, it had been so severely damaged and in such a prominent place that there had been a local news story on it. This was not the first time that the playground had been hit, but it was an escalation in the severity. I remember wondering why they always seemed to focus on the area of the playground that I happened to like best. I remember trying to understand why anyone would do something like that. She got very defensive. The more I tried to understand why someone would do something just for meanness that they could not get anything out of, the more irritated and defensive she got. She repeated several times that I was just lucky I didn't feel like I needed to do stuff like that.

This was a theme for her. She would often play the victim when confronted with something she'd done. The narrative she'd convinced herself of seemed to be that anyone who didn't experience cruel impulses or who chose not to act on bad impulses had it unfairly easy. In her narrative, she could steal from people, brutalize people, sabotage people, or destroy property, and those people were just lucky that they were not inside her head. This was her approach not just to the playground destruction but also to much more serious behavior. Often, with outright traumatizing behavior, the message was still the same.

4. Crime Framing

About

<u>About Crime Framing & MBP</u>

Crime framing connects to FDIA behaviors in several ways:

- It can be motivated in part by sadism.

- It involves sick stories (crime as a societal sick story).

- It involves telling dramatic stories of tragedy, such as death stories.

- If others are accused of a crime, it distracts from the crimes the perpetrator is actually committing.

- It fits a pattern of placing feelings about oneself or aspects of oneself onto others and casting oneself in opposition to that. For my mother in, specific feelings about herself or aspects of herself that she did this with included: sickness, scandal, hunger, humiliation, terror, physical pain, ostracization, addiction, judgment, powerlessness, badness, shame, mental illness, infantilization, invalidation, stupidity, dirtiness, and criminal tendencies.

- Other MBP cases involving this pattern: In Sickened by Julie Gregory, she describes her grandmother telling a made-up story about an African American man who gave her a popcorn ball, which she later claimed was poisoned. This connects to the crime framing section and the societal sick stories section because of her involvement of race in the story.

The Aquarium

<u>Incident Tags/Trigger Warnings</u>

Crime framing

<u>Incident</u>

When I was a small child, my mother would take us to the local aquarium. My favorite part was this large cylindrical tank that housed a variety of fish, sharks, and rays. It was a popular attraction. Visitors would crowd around it to watch feedings. It was packed with kids and parents trying to get a look. Pick pockets would sometimes take advantage of this to grab some wallets. It was a good opportunity for them because the area was dimly lit, everyone was looking in the same direction, and everyone was pressed together so that they wouldn't notice or think anything of it if one more person bumped into them. On one occasion, a woman near us called out because she caught a man with his hand in her purse. This caused a commotion as everyone turned to look. People began shouting. It caused quite a stir.

The next time we went to the aquarium, a strange thing happened. We went back to the same location. A man came through panhandling as sometimes happened there, especially on free days. My mother took her entire wallet out of her purse and handed it to him. He was immediately suspicious and hesitant to take it. He struggled between financial desperation and how off my mother's behavior was. At first, he refused to take it, telling her he only wanted a few dollars and that she should keep her wallet. She refused to give up or be talked out of it. She kept insisting that he take the entire wallet, remove the money, and leave the rest of it in a specific place she described to him. He kept refusing. She kept insisting. They went back and forth. He was hungry and probably too badly in need of money to walk away from the interaction entirely. He looked alarmed, but she was smiling reassuringly and exuding confidence. Eventually, she convinced him, and he went on his way with her wallet.

I did not understand the interaction. I was too young to understand that she was attempting to set him up. I was still at that age in which the vast majority of adult behavior is just lumped into an inexplicable tangle in a child's mind. I asked her about why she did that at the time, but she brushed off the questions repeatedly until I let the subject drop.

We lingered at the aquarium, visiting different exhibits until the police approached us. Someone had reported my mother's wallet found on the counter of the men's bathroom. They caught the man who had been seen with it and were preparing to take him back with them to be booked. My mother acted surprised and claimed that she hadn't even felt anyone's hand in her bag. He protested that he had done as instructed, but no one believed an obviously ridiculous and nonsensical story like that.

I was so young and naive that I still didn't realize what was happening. As the talk between the adults escalated, I believed I knew what was going on. I believed she had genuinely forgotten that this was what she had instructed him to do before. I piped in and reminded her. She attempted to brush this off, and I tried harder to remind her. I described the events in detail in an attempt to remind her. The dynamics then changed quickly. The police let the man go and continued talking to my mother. Eventually, the police left, apparently having decided not to document the behavior.

<u>Commentary</u>

Crime framing is another FDIA behavior that can quickly ruin lives or even turn deadly. Whether you are law enforcement, a witness, or a victim, please document the behavior and do what you can to make sure that documentation is visible across jurisdictions. This documentation could save someone's life in a future case.

The Dog

Animals, animal abuse, crime framing, sex toys

<u>Incident</u>

It was a cold winter day. I was a teenager. I walked along a row of shops in our neighborhood with my mother. We usually just passed by if we saw a dog tied outside a shop. It was a pretty common occurrence. She pointed one out, which was unusual. I just kept going, as that's what we usually did, but she insisted on stopping. At first, I urged her to just keep going. It was cold, and the owner was just inside for a moment, as usual, when people stopped into shops with dogs along that stretch. I wanted to move along. She displayed an unusual fascination this time. She insisted that the dog had been left out a very long time in the cold, long enough that it could be dangerous. I knew she didn't know this because we'd just come upon it. I told her this, but she brushed it off. After I kept on repeating this fact, she insisted that she had been out walking earlier and had seen it in the same place hours before. That wasn't plausible. The shop was small, and no one would have spent hours shopping in it. She also had not mentioned walking along the same stretch hours before until that moment.

She took a small plastic shopping bag she'd been carrying and tied it to the dog's leash. I asked her what it was and why she'd tied it to the dog. No matter how many times I questioned her, she insisted that the bag had been tied to the dog when we found it. She began to make a fuss and draw a crowd around us. This row of shops was popular around the holidays, and a crowd gathered easily. She began suggesting that maybe we could find some clues as to the owner of the dog if we looked in the shopping bag attached to it. People were generally reluctant to violate that privacy, but she kept up the act and tore the bag open. I did not recognize the object in the bag, but the adult's reactions told me it was something they were weirded out by. Someone explained that it was some sort of sex toy.

The dog owner exited the shop, probably wondering what the crowd was about, and saw the commotion. He was clearly concerned when he realized what was happening. He angrily told my mother to get that thing away from his dog. An argument ensued, with the stunned onlookers trying to figure out who was telling the truth. I got the impression from him that he had dealt with her before and knew that she was a problem, though I didn't get any details. Someone in the crowd asked me if I had seen and I said that she'd tied the bag on. He left with the dog, and the crowd dispersed. We continued on our way, my mother still insisting on her version of events.

The Pick Up

Incident Tags/Trigger Warnings
missing children, kidnapping, crime framing

Incident

When I was a little girl, I had a friend in the building next door. I'll call her Jamie, although that was not her name. One day, while Jamie, Jamie's mother, my mother, and I were hanging out, Jamie's mother told my mother a story about a scare she'd recently had. She had gone to Jamie's school at the usual pick-up time, but Jamie wasn't there. The school didn't know what had happened. In those days, schools weren't always as careful about who little kids were picked up by. She, of course, was beside herself with worry. It took some time to figure out what had happened, but eventually, it turned out that Jamie had been invited to get into a car with a friend without notifying her parents. The friend's parents had apparently not seen any problem with this. Being so young, Jamie and I didn't really understand the level of concern she displayed. It was obvious that this was something that was a big deal to grown-ups, though. Jamie's mother had told the story to various moms and had gotten a lot of sympathy and reaction. This was not what she was going for. She was simply sharing the story as one would, but naturally, parents had a reaction to the story.

A few days later, I was at home with my mother when she asked me to run an errand for her. She usually practiced coercive control and was less likely than the average parent to let me out of her sight. This time was different, though. She wanted me to go downstairs alone, out the lobby, and across the driveway to return a rental video in the strip mall next door. The entire journey from the lobby to the video store would be visible to her from the window of our apartment. This was unusual because we usually checked out and returned videos together.

As I exited the lobby, two people in the driveway waved and called to me enthusiastically. I recognized them from the building. They lived there, and we often saw them in the common areas. She was a single mom, and he was her son. I'll call them Olivia and Oliver (not their actual names). They invited me into the car. I told them no. I wasn't allowed to go off with third parties even if I knew them. That much had been made very clear to me after the story involving Jamie. They kept on insisting that I get in the car with them and that we go to the movies together. They seemed to be under the impression that we had a play date, which, as far as I knew, wasn't true. My mother had just told me to go return the VHS tape and come right back without talking to anyone. Still, this mother and son thought we had been planning on going to the movies together. I couldn't understand why they thought that. It was just too strange for any of us to think that we were walking into a setup, so we each believed the other was mistaken.

I eventually continued on my way to the store, dropped off the tape, turned around, and returned to our apartment. My mother then asked me who she had seen me talking to in the driveway as if she hadn't led them to believe that they were meant to pick me up in the driveway at that time. Can you imagine what could have happened to them if I had gotten into the car?

<u>Advice for Victims</u>

Today, you have a way to protect yourself from this type of behavior that you would not have had back then. Always send a text confirmation of plans, especially if kids or vulnerable adults are involved or if you just feel that a person is off. If you have to talk to the police later because someone like my mother set you up, you are going to need that text. Don't just reference plans. Reference what they said. For example, thank them for an invitation, clarify what they meant by a meeting location, etc. These abusers are 100% responsible for their behavior, and the victims are not to blame. Still, it's best to protect yourself as a default behavior whenever you can.

The Graffiti

Incident Tags/Trigger Warnings

crime framing

Incident

About a year before we moved out of our apartment to a house nearby, some new neighbors moved into the building on our floor. My mother took an immediate dislike to them. They were young parents who had gotten their apartment with the help of their parents. They were about half my parents' age. I'm not sure what the source of the conflict was. My mother may have resented that they had achieved a very similar lifestyle much earlier on in life. It may have been that they had said something completely harmless in conversation that my mother had taken the wrong way. Both envy and falsely perceived slights were very common reasons for my mother to take a dislike to people. She would make fun of them, bad mouth them, and talk about them as if they were below us when we were alone in the apartment, out of earshot. This went on for quite a while. The tension seemed to grow as the months went on, though I'm not sure if that was mutual or one-sided. I was always kept away from them, so I never found out.

One day, my mother pointed out some fresh scratch marks carved into the wood paneling in one of the elevators. It was the name of the young father she disliked so much. She told me that he had carved his name in. She held it up as proof of his character. I wondered why he would want to do that, and I also wondered how he could be so stupid as to carve his own name into wood paneling just below an elevator security camera.

A while later, we were in the elevator again, and I noticed the Graffiti again. I wondered why they hadn't replaced it and billed him for it. She said that they didn't think he did it but that they thought she did it. I wondered how they could think that she did it when it had been done just under the security camera, and all they had to do was check the footage. Shortly after, we began looking for a new place to live. I believe that management had gotten tired of dealing with her over the years and that this was the opportunity they needed to get us out of the building. I don't know this last part for sure, but I think it's likely.

<u>Points To Make</u>

This, like many incidents, could be placed in more than one section. I put it in crime framing, but it could just as easily have fit in the creepy toward neighbors section. If she was trying to prove that he was a bad guy, it could also have been placed in the hurting to be right section.

<u>Advice for Victims</u>

Does your building or neighborhood association have cameras? Do you have cameras? You may end up dealing with someone like this indefinitely if you don't have proof. Security cameras aren't just for keeping creepy people away from you. They can also help clear your name when you're faced with a wrongful accusation. They can save you hassle and money in the long run.

The Christmas Ornaments

Incident Tags/Trigger Warnings

stealing, crime framing, gossip

Incident

When I was in high school, my mother decorated the trees in front of our house with blue ornaments for Christmas. They were the shiny ball ornaments, but there weren't enough of them to look good or make sense. These were not evergreen trees but trees that were bare except for a smattering of bulb ornaments. She claimed that there had been more ornaments but that a neighbor boy had stolen them. She wove an elaborate story of him going through a troubled phase. She claimed that she had seen him. She claimed that she had found the ornaments later in the front yard of a house in between his and ours. No one really seemed to believe her. She later made a point of taking me for a walk and then, at a point in the walk, pretended to have found more to point out to me. Others later claimed that she had placed them there herself. The people claiming she had done it were our family members and family friends. I'm not sure if the boy and his family ever found out about it. I'm not even sure if the boy she told the story about ever actually existed.

The Clothes

stealing, crime framing

<u>Incident</u>

One day, I noticed my favorite clothes missing from my closet. I asked my mother about them, and she told me that someone had broken in and stolen them. Later, she took me for a play date at the playground by our building. One of the little girls at the play date was wearing the clothes she had told me were stolen. I immediately accused her of stealing my clothes. We began to argue. The whole story came out in front of the other kids and parents present. The other mother, realizing what had happened, became extremely uncomfortable. She had words with my mother, then left. I didn't realize what had happened until looking back on the incident when I was older. I'm not sure what the motive was here. It may have simply been to cause a fight and cause others discomfort.

5. Physical Sadism

About

<u>About Physical Sadism & MBP</u>

My mother was, in large part, motivated by sadism. Although not all MBP abusers are primarily motivated by sadism, all have a tolerance for other's suffering that goes well beyond that of the average person. I believe sadism is a more common motivation behind MBP than most think. Sadism is the 2nd most populated column in the pattern chart, second only to the stealing/fraud column.

- Examples of other MBP cases involving this pattern:

- Others recalled Nurse Cullen killing and abusing animals prior to his crimes against humans. After he was caught, he attempted to argue that he was a mercy killer, but this was clearly a lie because he sometimes killed healthy people who were about to be discharged from the hospital. In addition, he often caused his victims pain.

- In Sickened, Julie Gregory describes the high her mother seemed to experience after a painful and embarrassing medical procedure performed on a boy in her mother's care.

- Christopher Duntsch purposefully botched surgeries, causing victims lifelong excruciating pain.

- For a longer list, please see the pattern chart.

Pushing Down Stairs

<u>Incident Tags/Trigger Warnings</u>

being thrown down stairs

<u>Incident</u>

I was in elementary school when my mother took me to visit my father's mother without him. I think he was probably away on business. We were staying at her house for a few days. It was a two-level house with a first floor and a finished basement below that, instead of a traditional two-level house. We were standing upstairs in the kitchen talking with my grandmother. I was going to go downstairs to the room I was staying in. I walked to the top of the stairs, but then my mother called to me, and I turned to address her. It was a trap.

Suddenly, she was right up against me at the top of the stairs. She informed me angrily that if I took one step down the stairs to put distance between us or tried to step past her back into the room, she would throw me down the stairs. This threat came out of nowhere. She hadn't been angry a moment before, and nothing had happened. She kept me teetering on the edge of the stairs. I had to tense my body to keep my balance. She was in a rage, yelling and hissing threats. My grandmother attempted to de-escalate the situation with words as if this was an argument between two adults and not a grown woman threatening a child with serious harm out of the blue.

I wasn't sure what was happening because I was too young to understand my mother's dynamic. I now realize that she was enjoying herself. She kept me there for what felt like an eternity. I was attempting to speak logic to her and calm her, not realizing that this would do no good. Eventually, she got tired of the production and threw me down the stairs. She tossed me with such force that I flew past most of the stairs, injuring my leg badly on one of the last few steps. I tried to pick myself up, but I was in pain, and my right leg wouldn't work. I yelled that my leg was hurt and I couldn't walk. No one came to help.

My grandmother yelled at my mother but did nothing to help me. This may have been a strategy to distract my mother and keep her away from me until she had settled down. Maybe it was a reaction to abuse in my grandmother's past. I don't know.

I believe I was in shock at that point, but I had also grown up in such an environment, so I reacted by trying different strategies to get my leg to work again and then going on about my day. I had a bad limp for a few days, but there was no question of going to the doctor. That would have triggered a call to the authorities, and no one in the house would allow that to happen.

Slamming Back

<u>Incident Tags/Trigger Warnings</u>
physical violence, turning a blind eye to abuse

<u>Incident</u>

When I was a little kid, my family traveled to Oregon to watch a relative compete in a sand castle contest. The night before the contest, we settled into the rental we'd gotten. There weren't enough beds, so someone had to sleep on an old day bed with a metal frame and an old mattress out in the living room. I volunteered. It was comfortable, and I was looking forward to a good night's sleep.

Just before I drifted off to sleep, my mother came out of my parent's bedroom, grabbed me, pulled me from the bed, and began to slam my back against the metal rail that supported the mattress. I couldn't get her to stop no matter what I did, and I was in terrible pain. I just started saying, "It's not fair" over and over again. It was my gut reaction to what was happening when I realized there was no escape and knew I had done nothing to deserve this. My mother was further enraged by this. It triggered something in her. She was angry that stuff was supposedly so much more unfair to her. She went on and on about this, about how it wasn't unfair to me and was unfair to her, as she continued to slam me against the rail. Eventually, she stopped, and I just crawled back into bed. There was nothing else I could do.

The next morning was supposed to be a good morning full of excitement about the contest. Relatives came over to our rental to socialize ahead of the contest and eat breakfast. I couldn't move. I couldn't physically get myself out of bed. I was in terrible pain. Everyone blamed it on the old bed. I was so hungry, but I couldn't get breakfast. They insisted that I could get up if I wanted to. I think most of them actually believed that because they didn't know what had happened the night before.

After a long time, I was able to get out of the bed with great difficulty. My body felt very old. I was stiff and could barely walk. I kept talking about how much my back hurt, but my relatives brushed it off.

We went to the beach to see the contest. It was cold and windy. The sky was blue with some wispy clouds. There were large crowds around. Areas where contestants were working were roped off. They had lots of those 5-gallon buckets for their work. I was wearing purple flower stretch shorts and an oversized top, as usual. What was meant to be a fun day was miserable. I was very hungry and aching. Those around me still believed I had chosen to stay in bed and skip breakfast, so they didn't pay it much attention.

At the end of the day, one of my father's relatives saw my back when my '80s oversized t-shirt slipped down, revealing some of the bruising. He was horrified. He yelled at my parents about how if they weren't his family, he would have reported them. He didn't report them, and as far as I know, he never spoke of it or addressed it in any way again.

<u>Points to Make</u>

If you're uncomfortable with addressing abuse in your family, you can make an anonymous report to the authorities. No one has to know it was you. Ignoring it doesn't make it go away, and yelling about it doesn't stop it. Some fail to report abuse because they are afraid of something bad happening to the abuser or because they're afraid of something bad happening to the family's reputation. In reality, failing to take steps to stop the abuse doesn't protect the abuser or the family's reputation. You can still wind up with a book like this written about your family. You can still wind up with a very public, very messy outing of the abuse after the child is grown. All failing to report really does is allow more years of abuse to pile up so that when it does come out, it is an avalanche of revelations that include both the abuser and the enablers. Think of how much shorter this book could have been, how many less horrifying things could have been in it if it had even existed at all. That opportunity has passed. If your abusive family member and your family reputation are really so important to you, then take steps to stop the abuse immediately.

The Inner Tube

Incident Tags/Trigger Warnings
Sadism, hurting children, drowning, water-boarding
Incident

I was a little kid, about four years old at the time. A neighbor from our building had dropped off her sons to play with us, and my mother had taken us to the pool. One of the sons was my age, and the other one was a toddler. We played in the water while the toddler floated alongside us in the little inner tube his mother had sent with him. My mother was in the pool with us.

Suddenly, my mother flipped the toddler upside down in the water so that the inner tube was floating upside down with his head underwater and his little legs flailing desperately. She laughed and encouraged us to laugh along with her, pointing to the frantic action of his legs. She did this multiple times. The lifeguard came over and scolded her. Amazingly, he did not call the authorities or the mother. She stopped because she did not want him to make a phone call, but he left the child with us and went back to his desk.

Later, when their mother came to pick her sons back up, I told her what had happened. She did not believe me. There was no possibility in her mind that she had left her child in the care of someone who would do that, and she would not be convinced otherwise. We never spoke of it again.

Legislation

Again, I will sound like a broken record: mandated reporting, mandated reporting, mandated reporting. Don't limit it to certain professions or certain institutions. It needs to apply to everyone.

Hot Baths

<u>Incident Tags/Trigger Warnings</u>

burning

<u>Incident</u>

When I was little, my mother often liked to make me take painfully hot baths. There was no real point in this other than sadism. She would fill the bathtub as full as possible with hot water and make me stay in for long periods of time. I would come out looking sunburned with a visible water line marked by an abrupt transition from pale white skin to bright red skin. My whole body would be a deep red.

Vengefulness

Incident Tags/Trigger Warnings
paranoia, vindictiveness, vengefulness, hostile attribution bias

Incident

My mother was always very paranoid and vindictive. She was hell-bent on revenge even when it wasn't rational to believe that anyone had actually done anything to her. She was always convinced. She always believed stuff had been done to get at her even when others logically couldn't have done it. I think this may have been tied to her sadism because if she believed that others were like her and had her motivations, that would mean that they would go out of their way to hurt her just for the fun of it. I think it was also tied to her sadism because it acted as a built-in excuse in her mind. It wasn't a valid excuse, but she treated it as one because she wanted one. Maybe she was a vindictive narcissist experiencing narcissistic rage. I don't know. I'm not a psychiatrist.

If my mother stubbed her toe, she would become convinced someone had moved furniture in a plot to get her to stub her toe. She would spend months doing the same in hopes of getting back at anyone who could have done it. Once wasn't enough. She'd found a behavior she liked, and she stuck with it. Every time someone stubbed their toe again, she got a payoff.

Once, she tore her clothes on the back of a chair. She spent weeks reaching over and sneaking edges of others' clothes over the rough spot that had snagged her until everyone else ended up with torn clothes. This wasn't enough. She kept doing it after everyone else had torn their clothes at least once. There was no end to her need to "get even." It didn't make sense for her to think anyone had done that to her in the first place, but she was convinced.

Once, when I was little, we were walking along a sidewalk together. She suddenly cried out in pain. There had been a sliver of glass in her shoe that had stuck her in the toe. I'm not sure how it had gotten there. Maybe it had been on the sidewalk. She suddenly became convinced that I had put it in her shoe. This was odd because I'd never done anything like this and because we'd been walking for some time before it happened. The fact that we had been walking for several minutes already didn't occur to her. I pointed this out. It was physically impossible because I hadn't even touched her or her shoe. I don't think there was a reason she blamed me other than the fact that she was looking at me when it happened and somehow associated it with me. Soon after this, I wound up with glass in my shoe.

I could go on with more examples like this, but they're all the same. She lived in a world inside her head where everyone thought like she did. This was miserable because living in a world with only people like her would be miserable.

Brushing

Incident Tags/Trigger Warnings
blood, scraping skin, scraping under fingernails

Incident

My mother loved to inflict pain by doing supposedly normal things so she could write it off as an accident if she got caught. This is what she was doing with the hot baths. She also did this with brushing. She had a few different tactics like this.

She liked to hit me in the head with the bristles as hard as she possibly could, raising her hand up as high as she could and bringing it crashing up on my head as hard as she could. She would rake the brush across my scalp and make me bleed. She was usually careful to get only the spots covered by my hair so no one would know or believe me, but occasionally, she would get carried away and slip up. Then, a tell-tale bloody scratch would curve out from under my hairline onto my forehead. I think her favorite part was doing it again before it had a chance to heal.

Other times, she would sneak into my room at night while I was sleeping and tangle up my hair, tying knots and causing snarls. I know this because sometimes I would fake being asleep so that I wouldn't get hurt worse. The next day, she would claim that I had let my hair get too messy and enjoy yanking my snarls with the hairbrush to snap my head back and pull my scalp.

She also had an old nail brush she liked to use on me to separate my nails from the quick. She would hold my hands under a faucet of hot water and scrape the brush bristles under my nails until she'd pushed back the line where my nail connected to the skin underneath. I knew there was something wrong, not just because of the pain but because she would do this even when my nails were totally clean. She refused to acknowledge this when I pressed the point in an effort to get her to stop.

Points To Make

A lot of times, I would tell adults about this behavior, and they wouldn't believe me, or they would think I was exaggerating. Abusers know this. It's why they choose behaviors like this. Do not brush off an accusation like this just because it sounds too weird to be true.

Nose

Incident Tags/Trigger Warnings

physical sadism, broken nose

Incident

When I was a little kid, my mother had a homeless friend we often saw in the park and at the beach by our building. He was a nice guy who was probably just ok with the fact that a lonely housewife wanted to talk his ear off. She would occasionally give him a dollar or some change, though, despite the repeated long talks, she never tried to get him off the street or help him figure a way out of his situation. She gave him some change, and he listened to her drone on.

One day, he wasn't where we expected him, and we didn't see him for several more months afterward. Eventually, he turned up again with a badly broken nose. Part of the bone or cartilage was sticking out the side of his nose through the skin of one nostril. He told her a long story I did not understand about what had happened to him. In these days, it was not unusual for a homeless person in our area to get poor medical care or no medical care. He probably didn't have many options but to let it heal wrong.

As they were talking, she suddenly reached up and grabbed and twisted his nose. He reacted in extreme pain. I couldn't understand what she'd done. He hadn't done anything to offend or displease her. I think it was the simple fact that the pain was so tempting for her. It was already such a bad injury, and it would be so easy to hurt him badly. A homeless person, like a small child, is vulnerable and is sometimes less likely to be believed by the justice system. We parted ways after that, and though he was around again, their friendship, of course, did not continue. He would be polite to her, likely out of fear, but he avoided her after that.

Twisting

<u>Incident Tags/Trigger Warnings</u>

twisting legs

<u>Incident</u>

When I was three or four, my mother came up with a new behavior she seemed to enjoy. She would sneak into my room at night and twist my legs into odd positions until I screamed out in pain. This would not stop her. She would just keep doing it. At that age, I didn't understand why she was doing it or why no one would believe me. Eventually, she stopped this behavior on her own. I'm not sure what changed. Maybe she decided that she was tired of dealing with a tired, cranky child during the daytime, or maybe she was afraid of being caught because I was talking, or maybe she just got tired of it. Maybe she didn't know why she was doing it or why she stopped.

Street Fair

<u>Incident Tags/Trigger Warnings</u>

head trauma, sadism, bribery

<u>Incident</u>

When I was a little kid, my mother discovered that she could get more swelling by hitting me in a part of my head that had been hit repeatedly before. She started aiming for the spots that got the most reaction.

One day, we went to a street fair in our neighborhood. My mother put me in the very front seat of a little kid roller coaster. It was just a little circular track with a couple of ups and downs suitable for small children. The front was a dragon head design. She went off to the side, slipped money to the operator, and had a word with him, which was odd because the ride was free, and no one else had paid him anything.

He started the ride up quickly, then quickly slammed it to a stop. My head slammed into the dragon head sculpture in one of her favorite spots that had been hurt a lot before and swelled more easily than other spots. She doubled over in laughter while one of the other workers yelled at the operator. It took her a while to recover from the laughing fit. She was beside herself. The swelling came back badly, as usual.

Tripping

skinning, re-injuring wounds

<u>Incident</u>

When I was little, my mother very much enjoyed tripping me and watching the injury. She especially enjoyed a bad injury she could re-injure. I would run along the sidewalk in the park, and she would stick out a leg and watch me go flying or grab my leg from behind, then claim it had not been her, though no one else was within range. She liked to wait until a painful injury was almost healed and then get me again. She would deny her behavior even as she continued to laugh. Once, some building workers saw her do it as we exited the building. They yelled at her, but she brushed it off.

One time, she got me, so I fell against a concrete wheelchair-accessible ramp to the sidewalk and went sliding with my body weight on one forearm. I wasn't being fed properly and was very skinny. With no fat for padding, the scrape went through my layers of skin down to the muscle. Her usual pattern played out. She was religious about taking me to doctors for non-existent problems, but if there was an actual injury, she would avoid that to draw out the pain, and probably in hopes of causing long-lasting damage.

It became clear pretty early on that this was not a typical childhood skinning. Because the injury went down to the muscle, the scab tore open painfully every time I bent or unbent my elbow, as this required movement of the injured and scabbed muscle. This gave her an opportunity for another of her favorite torture techniques. She liked to poison or cause an injury and then insist to everyone else that I was faking so that I would be left in pain without the help people with a conscience would normally give to a kid in that situation.

She signed me up for a day camp that required swimming. Although it was owned by adults, we rarely came into contact with adults. Those in charge of the children were surly teenagers who clearly wanted to be elsewhere. She convinced them that I was just being a baby about my arm and that they needed to make me swim. I was made to get in the water on such a regular basis that my arm never had a chance to heal. I would feel the chlorine water soak in. Because it wasn't a regular skin scab, it was terribly painful. In addition, I had to keep moving the arm to stay afloat. Several weeks into this, one of the adults who actually managed the camp came by and saw what was happening. He yelled at the teenagers who'd been young and naive enough to fall for my mother's act. That was the end of swimming that summer.

At the end of the summer, we had to do the annual before-school doctor's visit in order to start the school year. My mother wasn't able to put off a doctor's visit any longer. When the injury and the story came out, my mother got another scolding. They seemed to think that would make a difference. It didn't. It never will. Only involving the authorities will stop a child abuser. Anything else just makes them more careful about getting caught.

Toenails

<u>Incident Tags/Trigger Warnings</u>

ripping nails off

<u>Incident</u>

When I was little, my mother enjoyed ripping my big toenails up. She wouldn't rip them all the way out by the root. She would rip them up off the quick so only the root was still attached. She would lay them back down and wait for them to heal a bit. Her favorite was to get one at a certain stage of healing and redo it just as I was starting to get some relief. I think the motivation was that it was incredibly painful and that she could hide the behavior. If my feet were in socks or shoes, people wouldn't notice. Even if they saw, she could claim I'd injured it somehow. She dropped this behavior when I got bigger. It was only safe for her to do when I was little and not able to kick her away.

There was never a pretense of any punishment for an offense. Instead, she would claim she hadn't done it, even immediately after the fact. When I cried out in pain, asking why, she would insist she hadn't done it even though she had just leaned down and ripped it up right in front of me. This was similar to her behavior in other types of sadistic actions that she did when no third party was around to see her. See 'The Music Box' in the Hurting To Be Right section for another example like this.

Sick/Not Sick

<u>Incident Tags/Trigger Warnings</u>
infection, peer pressure, starvation, vitamin deficiency

<u>Incident</u>

One of my mother's favorite tactics was to combine physical and emotional sadism by tricking others into participating in what was happening to me. Sometimes, she would poison me or infect me with something, then tell others I was faking sick. She especially liked to do this at parties and extended family functions and act like I was the one ruining the time. Other times, she would withhold food from me for days on end, take me to a social gathering centered around food, and not allow me any, claiming that she had fed me before. Sometimes, she would physically injure me in a way that couldn't be seen with clothes on and then insist I was making it up. This would usually be accompanied by some sort of physical activity that would be painful because of the injury.

I think she liked combining physical and emotional sadism, but I think that something else was going on here, too. I think that a lot of times, she was trying to contain things she didn't like about herself in her victims. Often, with her, every accusation was a confession, and every story of someone being mentally off was about her own mental experience. I don't know if she was conscious of this motivation or not, but looking back, it seems pretty obvious. I think this was also what was going on with a lot of her crime framing. My mother is someone who felt sick, scandalous, hungry, humiliated, scared, pained, ostracized, addicted, judged, powerless, bad, shameful, unstable, infantilized, invalidated, stupid, dirty, and criminal. I think a lot of what she did boiled down to trying to place those feelings outside of herself on a scapegoat. She wanted to feel less of those things in comparison to someone else. Of course, by doing the things she did to place those feelings on others, she actually became more what she desperately didn't want to be. Someone who does those things is sick, scandalous, bad, shameful, unstable, invalid, and criminal. She became those things more so, then tried to place those things outside herself on others more, then became those things more so, and so on, and so on. It would never be enough, and it would never be over.

6. Emotional Sadism

About

<u>About Emotional Sadism & MBP</u>

Many of the comments in the section about physical sadism also apply here. If you have not already looked at the introduction to that section, it is worth looking at for a better understanding of this section, too. The pattern chart also helps illustrate how common sadism is amongst such abusers. Medical abusers, in general, seem to have a much higher tolerance for other's suffering than the general population, even when that is not their primary goal. I have divided physical sadism and emotional sadism into two different categories in this book for clarity, although I'm not sure if sadists actually see them as two separate categories. Often, physical and emotional suffering cannot be totally separated. For example, an abuser may cause a victim to experience a physically painful death and then also participate in the grief of those who are genuinely mourning the death of their loved one.

Death

<u>Incident Tags/Trigger Warnings</u>
death, strangling, smothering, suffocation

<u>Incident</u>

My mother enjoyed cultivating a strong fear of death in me and then taunting me with it. From a very early age, she insisted on a version of reality without God or the afterlife. The message was very clear. She was insisting that she could annihilate me, that she could end my existence and totally destroy me. A sadist does not want victims to have hope. She wanted total control. That is not something that a version of reality with God and the afterlife would allow for. She was always very condescending and derisive whenever anyone mentioned God or the afterlife. When I was five, my father's father died. She insisted that he was dead in the ground and that this was the entire end of the story. Another viewpoint would not be tolerated.

My mother would often strangle me unconscious or smother me unconscious. I remember often thinking how unfair it was that it would be my last moment of existence and that this would be the last thing I would ever feel. I badly wanted to live, but I felt it was so unfair that if I had to die, I couldn't at least die in peace.

My mother also liked to insist that I was suicidal. Given everything else that was happening, this was inherently threatening. At the same time as she was insisting I wanted to die, I was desperately fighting to live.

Eviction

Incident Tags/Trigger Warnings

Eviction, manipulation

Incident

We had a neighbor in our building who we were friendly with. He was an older man. For years, we would say hi to him and chat with him. My mother was fond of him. At one point, something changed. Maybe she just wanted someone to pick on, and he was an easy target.

One day, he knocked on our door, very upset. I answered, expecting a usual pleasant interaction. I was a little kid and didn't understand everything that he was saying. He wanted to speak to my mother. When she came to the door, she acted oddly. She was enjoying herself.

The man was being evicted because of something my mother had made up. She had come up with some sort of manipulation, and he knew it was her but couldn't prove it. The eviction was sudden. He didn't have time to find a new place. He didn't have anywhere to put his stuff. He had no moving truck and no time to plan, and he was beside himself. His stuff was on the sidewalk outside, being picked over by random passers-by. He yelled, and she remained calm. The more he yelled, the more she seemed to enjoy herself. He told her she was a bad person, and of course, he was dead right. She was simply enjoying the evilness of it all.

Related Sections

Creepy towards neighbors

The Button

Incident Tags/Trigger Warnings

wetting pants

Incident

The week after I started the first grade, my mother put me in the after-school program at school. I was excited because other kids who'd been to the first week talked about how fun it was. The day I was to start after school, my mother did something differently when I got dressed in the morning. She insisted that the button on my uniform shorts was going to fall off and took a needle and thread to it after I had already put them on, even though it seemed fine to me. That day, I couldn't open my shorts to go to the bathroom. I tried all day long. I complained to the teacher and to the school nurse, who had an office just off the first-grade classroom by the bathroom. Neither of them understood what was going on.

I made it all the way to the end of the school day before wetting my pants, still trying to unbutton them in the bathroom before the after-school program. The nurse heard me crying and attempted to assist. That's when she and the first-grade teacher realized what had happened. My mother had sewn the button shut. They had a stern talk with her, but as would become a pattern, they did not report her behavior.

Points To Make

This was about sadism, but it was also about isolation. My mother knew I was looking forward to making friends in after school.

Christmas

<u>Incident Tags/Trigger Warnings</u>

holidays, ostracization

<u>Incident</u>

One Christmas, when I was a little girl, my mother hatched a plan to enjoy some sadism. She got everyone else up very early but left me sleeping. She gave away all the presents and food before I woke up. I came out of my bedroom on Christmas morning to find everyone happy and enjoying themselves. She had spent Christmas morning convincing them all that I had selfishly refused to get up and join them. I sat hungry, listening to everyone else talk about how good the Christmas breakfast was, watching the others play with their toys, and listening to the others talk about how fun the family time had been. She had them show me the toys in my stocking she had divvied up between them since I wasn't up in time and how much fun they were having with them. They insisted that I should have gotten up earlier. When I asked how they had managed to get up that early, they all explained that my mother had gotten them up.

Gifts and Compliments

taking back gifts

Incident

I learned from a very early age not to show excitement or pleasure over gifts or compliments. They were always a setup for hurting me later. The compliments would be followed by abuse and put-downs. The gifts would be taken back or broken if I showed I liked them. When I was three, a hospital gave me a teddy bear after surgery. I was very excited about it and was careful to act like I didn't care about it. My mother was angry they hadn't asked her permission to give it to me. She didn't want me to have it but couldn't be seen taking it away. I still have a photo she took of me with it. In it, I'm totally expressionless, careful to look unenthusiastic about this special bear that she would never have given me that I didn't want to be taken away.

Advice for Medical Professionals

It's common for children's hospitals to give a bear or something like that to kids coming out of surgery. Some medical abusers will go along with this and be perfectly happy about it. This does not mean you should rule them out as medical abusers. On the other hand, a parent reacting badly to this gesture should be considered a red flag. It does not necessarily mean that they are medically abusive, but it does mean that there is some dysfunction going on, and you should look for other signs that you may need a social worker to have a look at what's going on.

Tuna Helper

Incident Tags/Trigger Warnings

Christmas, holidays, hunger

Incident

Every year, my grade school collected Christmas presents and food for needy families. Each class got a family and a request list. They were often very modest requests for basics that most people take for granted. It was usually groceries for Christmas dinner, clothes for growing kids, and things like that. Each student would be assigned an item or two to bring in on the list.

One year, I was assigned to bring in hamburger helper. The family had requested any helper except for tuna, noting that someone in the family had an allergy to it and would not be able to eat dinner if it was tuna helper. I brought home the written instructions the teacher had given me. They explained this, but I repeated it to emphasize the point, wanting to make sure they got the right Christmas dinner.

At the grocery store, my mother made a point of buying tuna and tuna helper. I was too young to understand that this was on purpose. I couldn't understand how she had misunderstood both the teacher's written instructions and my verbal instructions at the same time. No matter how many times I tried to explain it to her, she insisted. I didn't have any money of my own and couldn't buy the right one for the family.

Looking back on this, I realize that this was about wanting someone to go hungry on Christmas. It was about the power she held over someone else to make them hungry on Christmas by giving them food they couldn't eat. See the malnutrition section for other examples like this.

The Doll

Incident Tags/Trigger Warnings
ruined birthday, making children cry, conflict

Incident

When I was little, there was an informal group of parents in the buildings on my street who coordinated holiday parties and birthday parties in the party rooms of the buildings. My mother wormed her way into this because she was a mother in the building, and even if some of them felt she was off, they couldn't exclude her entirely.

One day, a kid in the building had a birthday. My mother had volunteered to coordinate with all the other parents to make sure that there were not duplicates of the same present. She didn't have anything against the child, but she liked hurting people, and children were easy targets. I heard her on the phone telling every parent to get the little girl the exact same "Rainbow Bright" doll. These were popular at the time. I attempted to correct her because I was too young to understand that she had been doing it on purpose. The parents couldn't hear me. She was on an old landline phone with her hand cupped around the receiver. I kept on trying to explain to her how she had messed up. She wouldn't hear of it. She brushed me off with confidence as if she was the adult and she knew better.

On the day of the party, my mother excitedly hovered over the children and socialized with the other parents. Then came the time for opening presents. On the first one, the little girl was excited to have a 'Rainbow Bright' doll. This immediately sparked words amongst other parents, though, as another parent watching realized that they had gotten the same thing. Each accused the other of being wrong. This was fun for my mother. She liked to make people fight with each other. What was even more fun for her was watching the little girl's face collapse a little more as each present was opened until, finally, she was in tears. The other parents focused on comforting the little girl instead of having words with my mother. They could do that later, and the little girl was upset at the moment. Some of them may have also correctly gauged that getting angry and yelling at my mother would only entertain her more at that moment. The child's birthday had just been strangely sabotaged by an off adult who they'd only invited out of obligation in the first place. They told her that she would not be in charge of coordinating presents again. They all knew it was on purpose, but they didn't want to cause a scene.

My mother was pretty sensitive to being ostracized and being the odd one out. It seemed to matter to her more than other people. This tells you just how much she enjoyed hurting people. As much as she wanted to be part of the in-crowd, she was still willing to sacrifice this to cause pain. These were the people in our building. She would have to see them all the time, and they could cut her out of events, but she just wanted to watch parents fight and a child cry so much more.

So Sensitive

Incident Tags/Trigger Warnings

yelling, berating

Incident

In the 'Reversing Parent Child Relationship' section, I have a subsection called 'Venting.' The behavior described here predates that section. She switched to that venting behavior after she lost interest in this behavior described in this section.

When I was a little girl, my mother used to have a routine for after school. She would pick me up, acting all nice in front of others, then take me home and sit me down in the living room. She would then make up some pretense for suddenly being furious with me. She would yell and scream for long periods of time, not satisfied until she'd reduced me to tears.

This went on until I learned that the key was to refuse to react. One day I did this. She seemed stumped. When she asked me about it, I explained how meaningless all her rantings were because it was always something, and she just wanted to make me cry. She denied this and tried a few more times. When she realized I wouldn't take the bait and take it to heart anymore, she stopped the behavior entirely. She was never actually angry. She just liked the power and liked making me cry. Shortly after this, the venting behavior started in its place. In this behavior, she would go on long rants about others, forcing me to nod along instead of doing my homework or playing.

Parties

<u>Incident Tags/Trigger Warnings</u>

fights

<u>Incident</u>

My mother very much enjoyed inviting people to parties who would fight. She especially liked to blindside them with each other's invitations in settings too intimate for them to avoid each other. She would then watch the screaming and rage and act like the calm bystander. There were no limits to her behavior. If she couldn't find a conflict, she would create one. Sometimes, she would claim that one person had said something highly offensive about another that they hadn't actually said. Once she had the person convinced, she would invite them both and watch the fireworks.

The Bears

<u>Incident Tags/Trigger Warnings</u>

mutilation

<u>Incident</u>

When I was a little girl, there was a show on TV called "Duck Man." This was a cartoon marketed towards adults that had some inappropriate stuff for young children. My mother had us watch it together. There were these two teddy-bear-like creatures on it that were sweet and that the main character hated because of their sweetness. He would always do things like put them in blenders and mutilate them in various ways. My mother always talked about how funny this was and how much they reminded her of me.

Birthday

<u>Incident Tags/Trigger Warnings</u>

birthday

Incident

One birthday, when I was a little girl, my mother made a big production of what I didn't deserve. The year before, I'd gotten a nice birthday because I had been going through some supposedly naturally occurring medical issues. At the time, she had warned me that I should not get used to this treatment or expect it in future birthdays. She had repeatedly emphasized that she was afraid I would grow to expect that in future years and that it was only because of the medical issues that year.

The next year, she laid a trap for me. She kept insisting I tell her what I wanted for my birthday but kept on telling me I had grown to expect too much from the last birthday, no matter how small the things I asked for were. I tried asking for very small things, but everything was met with an angry response that I thought I deserved too much and that they'd spoiled me too much the last birthday. I tried to say I wanted nothing, but she didn't accept this either. It was about making me list stuff I would like so she could tell me I didn't deserve it.

Waiting

<u>Incident</u>

My mother always wanted to keep us waiting, make us miss trains, make car rides longer, and make other types of waiting longer, especially when anyone was tired or needed a bathroom. She liked this even if she had to hurt herself too in order to get other people's pain. She would rather have to wait uncomfortably than miss the opportunity to make others wait uncomfortably. She would rather be tired, needing the bathroom, bored, or otherwise inconvenienced and watch others experience this than miss the opportunity to watch others experience this. She took this to extremes. The piddly little power trip was always worth more to her than her own comfort or time. Sometimes, she would pretend to be lost. Sometimes, she would purposefully lie about a call from a travel agent. Sometimes, she would purposefully get times wrong. She was wasting her own time, too, but apparently, there was nothing else she would rather do with her time than that.

7. Hurting to be Right

About

<u>About Hurting to be Right & MBP</u>

Central to my mother's behavior and to the behavior of all abusers is a double standard between the abuser and everyone else in society. She thought nothing of correcting others quite rudely, as you will see many examples of in the section on faking authority and intelligence. If someone, however, even disagreed with her politely, she would often become enraged and lash out.

Although not all MBP abusers may act out in the way covered in this section, it's important to note that all MBP abusers engage in physical harm of others in order to push their narrative and in order to convince medical authorities of their correctness that something is wrong.

Incidents from other sections that could also apply to this section:

'The Transformer' in Infrastructure and Transportation Sabotage

The Music Box

Incident Tags/Trigger Warnings

Cutting, blood

Incident

When I was a little kid, my mother had a music box she was fond of. It was a little copper-colored sculpture of a wire man playing a piano. You could see through a little clear window in the front of the piano and watch the gears of the box move to make the music. I believe now that this was a very emotionally loaded object for my mother. Her adoptive mother was a piano teacher. She would often rant about how much she hated her mother. Her attitude towards the music box shifted over the years and from time to time in ways I don't think she understood.

She initially fawned over the music box and brought it out when she was happy. I initially associated the music box with my mother being in a good mood and being safe to be around at the moment. One day, without explanation, my mother put the box up on a high shelf I couldn't reach. After that, I would sometimes ask her to take it down, but she would refuse.

One day, after quite a while, I thought of it again and bugged her to take it down and let me play with it. She told me no because I would cut my hands open on it. It was a strange thing to say because she'd let me play with it when I was much younger, and that had never happened. It was physically impossible. The metal was dull and crimped around the edges to make it safe. When I argued this point, she took it down and gave it to me.

When I was done playing with it, she told me to hold out my hands palm up. I wasn't sure why, but I agreed. She sliced my hands open all over with a bunch of quick movements of a craft knife. Blood poured out. I screamed and cried. She insisted that I had cut them open on the music box and refused to acknowledge that she had done anything to cause the injury. This wasn't just about staying out of trouble for what she'd done. She didn't just deny this around others. She did this even when we were still alone together, even though I had been looking right at her when she did it.

Slip and Slide

<u>Incident Tags/Trigger Warnings</u>

Blood, cutting

<u>Incident</u>

When I was little, there was lots of advertising for these backyard toys for playing in the water. There are various brands and names, but they're all about the same. They involve a long strip of plastic with a water outlet to allow kids to run and slide along the strip of plastic. I always wanted one, but my mother insisted that we would hurt ourselves.

One day, we went to visit another family with kids. They had one of these toys out in their yard and invited us to play on it, unaware of my mother's rule. I hesitated, but they insisted it was safe. They played on it all the time and never got hurt.

As the adults socialized in the yard, the kids played on the toy next to them. Occasionally, my mother or another adult would help adjust the plastic or make sure there was enough water or something like that. My mother took part in this, too, which confused me because she had been against this. I couldn't figure out why she was being helpful with something she'd been against.

Suddenly, things went wrong. One kid hit a rock. Another got a long bloody scratch all the way up and down his torso from his chest to his stomach. One by one, all the kids started getting hurt by debris they'd never been hurt by playing on the toy before. Most suspiciously, they had been playing on the toy before we arrived and hadn't been hurt. If those things had been in the way of the toy that day, the injuries should have happened before we arrived.

The kid with the long bloody scrape started insisting that my mother had done this. His mother insisted that this could not possibly be true. She was trying to help. She believed what she was saying. She simply couldn't imagine that anyone would act like that.

<u>Points To Make</u>

Adults often assume that kids don't really know what they're talking about. The "Martha Mitchell Effect" (discussed in "Missing What's Right In

Front Of You") is often amplified for children. If a child is expressing distrust of another adult or discomfort with that adult, even if it sounds strange, listen. Don't automatically try to talk them out of it.

The Beach

Incident Tags/Trigger Warnings
Drowning, physical abuse, dragging

Incident

When I was a little girl, we went out to the beach one day. I was excited because I liked the beach. I liked playing in the waves. My mother told me not to go too far out. I waded in, and she told me I was going too far out. This was unusual because I often went out farther than that with no objection from her. I could still stand in the water, and she often let me go far enough out to swim without being able to touch the bottom. I was standing in the waves, enjoying myself and wishing that I could go farther out as usual. I waded a bit more but still didn't go out as far as I usually got to. She continued to go back and forth with me about it, warning me that an undertow could get me and I would drown. I don't know why this was an issue for her only on this particular day. The shallows went on for a while, so you could wade several feet before needing to swim. I did this often.

I was looking wistfully at the area where I was usually allowed to go swimming when suddenly, a huge force I couldn't see hit me from behind. I felt someone grab my ankle and pull it up. My face hit the water hard, went under, and dragged along the sand, rocks, and shells. I couldn't breathe, and I couldn't get loose. I was being dragged with my feet up in the air and my head down in the water. I clawed at the sand with my fingers, but there was nothing firm to get ahold of and push my head up above the water with. I hoped for it to stop soon. There was nothing else I could do. I had gone too long without air, and I knew I couldn't last much longer. Just as I was about to lose consciousness, I got a breath of air. I was up on the shore gasping and spluttering. There was a fuss around me. People were yelling angrily at my mother. They screamed at her, but she ignored it.

I asked her why she did it, but she denied that she had done anything. Despite the fact that people on the beach were screaming at her, despite what I had felt, despite the fact that she was standing over me where I was dropped, she simply calmly denied that she had done anything. She told me that I had been too far out and that the waves had gotten me like she'd told me they would. No matter how the other beach-goers screamed or I argued, she would not acknowledge the obvious but simply repeated the lie that exactly what she'd warned me would happen did.

<u>Points To Make</u>

Nothing ever came of this incident. Despite the reaction of everyone at the beach, nothing was actually going to be done, and she knew that. Today, things are different because everyone has a phone on them. If you see something like this, please get a picture or video of the adult after the child is out of immediate danger. This could have made a difference, especially if a number of the witnesses had come forward together.

Pizza

Incident Tags/Trigger Warnings
burning, hot food, hunger

Incident

When I was little, my family used to go out for pizza at a particular pizza place in the neighborhood with some of the other families in the building who had kids at the same time. It was a regular thing I looked forward to. One day, we just stopped going without explanation. I really liked the pizza there and the people, so I would occasionally whine about why we never did it anymore. My mother would respond by telling me that I didn't like it there and that I didn't like the pizza there. It was like she thought that if she repeated it often enough, I would just start to believe it.

One day, she announced that we were going back. I was very excited. We met up with some of the families we used to go with. I was hoping she would remember how much she enjoyed this and that it would become a regular thing once again. She behaved differently that night than she used to at that place, and I couldn't understand why. When the pizzas the other families had gotten arrived first, she wouldn't allow me any even though the parents offered. Finally, our pizza came out, but she wouldn't allow me any of that either as she ate it. I was hungry, and I couldn't understand why I wasn't allowed to eat. She told me I didn't like it. Finally, the other parents objected too much, and she didn't have a choice but to feed me.

She told me she would give me one, but I would see that I didn't like the pizza there, just like she had told me. She insisted that's why we never went there anymore. She took a piece and began to do something to it on the table. I insisted that she didn't need to do anything to it, just give it to me. I liked it just the way it was. She insisted that she needed to fix it and that I didn't know what I was talking about. The other parents began to object, telling her to stop what she was doing. She ignored them and kept on doing it. I couldn't understand it at the time, but I now realize she was covering the piece with all of the hot sauce and hot pepper flakes on the table.

Over the other parents' objections, she handed it to me. They told me not to eat it, but I was starving. I took a big bite and felt the pain. I asked for a normal piece of pizza without all that stuff on it. She refused, insisting that I wouldn't like any of the other pieces since they all came from the same pizza and that she had told me I didn't like it. I sat there in pain, forlorn, and extremely hungry. The other parents offered me some of their pizza, but she wouldn't allow it. After a few meek attempts, they gave up, too cowed by her. As often happened, I went to bed hungry, and we never went back again.

Broken Glass

<u>Incident Tags/Trigger Warnings</u>

broken glass, cutting

<u>Incident</u>

When I was a little girl, there was a girl a bit older than me in the neighborhood who I looked up to because of her age. One day, my mother and I met her and her mother at the beach. We were walking and talking when we reached the end of the beach. The edges of the beach always had mounds of stuff the beach combing machines had cleaned out of the rest of the sand. It mostly included things like cigarette butts and shards of broken glass. It was quicker to climb up these piles onto the cement blocks that marked the end of the beach than to go all the way around to the ramp. The little girl did this and motioned me to follow her. My mother told me no because I would get cut on the glass. I had done this before many times without being cut, and I reminded her of this. We had a back-and-forth about it, and then I scampered up after the other girl as my mother had instructed me not to.

My mother insisted I show her my foot to see where I had been cut by the glass she warned me of, but I had not been cut. She wouldn't let the point drop. She fussed until she got ahold of my foot. The next thing I knew, there was a shard of glass protruding from the top of my toe and dark red blood streaming out. I screamed in pain and asked her why she had done it. She insisted that I had cut myself on the glass as she'd warned. She denied the reality that my foot had been fine in the time between the climbing and the end of the argument. She denied the reality that stepping on glass would not wedge it into the top of my foot. The other little girl chimed in and insisted that I had been fine after climbing. Her mother hushed her. I think she was scared of what my mother might do to her daughter. That was a reasonable fear, but she still should have called child services after they got away from us.

8. Hurting Animals and Talking to Animals

About

About Animals & MBP

This section covers two subjects: hurting animals and talking to animals. Hurting animals fits the general pattern of MBP. Talking to animals and experiencing them talking back does not. I include those incidents anyway because they help paint a more detailed picture of my childhood. Although talking to animals does not fit MBP, being seriously mentally off in a variety of ways does fit MBP. This will look a bit different in every MBP abuser. It does NOT (and I cannot emphasize this enough) excuse MBP or any form of abuse.

For a lot of you, this is going to be one of the more difficult sections for you to read. It's one of the more difficult sections for me to write. You need to give yourself permission to skip this if you want to.

Hurting animals connects with MBP in many ways:

1. MBP abuse isn't specific to human victims. Most of the reactions that a person can get out of others for a sick child, a person can also get out of others for a sick animal.

2. There's a lot more sadism involved in MBP than people would like to think. It's not all about attention and sympathy. In fact, there were several times when given the choice between satisfying a desire for sadism and a desire for attention or sympathy, my mother chose to satisfy her sadism. Sadistic people often target animals. Sadists get a 2 for 1 of sorts if they can hurt an animal and make a person who cares about the animal aware of the animal's pain or death.

3. Animals can't tell you what someone is doing to them. Once a child gets old enough, an MBP abuser must trick the child into believing that they are genuinely ill or that the abuser would never poison them. They know they can skip this step with animals.

4. Abusers know that if a series of children die, it will raise questions and lead to an investigation.

5. In researching other forms of abuse, you will often hear of abusers holding power over their victims by threatening their victims' pets. This is such a strong pattern that in some states, lawmakers have enacted laws to make sure that people can take their pets with them to domestic violence shelters.

- Other MSBP cases involving this pattern:

- Nurse Cullen is said to have tortured and killed animals in childhood.

- In Sickened, Julie Gregory describes her parents allowing their dog to burn to death as part of an arson and home insurance fraud scheme.

- Lacy Spears took hundreds of death photos of her son after killing him. Although this has nothing to do with animals, it's worth noting the similarity between this and the photos in the red tide incident.

Further reading:

Munro HM, Thrusfield MV. 'Battered pets': Munchausen syndrome by proxy (factitious illness by proxy). J Small Anim Pract. 2001 Aug;42(8):385-9. doi: 10.1111/j.1748-5827.2001.tb02486.x. PMID: 11518417. Available at https://pubmed.ncbi.nlm.nih.gov/11518417/[1]

Star Gazing (cats)

<u>Incident Tags/Trigger Warnings</u>

dead kittens

<u>Incident</u>

One day, when I was little, we made a long drive out from the city into the country to join a group of stargazers. My mother had made friends with someone who had invited some people out to use their telescope to look at constellations you usually couldn't see from within the city with all the light pollution. We were in a field with tall grass, and a group of people were clustered around. We met shortly before sunset.

One of the little girls in the group had brought some new kittens with her, and they were allowed to wander around us. I was more excited about this than the star gazing. I asked to play with them, but I had to stay with my mother, who was around the stargazers. She told me I could play with them later. Eventually, I was able to wander off and look for them, but I couldn't find them. Bored, I went back to the stargazers, but my mother wasn't there anymore. I wandered around the group for a while, trying to entertain myself.

Hours later (or maybe what felt like hours to me as a young child), my mother came and told me we were about to leave. I protested because I hadn't gotten a chance to play with the kittens yet. I asked where they were. My mother said they were gone. I objected. No one had left, so they couldn't be gone. I asked others around where they were. No one knew. People went looking for them.

After a few minutes, one of the other people there came up to us, very upset. The kittens had been killed in a manner that made it obvious that a human had done it. I didn't understand who would possibly do such a thing and why. We were the only new people there, and the rest of the crowd had put the facts together. I hadn't. How had my mother known they were gone? It just wasn't a possibility my mind would entertain.

Grooming (cats)

Incident Tags/Trigger Warnings

cats, cutting, mutilation, torture

Incident

My mother was grooming the cats one day. She explained to me that it was very important to slide a comb between a cat's skin and a mat she was cutting out so that she didn't accidentally cut the cat's skin in case it had been pulled up into the mat. She told me a story about how she had 'accidentally' hurt our old cat like that once. This story didn't actually make any sense since this old cat we used to have was a short-haired cat who didn't get mats. His hair wasn't long enough for that to happen. She told me she had accidentally cut a quarter-sized hole in his skin on his abdomen.

This story made quite an impression on me, and I asked my father about it as soon as he got home. He confirmed the story but insisted that she had done it on purpose.

Her Childhood Cat

<u>Incident Tags/Trigger Warnings</u>

dead cat

<u>Incident</u>

My mother would sometimes speak of her childhood cat, Silky, wistfully. She said that Silky was a Ragdoll cat. I had never heard of this breed before. She told me that it was a wonderful, very docile breed that was good with children but that the problem with them was that they were too docile and didn't defend themselves if children were being mean to them. She told me that the breed didn't exist anymore because they had stopped breeding them because of this problem. This is not actually true. They do still exist, and as far as I know, they are not generally known as too docile.

She told me that Silky had been killed by a neighborhood boy who had gone around killing a lot of the neighborhood pets. Later on, she referred to the neighborhood child who had killed her cat as a girl. I questioned her about this, and she evaded the question. I kept on asking, and eventually, she told me that it had been a girl and that she had lied earlier when she told me it was a boy. When I asked her why she had told this lie, she told me, "Because I didn't want you to think that it was me." I didn't think it at the time. I do now. Of course, it was.

Dog

<u>Incident Tags/Trigger Warnings</u>

dead dog

<u>Incident</u>

When I was a little kid, there was an older lady in the building we were friendly with. She had a little toy poodle she was always walking in the park. I always loved to go say hi to her and the poodle. She was friendly and would chat with us. This went on for years.

One day my mother told me a story that this woman's little dog had been killed in the park by a bigger dog who had rushed up to them and raped the little dog until it died. I was well below the age that this would be an appropriate story and level of detail to tell a child.

My mother instructed me not to mention it at all or even mention the dog if I ever saw the lady again. I didn't realize it at the time, but this was a giveaway whenever my mother was making up a story. She always insisted that a story was too sensitive to ever bring up whenever she was making up a story. This was to try to avoid people comparing notes and finding out she was lying and making up elaborate, bizarre, sick stories.

It was much longer than usual until the next time that we saw this lady in the park. I was so glad to see her again and began to approach her enthusiastically. My mother kept telling me to stop, but I disregarded this. I called to the lady and ran towards her. My mother followed me towards her.

When she noticed my mother approaching, she reacted in terror. I couldn't understand what was happening. I called out to reassure her that it was just us. I thought maybe she had mistaken us for someone else at a distance. She moved to protect her new little dog and kept saying things like "no" and "stay away." Her body language indicated that she was physically afraid. She left hurriedly. I couldn't understand what had happened.

In the days that followed, I kept on asking my mother about this. I couldn't understand why we'd lost a friend. Eventually, she told me that the little dog hadn't been killed by another dog. The little dog had been killed by a person who suddenly ran up to them and killed the little dog with their bare hands. I still didn't understand what that had to do with us. Now, of course, in hindsight, from the perspective of an adult, the answer is obvious.

Red Tide

dead fish, dead sea creatures

Incident

When I was a kid, we would usually go to see our relatives in Florida about once a year. One year, we could not swim at the beach as usual because of red tide. We went to the beach anyway. My mother was thrilled. She kept on exclaiming over how fascinating she found the dead creatures on the shore who had been killed by the red tide. She went on and on about it. She began taking pictures. This was back in the days before digital cameras. She spent up several roles of film all on dead sea creatures. It was all the same thing over and over. They had all died the same way, and all looked the same, but to her, each one was unique and fascinating and needed to be photographed even though she'd already photographed many just like them. I kept on asking her what was so fascinating to her about it, but she couldn't explain it to me. She just thought it was obvious. I trailed along, bored and annoyed, as she went on and on for ages, exclaiming about how neat it all was and taking photos.

Similar Cases

See the case of Lacey Spears (mentioned in the pattern chart). She took and posted hundreds of photos of her son after she had murdered him.

Ant Farm

Incident Tags/Trigger Warnings

dead ants

Incident

When I was little, I wanted an ant farm very badly. I'd seen TV characters who had them, and I'd seen commercials for them on TV. I would bug her about it. She would always give me the same answer when I asked why I couldn't have one. She would tell me that kids couldn't resist smashing them and killing the ants. I couldn't understand this response. I couldn't imagine wanting to do this. I kept insisting that I would never want to do that, and she kept insisting that I would.

One day, she finally relented. I couldn't believe it. I was so excited. We got the ant farm and put it together. It was two panes of clear plastic with sand wedged in between. It had a stand and a bit of ant food. For some reason, my mother insisted that it would go in our bathroom. I would look at it often, eager to see any progress in their activity.

One day, I found that the ant farm had been smashed on the floor. It was broken into pieces, and the ants had been killed. I was so sad. I asked what had happened. My mother had smashed it and killed the ants. She reminded me of what she had said when I first asked for one. If I'd known that she was really talking about herself and that she was going to kill them eventually, I wouldn't have asked for them.

Many Legger

Incident Tags/Trigger Warnings

pulling legs off bugs

Incident

The area I grew up in got pests, some called 'manny leggers.' I still don't know the proper name for them. They were technically a type of arachnid with 88 legs. They were kind of a tan color and scurried quickly. You could usually find them in basements and on the first few floors of buildings throughout the region. Some, including myself, called them 'centipedes,' although this was not accurate. They are not actually related to centipedes at all.

One day, I went into the bathroom in our house after school and found a strange sight. There were many legger legs all over the place. They were too high up to have simply scattered when someone smashed one or stepped on one. They also weren't in any pattern that the cats would have left them in if the cats had killed one. One leg was hooked into the fibers of a towel high up on a rack. A few were scattered on the floor, a few more on the counter across from the towel rack, a few more in some of the toiletry baskets, and a few more here and there in various areas of the bathroom too far apart to be explicable.

Someone had methodically pulled off all of the many leggers' legs and put them all over the bathroom.

The Bat

dead bat

Incident

When I was in elementary school, my mother came to pick me up one day, holding a zip-lock baggie containing a dead bat. She seemed very excited about it. She seemed to expect me to find it as exciting. I didn't understand where it came from, why she had it, or why it was such a big deal to her. It was a cold winter day, and she claimed that it had frozen to death. I have never before or since come across a frozen bat in the middle of a city. I'm still not sure where she got it from or what she did to it. She started talking about me bringing it in for show and tell. Although I was still in elementary school, I was past the age at which classes still did show and tell. She already knew this, and I reminded her of it. She wouldn't let the subject go. It was clear the subject wasn't going to drop until I agreed. I reluctantly agreed, and she brought the bat home with us and put it in the freezer with our frozen foods and ice cubes.

I don't know how she talked my teacher into allowing me to bring the bat in, but she did. Maybe the teacher was scared of her or just didn't feel like arguing. This certainly had to have been a health code violation of some sort. At the teacher's prompting, I went up to the front of the class and said a few awkward words about it. Classmates expressed disbelief at my mother's story. Even at that age, they could tell that there was something wrong with the story and something wrong with the whole scenario.

I brought the bat back home at the end of the school day as instructed by my mother. She kept it in the freezer for years afterward. Every time we opened the freezer, there it was. I tended to avoid the stuff in that area of the freezer.

Buffalo Skull

<u>Incident Tags/Trigger Warnings</u>

death, decay, bugs, skull

<u>Incident</u>

Hanging over the couch by the TV was a buffalo skull. This was not of cultural significance to my family. It was simply a part of my mother's fascination with death. She avoided questions by redoing the upholstery to a southwest pattern at the same time as she got it so it seemed to be a part of the decor.

One day, my mother announced that she would be redecorating the living room. She made a big deal of the project, flipping through magazines and showing me patterns. She decided on two southwest-looking patterns that clashed with each other. She had half the living room set reupholstered in one and the other half in the other. She also ordered a buffalo skull to hang on the living room wall over the couch.

This was a big production. First, we waited for it in the mail. Next, she explained that you could get them already cleaned and ready to hang but that she had opted for an uncleaned one instead. She ordered the unclean one with some carrion beetles to clean it. She wrapped it in a bag full of beetles and placed it on the floor between the back of the loveseat and the dining table. There it was for weeks, sitting there as the beetles cleaned it. It was just behind me while I watched TV and just next to us as we ate. She was thrilled with it. I just wanted it away from me.

After several weeks, it was clean. She unwrapped it and hung it on a stud over the couch. It hung there for years. She was able to pass it off as just a bit of 90s-era cultural appropriation. I now realize that this was part of her fascination with death and dead animals.

Crawfish

<u>Incident Tags/Trigger Warnings</u>
dead animals, decomposition, playing with dead animals
<u>Incident</u>

My family used to go to a cabin in Wisconsin for a week every summer. The cabin was one of several rental cabins by a little freshwater lake. The owners and the visitors would often socialize while wading in the shallow water. The water had some small fish and some creatures we called crawfish or crawdads. I don't think that's actually what they were. I think they were something native to the area that looked similar. They were some sort of a small freshwater crustacean. The water was very clear, so I could look down as I stepped through the shallows to make sure I wouldn't accidentally step on one. Occasionally, there would be a dead, decomposing one in the shallows. This disgusted me, and I would take a wide path around one to avoid the possibility of the movement of the water brushing one up against me.

As we stood around chatting with other visitors and the property owners, my mother would step in these decomposing ones and squish them between her toes. The rotting flesh would move around her feet, and the bones would sometimes poke up from between her toes. At first, I thought this was an accident she had not noticed. I pointed it out to her. I thought she would be horrified as I would be, but I figured she would want to know to get her foot out of it. At first, she pretended that she did not know and thanked me, but she didn't really move her foot enough.

As time went on, it became clear that she was stepping in them on purpose. She tended to favor the more rotten ones over the fresher ones that had died more recently. I asked her why she was doing this. She told me that it was an adult thing and that when I was an adult, I would understand. I'm not sure if she actually thought this was true or if she was just trying to get out of giving an explanation.

Opossums

<u>Incident Tags/Trigger Warnings</u>

dead animals, playing with dead animals, starving animals

<u>Incident</u>

When I was 16, my family moved from an apartment to a house a few blocks away. We had a new next-door neighbor who we already knew from our old K-8 school. They had an old, dilapidated garage on the back of their property by the alley. There was an area where opossums and stray cats could get in, and they allowed this instead of sealing up the area they had been getting in. I think they were animal people and didn't want to take away their shelter from the harsh winter.

My mother told me a story one day about this situation. She found it very amusing and thought that I would as well. She told me that the family next door had sealed up the garage but failed to check if animals were inside and simply left it that way. Over time, the animals starved to death in there, and they found a bunch of dead animals when they opened it back up. She then went on to describe a game the man of the house had played with the dead opossums. She claimed that he had taken their stiff, desiccated bodies and hooked them together so that they dangled in a line, looking like they were holding paws. She was essentially inviting me to judge his weirdness and laugh at it. I found the story upsetting, as most people would.

A few days later, we ran into him in the yard. She pushed me to bring up the story she'd told me and ask him about it. That's when it all came out. She had reversed the story. She had sealed up the garage without the neighbors' knowledge. She had allowed the animals to starve in there, with the family next door unaware. She had played the game with the dead animals. He was upset about it. She had pushed me to bring it up with him, knowing that he would react. I think she was just enjoying his sadness about what had happened to the animals while he was just a few feet away, unaware they needed help.

<u>Legislation</u>

Some jurisdictions have recently changed animal cruelty from a misdemeanor to a felony. This is not just to protect animals, although that is a good cause. It is also to protect people. There is a strong link between the abuse of animals and the abuse of people. Strong laws against animal cruelty also help protect people. If your area has not made this change yet, you may want to consider advocating for such a change. Humane societies often help push for such legislation and may already be aware of such efforts in your area.

Rookery

<u>Incident Tags/Trigger Warnings</u>

cruelty to birds

<u>Incident</u>

When I was a little girl, I loved the rookery in the zoo we visited most often. It was a special place for the migrating birds to rest in the middle of the city. Sometimes, it was closed when the rest of the zoo was open, I suppose depending on seasonal nesting and migration patterns.

One day, we went to the zoo, but the rookery was closed. My mother told me to wait outside while she went inside. I dutifully stood around outside while she snuck in past the sign telling visitors to keep out. I was too young to register this as bad since I didn't understand what she was up to. I did register it as weird since we always went in together, and she'd left me standing alone out there for quite a while. Eventually, an employee came by and asked about why a young kid was out there alone. I explained that I wasn't alone and that she was in there. He went in to investigate.

A few minutes later, they both came out. He was still yelling at her as they walked out. I couldn't figure out what had happened. He was yelling at her about the welfare of the birds, about how they needed a place to be safe. He told her that if it happened again, he would call the police. I never did find out what she was up to during that long time I was waiting outside, but I can't imagine it was anything good.

The Crane

Incident Tags/Trigger Warnings

hallucination

Incident

My family was on one of our yearly trips to my father's family in Florida. We were sitting in a restaurant on the water. It was one of those tourist restaurants that is open-air and ocean-themed. The seating was over the water and sometimes got wildlife wandering through.

We were all sitting together and chatting when a crane wandered in. Most of the restaurant patrons were delighted, as was I. My mother was very upset. She started screaming at it as if they were in a two-way argument that it had started. No one else but her could hear what she believed was the bird's side of the argument. She was being defensive and saying things that sounded like she thought it was insulting her.

I was so young that I thought she was being silly for entertainment purposes. I was still at that age where an adult might put on a pantomime with a hand puppet or act silly like that for a kid's sake. I thought she was just joking around like this. Everyone else at the restaurant got what was happening. Looking back on it now, I can see this from their reactions. At the time, I laughed and simply didn't understand why others were acting so upset about what I believed was her joke. This laughter probably aggravated her further. No one ever explained to me what was actually going on. I think they were just all too uncomfortable.

Shorts

Incident Tags/Trigger Warnings

Munchausen, MBP, animal abuse

Incidents

The following are incidents that would also be in this section if I'd done a full write-up of them. Each one gets a short blurb. Some are so straightforward that they do not need a full write-up. Others are ones I cut from a full write-up for length because they are similar to others I have already done a full write-up of. Others are short because there is no point in putting myself or you, the reader, through all the gory details simply to get the information across. This is not a complete list because some are just too upsetting to talk about and because if I mentioned everything, it would just go on forever.

Zoos and Sanctuaries

My mother would sometimes talk to animals in zoos and sanctuaries as if she were in a two-way conversation with them that only she could hear the other half of. It sounded like when you're hearing only one end of a telephone conversation. There was an incident like this with the elephants at the zoo and another incident with birds in a sanctuary. She also bought cassette tapes of bird calls and laughed as if they were telling jokes. Occasionally, a zoo staff member would chastise her for showing up clearly very inebriated with a kid in tow. When that would happen, we would just move on to the next thing. My mother also claimed that bird calls would wake her up too early. We lived on the 21st floor. There were no birds nesting up there or anywhere near. I never heard any bird calls up there.

Cat's Eyes

My mother liked to do things to cause chronic issues with cats' eyes. This was an issue with one of our cats. I didn't realize she'd been the one doing it. One year, we went to a bed and breakfast that had cats. My mother mentioned that one of the cats had really messed up eyes. I'd seen the cat. Its eyes were fine. Later, the cat developed a terrible eye problem, just like our cat. The lady who ran the bed and breakfast yelled at my mother and told her she'd seen what she'd done to the cat's eyes.

Barfing Blood

One day, when I was a little kid, one of our cats was hiding in a bathroom cabinet, barfing up blood. My mother seemed unconcerned. I asked her if we could help him, but she said there was nothing to do. My father came home, asked my mother what she'd done to the cat, and yelled at her. He didn't give the cat to a safe home, though, and he didn't seem concerned about her doing similar stuff to me.

Cats and Water

My mother had a thing about torturing cats with water. At one point, when we were in the house we lived in when I was 2 to 4, she held our cats underwater in a hot tub, insisting it was part of a flea bath. That is not at all how a flea bath is done. In other instances, in the apartment, she would hold our cats' faces under a bathtub faucet running full blast. She tried to retell this story as if it had been someone else from their past, but that didn't even make any sense.

Stealing Pets

I think a lot of the pets we had were stolen. My parents would talk about how it had been a good thing they'd moved right after they got a certain pair of cats because they looked just like cats that had gone missing in the neighborhood, and they were afraid people would ask questions. In one incident, my mother presented me with a gerbil when I got home from school and told me an elaborate story about how it had been found wandering the halls of the building alone in a gerbil ball. Later, building workers came by asking if she was the one who had it. They told her she wasn't in trouble; they just wanted it back.

O.D.

My mother named one of her cats O.D. for 'Oh Damn' because she claimed that she'd discovered the cat had terrible intestinal trouble right after she adopted her. In reality, I think the cat was fine up until my mother got her. My mother couldn't get away with naming a child for a medical issue, but she could get away with that with a cat.

The Gator

At one point, my father's brother's cat disappeared at the same time as my parents were visiting him in Florida. When I asked about where the cat was, my parents made up a story about him getting eaten by an alligator. I later asked my uncle about it and found out that wasn't true and that he'd always suspected my parents had something to do with it.

The Bird

When I was young, my mother took me on a trip to the Southwest. One morning, we saw a little baby bird on the sidewalk. She scooped it up, took it into our motel room, and made it a nest of tissues on the counter. She said she wasn't sure if it would survive. The next morning, it was gone, and she told me it had died. Later, in the main area of the motel, some other guests yelled at her about what they'd seen her do to the bird. Why would she bring it in and care for it just to do something terrible to it later? I don't know, but it was similar to her pattern with me.

Lizards

One year, when we went to visit my father's mother, she was very excited about some little lizards that had taken up residence in her bathroom. She showed them to all the family members staying in the house and told everyone to be very careful where they stepped. My mother smashed one of them on the floor on purpose. She left it there and waited in the area just outside the bathroom to get my grandmother's reaction when she found it.

She then told her that one of the grandkids must have accidentally stepped on it.

Dead Rats

My mother sometimes liked to get a dead bloated rat on the edge of a body of water and lead me to it, then tell me it reminded her of me. This happened on two occasions in my childhood. As an adult, I woke up to find a dead rat on my doorstep shortly after I'd outed her about the abuse. It was not a kill left by a cat. It was not bloody but cleanly laid out with its nose against my door and not a mark on it.

Jelly Fish

My mother was not alone in her cruelty to animals, though she was much more enthusiastic about it than my father and did it a lot more. In one incident, when I was little, he scooped up little bitty jellyfish the tide had brought into the shallows at a beach resort where we were staying. We would look at them swimming in the water cupped in his hands for a moment; then he would suddenly close his hands and burst them for comic effect. He got yelled at by a resort staffer for his behavior.

9. Sexual Abuse and Inappropriateness

About

There is a lot about sexual abuse in this book. I have given sexual abuse its own section in this book that you can skip over if needed. Although this section is useful for a more thorough understanding of abuse dynamics that can include medical abuse, it's not necessary to read this section. Give yourself permission to skip over it or any other section of the book if you need to.

This would be one of the larger sections of the book besides the section on MBP abuse itself if I included all the memories I have of sexual abuse. Like most of the sections in this book, the incidents in this section are only a small fraction of the incidents in my life, which would be in this section if included.

Not everyone who has been through MBP abuse has been through sexual abuse; however, there are undeniable parallels. Both reflect a willful disregard for other people's bodily autonomy. I believe that anyone morally bankrupt enough to be capable of MBP abuse is morally bankrupt enough to be capable of sexual abuse and vice versa. If a sexual abuser didn't commit MBP abuse against anyone, it was simply because they didn't feel like it. If an MBP abuser didn't commit sexual abuse against anyone, it was simply because they didn't feel like it. They have already proven it is a line they would be willing to cross.

Other MBP cases involving this pattern:

- Sickened by Julie Gregory includes a description of an incident involving a setup for an underage wet t-shirt contest.

- Deedee Blanchard had her daughter when she was 24, and the father was 17.

- There was a sexual component to the abuse nurse "Jolly" Jane Toppan inflicted on others.

- There was a sadistic sexual component to the abuse medical orderly Donald Harvey inflicted on others.

- In addition, both the Rajneesh cult and Jim Jones cult (both included in the pattern chart because of poisoning) engaged in sexual abuse.

The Monster

Incident Tags/Trigger Warnings

sexual abuse, strangulation

Incident

When I was a little girl, my mother would sometimes strangle me unconscious with one hand while molesting me with the other. Other times, she would sit on my face without underwear so that I was unable to breathe. I was so young that I believed a monster to be doing it. I would hear someone coming, fear it was a monster, and freeze with my eyes closed. I now realize who it was because she was the only one in the apartment. I learned that the best way of surviving was to play dead. This caused the monster, whom I later realized was her, to lose interest.

Sometimes, I would later describe the incidents with the monster to my mother, hoping that she would help protect me because I did not realize it was her. I remember once describing the monster as "slimy and fat." She reacted as if she was hurt by this, and I couldn't understand why. At this age, it was inconceivable to me that it could actually be her. When I asked her about her reaction, she refused to explain it.

At one point, a child who had slept over at our apartment described the same thing happening to her to an adult in her life. I was accused. The room was dark, and they just knew it was a female. The adult told my mother, who acted shocked and innocent. I told the adult I hadn't done it, and the same thing was happening to me. I asked her to help me stop it from happening to me, too. She flat-out refused to believe me and considered the matter settled. Meanwhile, some at school had figured out what was actually going on, but they refused to help me and just kept pocketing the tuition money and donations.

In retrospect, I don't think it was rational that the adult in this case believed my mother. I hadn't been through puberty yet, and the attacker clearly had. I think she simply could not see my mother this way. Maybe she felt like she would have to report an adult, and this was too frightening for her to conceive of.

<u>Points To Make</u>

Never ever consider something like this to be handled and settled privately. If you have not contacted police and social services about a sex crime you know happened to a child, you have not handled it correctly. This person probably thought that she was also protecting me from consequences or a juvenile record. In fact, had she reported what she believed happened, there would have been an investigation that would have caused the actual truth to come out. I would have been rescued. If you are not law enforcement or a social worker, do not presume yourself capable of taking their place and doing their job.

Mutilation

Incident Tags/Trigger Warnings

mutilation, genital mutilation

Incident

Sometimes, my mother attacked my private parts in a way that was pure sadism. She would cut me and stab me, sometimes with scissors, sometimes with I'm not sure what. I won't go into detail here.

At one point, I was in a camp program affiliated with the public school system, and they caught on that she had done something to me in their bathroom. They tried to stop her, but she rushed me away before they could, me still bleeding with a hole torn through my tights and underpants. If I'd been enrolled in the school as a student, they would have known where to direct social services and police, but they didn't have as much information on kids just attending their side programs. We never went back, and I didn't know how to get back there for help on my own or contact them.

Why would she take this risk? She took a lot of stupid risks. She often worried about how to get out of a problem after the fact. She also may have been surprised by the fact that they didn't look the other way like the Catholic school she was sending me to did.

Santa

<u>Incident Tags/Trigger Warnings</u>

sexual abuse

<u>Incident</u>

One year, my father insisted on playing Santa at the building holiday party even though several of the parents were uncomfortable with this idea. They felt unsafe about having their children in his lap, and some of them refused to let their children sit in Santa's lap that year because they knew it was him. He'd also had inappropriate sexual behavior towards children at another building function, and I'm sure that was on their minds.

At some point, it seems he did act sexually inappropriately while playing Santa. I'm not sure what happened, but I remember, at one point, people pulling their children away from him and shutting it down. No one called the police. I don't care how many other people were in the room at the time who also didn't call the police or who maybe would call the police later. If something like this happens, you call the police. Unsurprisingly, this was not the last building event where he acted sexually inappropriate towards children. He was later caught molesting a boy, but again, no one called the police or social services.

Sponsoring Children

Incident Tags/Trigger Warnings

child sexual abuse

Incident

When I was young, my mother sponsored a child through one of those many charities that allows people to sponsor a child in another country and become a pen pal with that child. Many people did that, and it was a way to engage with more children that didn't raise any red flags. My mother would sit at the dining table and spend time poring over letters, reading them, and writing them. It was standard for the people on the other end to send photos of the child and describe the child's life and how the money was being used. I never saw what my mother wrote, but she sometimes showed me the pictures of the child and the letters the charity had sent, including a note from the child.

One day, the tone of these letters and photos changed drastically. The child and an adult standing protectively with her scowled at the camera. The letter said that she was sending the photo to show my mother how unhappy she was with what my mother had done and that she had adults who would protect her. They would, of course, not be providing the photos my mother had asked for. The letter spoke of how disappointed they were and went on about bad feelings. I was confused as to what happened. My mother wouldn't explain it. I was too young to read between the lines, even after what I'd gone through myself. The adult reaction to protecting her didn't clue me in because that wasn't the adult reaction I had in my life.

I asked my mother to explain it. I didn't understand why they were so unhappy. My mother told me they were not unhappy. I pointed out their faces in the photos. She told me that part of the underprivileged nature of the part of the world they were writing from was that they knew less than us about a lot of stuff, including social interactions. She explained that they didn't know about smiling in photographs. Even at that age, I knew that was not true. I pointed out that they had been smiling in all their photographs before.

My parents stopped sponsoring the child, but the organization never seemed to have reported them. No one from law enforcement or social services ever followed up with us. Several years later, a scandal broke when it came out that several charities like this were leaving letters like this unreported to authorities.

Premeditation

<u>Incident Tags/Trigger Warnings</u>

sexual abuse

<u>Incident</u>

Throughout my childhood, my parents said things that made it very clear that they had both premeditated abuse, including sexual abuse, against me since before I was even born. My mother repeatedly told me how my father's first choice for a name for me before I was born was to name me after his favorite French maid character from their sexual role-playing. She didn't want to do that, so they compromised by giving me a different French name despite the fact that we have no French ancestry and it was not a family name.

She would also often say that they'd had kids because they knew I would be fun when I was older, but they hadn't realized how fun I would be right away as soon as I was born. This had particular overtones because of the abuse. She would also sometimes say that it wasn't fair they'd gotten stuck with kids just because they'd wanted to have sex. My parents used birth control for years before having me. In this context, it's clear what this comment means.

Screaming

<u>Incident Tags/Trigger Warnings</u>

sexual assault, lost time

<u>Incident</u>

When I was in junior high school, I was spending an evening in front of the TV with my family. I went into my room to get something. I sat down on my bed for a moment and forgot what I was looking for. I walked back into the room where everyone else was, and I was surprised to find that I'd just lost an hour of time. I asked them about it, and they seemed uncomfortable. They said they'd seen my father follow me into my room and heard me screaming for help but hadn't gone in because they were too frightened. I had no idea what they were talking about. They apologized. They said they knew they should have helped me but were just too scared. I still had no idea what they were talking about. This was about thirty years ago now. My memory of this incident has not changed since. I still remember exactly what I remembered that night and nothing more. In context, though, it's clear what happened.

The Vest

Incident Tags/Trigger Warnings

child sexual abuse

Incident

At one point, my mother decided that she wanted a big fly fishing vest with lots of pockets for her "volunteering" in the museum. She said she wanted to use it to hold lots of stuff that it would be ok for the museum visitors to touch. Some museums have pieces of exhibits or examples that it's ok for visitors to touch. These are usually inexpensive replicas, examples of raw materials, or stuff used for demonstrations as opposed to the valuable stuff behind glass or ropes. She claimed that she had lots of stuff like this for her volunteering and that such a vest would allow her to organize it all and keep it on her without having to carry a bag or case. On the surface, this seemed plausible enough.

My father bought her one for Christmas in green. After a screaming meltdown she pulled at the mall trying to exchange it for a tan one, she was off to the museum in her tan fly fishing vest. At first, everything seemed ok. She would go off to the museum in it from time to time and come back with stories about using it in the dinosaur hall. Someone told me that there were no touch exhibits in the dinosaur hall, but I didn't think much of it, figuring they must have been mistaken.

Eventually, my mother got in trouble and had to stop her behavior. She would apparently invite people to reach in and guess what was in the pocket without looking. Some of the things in her pockets were inappropriate. In other cases, it seems she had simply cut the ends of the pockets out in strategic places and invited people, including children, to keep on reaching until they figured it out.

As usual, she was simply made to stop, not actually held responsible, probably because others were afraid of her or afraid of public backlash if the story got out. I'm not sure what happened in terms of reporting in this case. It's possible that people reported it to the museum instead of to the authorities. It's possible that they did report it to the authorities and that the authorities didn't have enough evidence or dropped the ball. I just know that she never faced consequences for this.

Shorts

Incident Tags/Trigger Warnings

Munchausen, MBP, sexual abuse

Incidents

The following are incidents that would also be in this section if I'd done a full write-up of them. Each one gets a short blurb. Some are so straightforward that they do not need a full write-up. Others are ones I cut from a full write-up for length because they are similar to others I have already done a full write-up of. Others are short because there is no point in putting myself or you, the reader, through all the gory details simply to get the information across.

Drugging

At a certain point in my adult life, it dawned on me that I'd been drugged unconscious a lot during the first 18 years of my life and that at least some of these incidents had involved sexual abuse. I was not one to experiment with drugs or sex as a teenager, so I had not figured it out nearly as soon as others might have. Given what I now look back on, I know both of my parents were involved in this.

Maintenance

At a certain point, the maintenance staff at the building stopped responding to my mother's calls alone because of times she had gotten sexually aggressive with them. At one point, she'd stripped down to nothing but nylons and refused to move out of the way of the door and allow the man to leave when he refused her sexual advances. As usual, she tried to pretend this was someone else in the building, but the truth came out.

Grabbing

My father frequently grabbed people inappropriately or rubbed up against them. He would grab at men, women, and children in public places and pretend like it was accidental, then flip the story around later.

10. Neighbors

About

<u>About Creepiness Towards Neighbors & MBP</u>

Vandalism, graffiti, stealing, breaking and entering, and other anti-social behaviors are not a phase or a stage when committed by an adult. They are a sign of a larger cluster of behaviors. Some kids may get into graffiti or breaking and entering when still in a developmental stage in which they can be taken in by the wrong crowd or act out until they've learned better coping. On the other hand, some serial killers, such as the golden state killer, started with break-ins.

How do you distinguish between these two groups? The difference is pretty obvious when you think about it. Breaking into someone else's home, though serious for a youth, is a completely different thing in a person of middle age who does not have a financial reason to steal. This is a sign of a dangerous person. I do not have any training in criminology or psychology. I make these observations as a matter of simple common sense. You have probably met kids who grew out of a troubled phase with some guidance, and you have probably also met adults who will only continue to escalate bad behavior throughout the rest of their lives. I think the average person reading this probably has a pretty good idea from their own lives of the personality types I'm talking about.

If someone in your building or neighborhood is displaying this behavior, do not brush it off. You probably don't have any idea how many people in your neighborhood the same type of thing has happened to until you start talking to people. Do not let people like this isolate you or stop you from comparing notes with others.

Please, please, please use security cameras and home alarms. Please change your alarm codes regularly. If this is what we knew about, what did we not know about? How many people's places did she get in and out of without getting caught? Did any of them later get sick from food in their fridge or from household toiletries? Did she have pictures or videos of them? Please protect yourself and your loved ones.

- Other MBP cases involving the patterns in this section: Beverly Allitt also engaged in shitting in public or community spaces. Donald Harvey also committed burglary.

- Other related incidents in other sections:

'Eviction' under Emotional Sadism

'The Christmas Ornaments' under Crime Framing

'Graffiti' under Crime Framing

'Cookies for Maintenance' under Traditional MBP

'The Transformer' under Infrastructure and Transportation Sabotage

Binoculars

Incident Tags/Trigger Warnings

Voyeurism, Stalking

Incident

When we first moved into our apartment, the lot next door, just to the south, was empty. A few years later, developers built a high-rise retirement home on the lot. My mother developed a new fascination with looking across at the building with a large pair of binoculars. She would do it very often and for long periods of time. She claimed to be watching falcons nesting on the exterior of the building, but I could never see them. She would describe seeing them rip apart pigeons. I don't know if there were ever actually any birds nesting on the outside of the building. If there were, I never saw them.

At some point, it came out that someone had been writing creepy letters to some of the residents in the retirement home, describing stuff that one would only know by looking through their windows. As far as I know, my mother never faced any real consequences for this, although I think they knew it was her. I'm not sure if she signed the letters or if they just figured it out on their own. Given the locations of the apartments targeted, it was probably a short list of suspects, and they knew from previous run-ins which apartment in our building had someone with those types of behaviors.

She told the story from the third-party perspective as she often did with stories of bad or embarrassing things she'd been caught doing. There was a particular tone she always used in these stories that gave her away. It was the same tone she used when describing a person in the board meeting complaining of alien abduction, or when talking about a person doing sex work down the street (See "The Acting Company" in Reversing Parent Child Relationships), or when accusing a security guard of racist comments. (See 'The Security Guard" in Non-Medical Sick Stories). It was this very exaggerated, put-upon, and condescending tone meant to separate herself from the incident as much as possible.

Legislation

Stalking laws have been increased in the last few decades. That's a good thing, but they could still be strengthened. They also need to be enforced consistently.

Breaking and Entering

Incident Tags/Trigger Warnings

Burglary, Voyeurism

Incident

When I was a little kid, my mother would often take me with her to sit around while she was working out on the exercise machines by the pool. One day, this went strangely. A young woman on one of the other machines confronted her about something she'd done. They both continued working out on their machines as the woman began describing what she'd done. I think the machines may have helped them channel their energy and stopped it from becoming a more aggressive confrontation. Third parties listened in amusement while I listened in confusion.

My mother had figured out that some apartments had the same keys. Through trial and error, she could get into some of the other apartments in the building by trying her own keys in other locks. She had walked into this woman's apartment and walked in on her sitting around in a towel after a shower. She hadn't attempted to make an excuse or talk her way out of it. She just gaped at having been caught and then walked back out without saying a word.

The conversation ended after the woman apparently decided that she'd had enough of chewing out my mother in front of other exercisers. She had already made a report to the building, so she knew that it was being handled. I think this conversation was more about speaking her mind and getting out her frustration, which was totally understandable.

My mother never let on that she was upset or embarrassed by the conversation. Maybe she wasn't. She may have enjoyed the other woman's discomfort. I don't know what her plans in that apartment would have been if she hadn't been caught or how many other apartments she did that to without ever having been caught. We weren't kicked out of the building, and that's amazing. Maybe she had managed to convince the building that it was an accident. More likely, she claimed something like that, and they knew it was a lie but couldn't prove it.

Shitting

Grose

Incident

One day, we were waiting for the elevators to reach our floor and take us downstairs. There was a metal ashtray fixed to the wall between the two elevators about waist-high to an adult. As we waited for the elevator, my mother mentioned that someone had shit in the ashtray recently but that it had been cleaned out since then. I did not believe her. It seemed implausible to me that anyone would do that. I couldn't think why anyone would. Everyone's apartment with their own personal toilet was just a few feet away. It didn't make any sense.

She explained that it hadn't been an accident or an emergency. They had done it because they wanted to. This was even stranger to me. She then began to talk about how difficult it was. I asked her what she meant. She pointed out the height. An adult would need to get a footstool or be on tip-toe. Even then, it was not a large surface easy to hit. It was fastened to the wall so it couldn't be taken down and put back up. I was confused by this conversation and didn't put it together at the time. Later, we ran into some maintenance workers in the hall who seemed very unhappy with her, and they had a word with her about it.

Similar Cases

See 'Public Defecation or Exposing Others to Feces' in the pattern chart.

The Move

<u>Incident</u>

When I was a little girl, a family in our neighborhood moved way out to the suburbs to get away from us. We showed up to the little girl's birthday at their new house uninvited. They included me when we showed up because I didn't know we weren't invited, and they didn't have the heart to tell me. At the party, every kid got a little flower pot to decorate and take home. My mother was angry because they had not ok'd this with her first. She had brought me uninvited but was angry I got something to take home that wasn't cleared with her. I think she was mostly angry because I was happy about it. As we were leaving, she "accidentally" broke it. They offered another plain one to replace it that I could decorate later. She said no. "I knew that was going to happen," one of the mothers said. I took home the broken pot, pasted it together, and kept it for years. I never saw that family again.

The Baby Sitter

Stealing, manipulation

When I was little, I had a particular babysitter who lived in the building, who I liked very much. She was a teenager and a good babysitter, and I looked up to her. At one point, she accidentally left her shoes in our place and walked back to her apartment in her sock-feet one night when she was very tired. My mother found them, claimed she had bought them for me, and gave them to me. Later, we had to return them. It was very awkward.

In another incident, my mother scammed this babysitter by pretending to have the authority to rent out another apartment in the building to her. She lived with her mother, so she rented the apartment for a night to have a romantic evening with her boyfriend. In fact, my mother had no authority to do this. The actual owner of the apartment walked in on the babysitter and her boyfriend. It was a terrible situation for everyone involved. I'm not sure if my mother's primary motivation was money or this awkward situation.

Sneaking In

<u>Incident Tags/Trigger Warnings</u>

Stealing, Burglary, Lying

<u>Incident</u>

The young man who lived next door to us in the building would sometimes prop his door open for fresh air. I think he felt safe doing this because there was a doorman in the lobby, but he never considered that creepy people might live in the building. As we came home one day, my mother saw the door propped open. She told me I needed to wait there and be quiet. She tiptoed in and came back out a little later with something in her hand. We then went back into our apartment. Later, he confronted her about it, and she tried to tell him that I had done it. He looked at me, a confused little girl, and at her and knew she was lying. He told her off but never pressed charges.

The Shoe Guy

Stealing, Burglary, Lying

At one point, a new guy moved onto our floor of the building, who everyone seemed to like. I'll call him Larry. That was not his name. The one person who did not get along with him was my mother. She went full blast with defamation behind his back, trying to turn everyone against him, as was her habit when she had a difference with someone. The problem seems to have started when she stole some of his belongings out of the storage area and got called on it.

Each floor in our building had storage space off to the side of the service elevator bank. It was a very dusty area that smelled like paint. It contained a series of cages that people could lock their belongings in. Most people kept things such as suitcases in there. Sometimes, my mother would go in there and fuss with the locks and swear. She told me that she had forgotten combinations, and I was young and naive enough to believe her. Larry was some kind of a salesman, and he kept a stock of high-end expensive shoes. One day, building security came to our door to ask about stolen shoes. From that day forward, she was out to get him. She would tell people in the building terrible stories about him beating his wife. There was no evidence this ever happened.

The Perfume Container

Incident Tags/Trigger Warnings
Stealing, Burglary, Lying

Incident

My mother was friendly with a flight attendant who lived in the building who sometimes chatted with us in the elevators. One day, this woman bought an expensive perfume that came in a special box she wanted. The box was Egyptian-themed and reminded her of her heritage. She wanted the box even more than the perfume and so splurged on perfume at the limit of her budget. I did not know any of this information at the time, though. My mother came home with an elaborate Egyptian box, telling me she had bought it for me. In fact, she could only have gotten it by sneaking into the woman's apartment. She later decided to rub the woman's face in it by prompting me to tell her about the box when I was still unsuspecting.

The Crying Woman

Munchausen, MBP, Lying

Incident

One day, when I was a little girl, we walked into the lobby of our building and saw a woman crying on the bench in the lobby while another woman consoled her. My mother took me aside and told me not to say anything to her because she was very sensitive about what had happened. I asked what had happened. My mother told me that she had been so badly sunburned that her skin would be messed up and ugly forever. This was strange because she didn't even look sunburned at all. I pointed this out to my mother, but she brushed it off with some sort of usual statement about her being older and knowing more. She told me to wait where I was, then approached the woman and told her she would be stuck like that forever. The two women on the bench acted as you would expect. They were in no state to be dealing with my mother's nonsense. They shouted at her, and the doorman told her to leave them alone.

Knocking

Incident Tags/Trigger Warnings
Manipulation, Conflict

Incident

When I was a little girl, we would socialize with other families in the neighborhood who had kids around the same age. One day, one of these families had enough of my mother and decided that they weren't going to deal with her anymore. She brought me over to their place anyway. She would normally knock on the door, but this time, she stood off to the side just outside of the sight of the door's peephole and made me knock. I could hear them talking through the door. They debated whether to open the door because they didn't want to deal with my mother, but couldn't see her and thought I might need help. They opened the door, and my mother barged in faster than they could do anything about it despite their angry protests. I think they did not have her thrown out by security or police because they did not want to make me observe that. I may have been upset at the time, but I would have been so much safer in the long run if they had done that.

Laundry

Incident Tags/Trigger Warnings

Stealing

Incident

My mother enjoyed stealing and messing with other people's laundry in the building laundry. It was a big room with lots of machines in the basement of the building. She would look around to make sure no one was around to see and then switch out her clothes for someone else's to save a quarter. She would dump their clothes on the floor in a heap. Other times, she would take clothes she liked. Other times, she would mess with clothes just for spite, even though she didn't need a machine or want any of the clothes. I remember building staff coming down to the laundry room to confront her about it in front of me.

The Car "Accident"

Incident Tags/Trigger Warnings

Bill Cosby, Car Accidents

Incident

My mother was fixated on a Bill Cosby stand-up routine about driving his manual transmission car in San Francisco and the "idiots" who got too close behind him at an uphill stop sign. This risked a fender bender because of the slight slide backward that can happen. She started repeating this story as if it were about the people behind her on the exit ramp for our building's garage. In fact, they were not getting too close. I would be seated in the back, and she would look in the rearview mirror and parrot his lines from the story word for word and fuss as if she was struggling hard to shift in time because the person was too close. They were fine. They kept a good distance from her, but that didn't fit what she was reenacting. This happened repeatedly.

Later, she got a talking to from garage staff about only going forward there. She had apparently slid far enough back on an occasion that she caused an actual accident. I was not there at the time, though.

The Management Office

Incident Tags/Trigger Warnings
Conflict, Locking out, Screaming

Incident

My mother used to be friendly with the people in the management office of the building, but one day that changed. She used to go in there to chat, but she would talk their ears off and never grow tired. They would have to politely excuse themselves, but there was no place they could go. The whole front of the office was glass. She could see if they were there. They had lots of work to do and could not afford to just sit around chatting.

One day, it was necessary for them to tell her more firmly that they couldn't talk because she hadn't taken the hint. She had a total meltdown. She started screaming at them and caused a scene. After that, she would try to go back in as if nothing had happened and she was just stopping by for another chat. They would not buzz her in, though. I think they didn't feel safe. She got bent out of shape, claiming they were snobs who thought they were better than her.

Mailboxes

Incident Tags/Trigger Warnings
Stealing, Mail Tampering, Conflict

Incident

When I was a teenager, the Mailboxes etc. store came to our neighborhood. My mother was immediately enamored with it. I couldn't understand what was so interesting about mailboxes and a selection of office supplies. She went there a lot and spent an unusual amount of time there. She often invited me to join her, and I declined.

One day, I finally agreed to go, just to see what all the fuss was about. When the man behind the counter saw us, he scolded her and told her that he'd warned her before about coming in. He told her that she had to leave other people's mailboxes alone. She didn't rent a mailbox there. She just went around trying to break into other people's mailboxes.

Shorts

<u>Incident Tags/Trigger Warnings</u>

Vandalism, Car Sabotage, Paranoia, Conflict

<u>Incidents</u>

The following are incidents that would also be in this section if I'd done a full write-up of them. Each one gets a short blurb. Some are so straightforward that they do not need a full write-up. Others are ones I cut from a full write-up for length because they are similar to others I have already done a full write-up of.

The Garage

(This is also in the Gremlin Mode section.) My mother liked keying cars and tried to teach me to do the same. I didn't understand what the point was. She acted like it was lots of fun. She would do it to cars near ours in the building garage and also to our own. When she was confronted, she pointed to the key marks on our own car, claiming that she would not possibly have done it to her own car, too.

Hot Dogs

When we lived in our house towards the end of my high school years, the larger neighborhood had a series of block parties every summer. On any given weekend, you could find several blocks in the city having their annual block party. She would tell me a story about the "hot dog guy." This was supposedly a man who was not all there mentally who went around to all of the block parties insisting they give him hot dogs until he'd had a bunch in a day. Later on, someone told me that she was, in fact, talking about herself.

The Therapist

When I was a little girl, my mother made a big to do about how another mom in the mom's group was uncomfortable around her because the other mom had issues. When I asked her about it, she told me that some people are very uncomfortable around psychiatrists because they're afraid that they will be able to pick up on their issues and know what they're thinking. This did not make sense as an explanation because my mother was not a psychiatrist. The other woman was.

11. School

About

<u>About Creepiness at Schools & MBP</u>

If your kid is at a school that tolerates behavior such as my parents' behavior, your kid is in danger. It's not just that your kid is in danger of that one particular person you are aware of. It's that abusers flock to institutions like these like flies do to shit. If they aren't going to report someone like my mother, they aren't going to report anyone else with any other form of inappropriate or criminal behavior around a child, either. Abusers talk. They figure out what institutions are safe for them to offend at. They spread the word. While the schools I attended were helping my parents get away with abuse, they were also helping others get away with abuse of other children, too.

Some will point out that in many places, such as public schools here in the U.S., schools are obligated to accept students. I will point out that they are not obligated to stay quiet - in fact, the opposite is true. A school should call the police and social services and warn parents and students.

You'll see more about how my parents were creepy towards people at my schools if you read the "Catfishing" section, the "Hurting Animals" section, the "Terror Threats" section, and the "Exposing Me To Substances" section. I will also note that this section here is specifically about how my mother was creepy towards people at the schools I attended in non-sexual or mostly non-sexual ways. There were also times when my parents behaved in sexually inappropriate and abusive ways towards my classmates, but I did not include those in this book.

The Parking Lot

physical attack

When I was in elementary school, a classmate passed on a bit of gossip to me one day. She claimed that another classmate (We'll call her Arla. That was not her name.) and Arla's mother thought they were too good for me and my mother. This student was a huge gossip, and there was no good reason to believe what she said, but I took her at face value because I was young and naive. I wasn't upset since Arla and I weren't friends, and the news seemed inconsequential to me. The gossip wouldn't let it go, pressing the point again, not having gotten the reaction she was going for on the first try. Looking back on it, I think it's likely that, in fact, the gossip was in some sort of conflict with Arla, which motivated this.

When I got home that afternoon, and my mother asked me about my day, the story came out since the gossip had made such a production about it. I thought nothing more of it, not realizing how extreme my mother's reaction to such a thing would be.

A while later, the class was buzzing with a story. Arla's mother had been physically attacked in the school parking lot. This was not gossip. The teachers confirmed it. Apparently, it was a particularly bad attack. At first, I believed it was a mugging. This was what it sounded like to me from the first version of events I'd heard.

Later, it came out that this was not what it was. Arla took pains to convince me that she and her mother didn't think they were better than me and my mother and she didn't know how we could have gotten that idea. I accepted this, though I didn't think much more about it than I had when told that they disliked us. I didn't understand why she kept pressing the matter after I'd already acknowledged that and told her I believed her.

Later, it turned out that the attacker had been my mother. That's why Arla had taken pains to convince me that there was no bad blood between us. People seemed to think that I was lucky that Arla's mother had agreed not to press charges. I was not lucky. Charges against my mother for physical violence could have made a huge difference in my life.

<u>Points To Make</u>

You are not doing kids any favors by deciding not to press charges against the adults who have custody of them.

This incident illustrates a loophole in some mandated reporting laws. If violence happens on school property, it should fall under the umbrella of mandated reporting regardless of whether or not it directly involves students.

Fixations on Teachers

Incident Tags/Trigger Warnings

Munchausen, MBP, Stalking

Incidents

My mother would sometimes develop fixations on people, and sometimes, these people were my teachers. Sometimes, she looked up to them, and sometimes, she disliked them and enjoyed antagonizing them.

She frightened my kindergarten teacher. The kindergarten teacher had befriended some of the moms but not her. Toward the end of the school year, the kindergarten teacher invited some of her friends, some of whom were moms in the class, to her house to plant roses. My mother crashed this event with me in tow. She brought a rosebush the teacher didn't want and planted it in a place the teacher didn't want it, despite the teacher telling her she would just dig it up later. My mother continued on as if all this was normal, then left with me when I guess she felt she'd accomplished whatever she thought she was doing.

She idolized my first-grade teacher and practically fawned all over her despite the fact that the woman herself had several inappropriate behaviors and was deeply disliked by everyone else in the school. A few years later, she dragged me to therapy, insisting I was suicidal, and kept bringing me back no matter how many times I refused to participate in the process. After more than a year of this, we ran into this teacher in the parking lot. My mother acted like it was a surprise, which, at the time, I thought it was. She attempted to chat with the teacher, who clearly just wanted to get out of there. To my mother, this was a social occasion, but the teacher clearly didn't see running into someone at the therapist's office as that. She got out of there as quickly as she could despite my mother's efforts. After she pulled out of the parking lot, my mother remarked to me that she couldn't believe how long it had taken us to run into her there.

Marcy

Incident Tags/Trigger Warnings

Munchausen, MBP, Manipulation, Inappropriate behavior toward children

Incidents

There was a girl in my class in the K-8 school I attended. We'll call her Marcy. That was not her name. My mother zeroed in on Marcy as someone easy to manipulate and got to work. First, my mother insisted, despite my protests, that she chaperone a field trip to go apple picking. Marcy was frightened because there were bees, which she was allergic to. My mother instantly had a project. A child who had actual allergies she didn't have to make up? It was a treat for her. By the end of the field trip, my mother was her hero and protector. Further, she had convinced Marcy, who was one of the popular kids, to instruct all of the other children to ice me out until I was nice to my mom. No matter how many times I asked my mother and Marcy what they thought I'd done to my mother, they would not explain themselves. It was a miserable day. This behavior continued after the field trip as well.

Sometime later, my mother came up with a new scheme. One day, Marcy came into school with a moving story of what a good deed she'd done. She had been at a shopping mall with her mother when they ran into a woman who was having a problem. The woman was very upset because she used to go shopping with her daughter, but her daughter had died. She just wanted to go shopping with her daughter again and asked if she could take Marcy shopping around the mall and if Marcy would just pretend to be her daughter for the day. This woman supposedly had a still-living bad daughter who had refused to indulge in this fantasy.

They agreed. Marcy was happy to help. They went around to all the shops, the woman calling her "Jessie" and her calling the woman "Mommy." At the end of the day, the woman brought her back to her actual mother and said, "Goodbye, Jessie." She said, "Goodbye, Mommy," and waved.

The class ate this story up, and she told it several times. I didn't realize that the woman was my mother. Of course, she'd never had a child die. When it became clear that I'd never had a sister, they became deeply uncomfortable.

I think this may have been a case of borrowing. I had at one Halloween been "Jenny" from the children's story "The Green Ribbon." This sounds very close to Jessie.

Rand McNally

Incident Tags/Trigger Warnings
Stealing, Manipulation

Incident

One day in junior high, my mother and I went to the school for some sort of special occasion. It was a field trip or retreat of sorts where people were carpooling. She met up with another mom in the parking lot, where they discussed directions. This was before even the most basic map websites existed, and both of them had their big Rand McNally map book of the U.S.

They agreed upon directions, and my mother took both map books and headed back to her car. The other mom objected, but it quickly became apparent that my mother was going to cause such an issue, insisting it was her book that the other mom decided to forfeit the expensive book that was clearly hers. It was identical to my mother's. This wasn't about money or a possession. I don't know what it was about. The other parking lot incident that had happened years earlier with my mother at the same school probably was in the other mom's mind as she made the decision not to pursue the matter, especially with her kid in tow. My mother kept both in the car after that. She would fondly mention it as from that incident. It was somehow a souvenir that meant something to her.

Creative Writing

Incident Tags/Trigger Warnings
Manipulation, School rumors, Inappropriate behavior toward children

Incidents

In high school, I had a creative writing class at one point and a political literature class at another point. Both had similar weird incidents in which my mother supposedly "helped" other students with their stories. In both cases, these were not even students I knew very well, and I'm not sure how my mother weaseled her way into this situation.

In the political literature class, we mostly read literature and wrote papers on it, but one assignment required that we write our own political short story. A kid in my class wrote a story he read aloud for the class about a supposedly perfect mother who one day poisoned her entire family's dinner and killed them all. The story ended with them all face down and her sitting at the table as the only one left alive. He later talked about how my mother had helped him a lot with it. I think the idea had been hers, and she had kind of taken over the assignment.

In the creative writing class, another student read part of a story aloud that my mother had helped her with. It was about a girl on a train who was embarrassed as a man was staring at her because he recognized her from somewhere. She didn't finish the story but alluded to the fact that the place he knew her from was a salacious surprise. When it was clear I had no idea what she was talking about, she accidentally let slip that she had thought the story was based on me up until that point.

Did their parents know what they were writing and that another parent was "helping"? As a parent, what would you do if you found out what your child's story was and where it came from? And that the school hadn't told you?

The Party

<u>Incident Tags/Trigger Warnings</u>
Inappropriate behavior toward children

<u>Incident</u>

One day, I came home from school, and something was different. There were kids in my house from my school, but not kids I knew well. I asked what they were doing there. One of them asked incredulously what I was doing there. I was thought of as kind of a goody-goody, and he was insisting that I should not be there and should leave. He seemed very uncomfortable with the fact that I was at the house. When I told him I lived there, he didn't believe me. Things were happening at that house that did not fit what he knew of me. I asked him what he was talking about, but he wouldn't explain. He insisted it wasn't safe for me to be there. This was a kid in my class, so although he was maybe less of a goody-goody than I was, he was still underage. What were my parents up to? I'm still not sure.

12. Exposing Me to Substances

About

About Exposure to Substances & MBP

This connects with MBP in the same way that sexual abuse does in that it connects to having no regard for other's bodily autonomy, health, and suffering. Once again, this behavior only makes sense in the context of MBP when you realize that MBP has much more to do with sadism, power, and control than it does with seeking love and approval from medical professionals. This again connects with sexual abuse.

Drug Muling

<u>Incident Tags/Trigger Warnings</u>
drug muling, exposing kids to substances

<u>Incident</u>
When I was a little girl, my parents took me on a yearly trip to Cozumel. They also occasionally went on other trips to Mexico, Central America, and South America, including Belize and Honduras.

One year, on our way back home from Cozumel, my mother was stopped at the airport. She had an entire suitcase filled with Tylenol with Codeine, which was sold over the counter in Mexico in those days. She insisted it was just her own personal medication even though it was the only thing in the whole suitcase.

In another incident, my parents went somewhere on a trip and brought me back souvenirs. This included "candy," which I needed to test first before them. They instructed me how to rub it on my gums because it was a special type of candy that worked like that. I now realize that they were probably testing cocaine on me to make sure it was safe before they took any.

One year, on our trip to Cozumel, when I was still very little, my mother bought some big grapes and told me that I needed to practice swallowing them whole to eat them in the authentic way they were meant to be eaten. I found it very uncomfortable, but she insisted. Eventually, she made me swallow other things as well. I think she was using me to mule drugs because she had been caught before. This also connects with my experiences going to the bathroom after we arrived back home, but you don't need to hear about that.

I believe at one point, there was a man who caught on and tried to help me. I don't know who he was. We had gone to a restaurant in Cozumel with a little 3-hole mini golf course in the back. He asked me if I was ok and tried to intervene. My parents quickly whisked me away from there. When I asked to go back to that place the next year, they told me it had been destroyed by a hurricane. Looking back at that time period, I cannot find any record of a hurricane.

Antibiotics

Incident Tags/Trigger Warnings

alcohol, dentist

Incident

When I was a little girl, I had to take antibiotics every time I went to the dentist because I had a small heart murmur. The regulations have since changed, and this is no longer required. One day before a dentist appointment, my mother gave me a glass of cola that she claimed had the antibiotic mixed in. I had seen her mix the antibiotic in on previous dental appointments, so I did not question this at first. I took a sip, and it tasted very different from the other times I had tasted cola with antibiotics mixed in. I told her there was something wrong with it, but she insisted that I drink it all.

I barfed immediately after drinking it, an incident she would later use to claim that I had a penicillin and amoxicillin allergy. I have since been exposed to both of these as an adult and had no allergic reaction at all. Looking back now as an adult, I realize from the taste that what I drank had a large amount of strong alcohol mixed in.

I felt very sick. I was dizzy and disoriented, and I felt like I was going to puke again. I told my mother I was too sick to go to the dentist, but she insisted we go and put me in the car. At the dentist's office, they could immediately tell I was very drunk and very nauseous. I gave them an earful about how unhappy I was with them overprescribing the stuff that had made me so sick. They scolded my mother and told her they would report her if it happened again.

Legislation

This is a case in which already existing legislation needs to be enforced. Medical professionals are mandated reporters. In addition, if you see something like this, you morally need to report it whether or not you are a mandated reporter.

Easter Bunnies

Incident Tags/Trigger Warnings

hallucinogens, drugging children

Incident

When I was a little girl, there was a cartoon on TV every year around Easter called "The Easter Bunny is Comin' to Town." I enjoyed this very much when I was young, but I started to get a little too old to be interested in it anymore. Apparently, this wasn't a stage my mother was ready for me to reach yet. She wanted to watch it with me and for me to react like I had when I was younger. She insisted on us watching it, and I sat down, ready to be bored all the way through it.

She gave me a snack and a drink, and after I ate it, the cartoon became fascinating to me. My perceptions of color and of the television changed wildly. It looked like the bunnies were coming out of the TV and painting eggs all over. I tried watching it again later and didn't have this experience again. I asked her about it, and she said this was because of what I had taken before I watched it the previous time. I hadn't known that I had taken anything. I was too young and naive to figure out on my own that I had been drugged.

Points To Make

This could also fit with the "Not ready for" section. I was getting too old for the bunny video. This could also fit with the "Hurting to be right" section. She wanted to be right about me still being an appropriate age for the video.

Party Punch

<u>Incident Tags/Trigger Warnings</u>

alcohol

<u>Incident</u>

One day, when I was a little girl, my mother brought me to a party in the building complex. This was a small gathering of kids and moms. She and the other moms set everything up, including snacks and a punch bowl, as they stood around chatting. When the rest of them turned their backs, she poured a bottle of something into the punch and then hid the bottle away again.

A few minutes later, the kids started complaining that the punch their mothers had served them from the bowl tasted bad. A few moms tasted it and realized that it was heavily spiked. They took the drinks back from their children and remarked that they knew who must have done it. She had just stood there and watched them serve their children without saying anything. The party broke up at that point. She never got in any real trouble for this.

Cheese Wheel

Incident Tags/Trigger Warnings

sadism, drugging children

Incident

When I was a little girl, there was a commercial on TV with a walking talking wheel of cheese. I liked this commercial. One day, my mother gave me something to eat and asked if I felt different. I said I did not. She said that I would. In a few minutes, she tried again. That commercial had come on air on the TV in the room we were in. She told me that this cheese wheel cartoon was now out of the TV and in the room with us. I told her that was ridiculous and not possible.

She insisted, and then I saw it upon her suggestion. I liked this cartoon, so it was not upsetting for me. She decided it would be more entertaining for her if it were upsetting for me. She told me that he had a knife and was going to stab me. I told her that was not true because he was nice. She kept insisting, and eventually, I saw it. I was screaming and cowering in terror. She just about died laughing.

Sleeping Juice

Incident Tags/Trigger Warnings

alcohol

Incident

When I was a little girl, if my mother wanted me to go to sleep and I wasn't sleepy, she would give me a special sleeping juice. This tasted terrible and burnt going down, but then it made me feel warm and sleepy. I now realize that this was juice with a lot of strong alcohol mixed in. This was her go-to drink for herself also. She would fill a glass most of the way with alcohol and then put in enough juice to color it so that it looked like she was drinking juice.

Xanax

<u>Incident Tags/Trigger Warnings</u>

benzos, drug-pushing

<u>Incident</u>

When I was in high school, my mother offered some of the other kids in my school who lived nearby a ride home one day. They all piled in the car with me. I didn't know them that well. Most I just recognized from the hall but didn't know by name. It was an unusual gesture for her, and I couldn't figure out why it was different that one day, but I shrugged it off.

When all of the other kids were gone, we pulled up and parked in front of our house. My mother was unpacking the trunk space in the hatchback when she called me over. She pointed something out. At first, I couldn't even see what she was talking about. She pointed out a little pill lying on the bottom of the trunk space. I shrugged it off. I couldn't have cared less if someone left a stray pill, and I couldn't understand why she thought it was worth pointing out.

She wouldn't let it go. I turned to go to the house, but she kept pulling me back into the conversation. She acted like it was a big deal. "Do you know what that is?" she asked. It was a Xanax. I had no idea what that was. She made a big fuss about it being a strong medication and suggested that only a really troubled person would be on it. She spun a story about one of the kids we'd just dropped off and how it must have been hers. She went on and on about how troubled the young woman must have been and how this was very serious. I didn't consider it any of my business and was bored and tired and moved again to go towards the house.

Again, she wouldn't let the conversation drop. Suddenly, her tone shifted oddly. She asked if I wanted it. I couldn't understand the shift, but I didn't much care. I said no and turned to go to the house again. Again, she kept the conversation going despite my obvious lack of interest. This went back and forth for a while. I couldn't have been less interested, and she wasn't willing to drop her plan. Eventually, she had no choice but to give up when it was clear I wasn't taking the bait.

This was not the only instance of her trying to get me hooked on benzos, and I later discovered that she had a very bad addiction to alcohol and benzos herself. She knew what power it had over her, and she wanted that power over others. (See The Racist Drug Pusher under Non-Medical Sick Stories).

<u>Points To Make</u>

Notice how this behavior often incorporates multiple motivations that serve multiple purposes. She got to tell a sick story about another person, as she very much enjoyed doing. At the same time, she got to try to get me hooked on something that would help her control me.

<u>Advice for Victims</u>

Do you suspect that there is a medical abuser in your midst? Be on the lookout for them to try to get people around them addicted to various substances. Addiction is yet another sick story. It can also cause other types of physical and mental illness. It's also a way they can try to get control over people using medication or other chemical substances. This is also a playbook commonly used by other types of abusers, like those committing sexual abuse or using coercive control.

13. Substance Abuse and MBP

230

About

<u>About Substance Abuse & MBP</u>

There are many times I can clearly point to in which my mother was committing MBP abuse with no chemical-substance-based payoff. There were times she committed this abuse even when she could not possibly get drugs, alcohol, or drug money from the behavior. There were also times in which she was multitasking and engaging in behaviors that served a Munchausen purpose and a chemical substances purpose at once. The psychiatric community defines this behavior differently depending on motivation and payoff. People who do this stuff purely for money as some sort of financial fraud are considered to be malingering. People who do this stuff for internal psychological motivations are considered to be Munchausen abusers.

In reality, however, things are often not as neat and compartmentalized as they are on paper. My mother sometimes engaged in this behavior for one reason, sometimes for another, and sometimes for multiple reasons. You can tell this by what she realistically could have expected to get out of various different fabrications. This is not the only case I have heard of like this. I believe it's especially common for these abusers to occasionally incorporate some financial grift into their behavior, even if that behavior did not start out as a bid for financial gain.

MBP abusers are forcing codependence on their victims and often on others in their victims' lives. This recreates similar co-dependent patterns that sometimes develop in cases of substance abuse. Are some of them recreating family patterns that started with substance abuse or some other form of illness?

Injuries

Incident Tags/Trigger Warnings

physical abuse, medical abuse, painkillers

Incident

My mother would sometimes cause others injuries and then take some of the pain medication they'd been prescribed as a result. She would sometimes do the same with unnecessary medical procedures. I'm not sure if these started out as bids to get pain meds or if they started out as Munchausen abuse and that she then simply happened to take pain meds because they were there. I know she committed a lot of Munchausen abuse in which there was no possibility of getting pain meds. Even if meds were a primary motivation, some of the time, they weren't a primary motivation all of the time. Maybe they were always an afterthought. I don't know. I just know that people, myself included, spent time recovering from injuries and medical procedures without medication because it had mysteriously disappeared around her. This may have served three purposes at once. It allowed her to get high, it allowed her to cause suffering, and it allowed her to gain attention for medical troubles.

Bad Back

Incident Tags/Trigger Warnings

Munchausen, drinking

Incident

When I was a little girl, my mother's back would occasionally "go out." This is a thing that happens to people and may even, on occasion, have been a thing that actually happened to my mother. Usually, however, in her case, this was a put-on. She would wait until I was watching to suddenly have it hit her and fall to the floor. This would only ever happen on the carpeted area near her bed. This would require her to get into the bed, lie down, and send me down to the market in the lobby for a large bottle of vodka.

Sometimes, if I looked away or left the room, she would suddenly and miraculously regain the power to move around as normal. If I asked about it later, she would make an excuse. She would claim that it was just starting to get better but then got worse again. I was young enough that I didn't catch on. I figured it was just adult stuff that I didn't understand.

I would go down to the market with the money and exchange it for the bottle she'd called down about, then come back upstairs to her. At first, the shop clerks would joke around with me about it. Once they started to catch on to how often it happened and how much vodka I kept coming back for, they became concerned and cut her off. I felt I'd somehow messed up. The shop clerk was careful to tell me that I hadn't done anything wrong, but that he couldn't give me anymore.

14. General Substance Abuse

About

<u>About General Substance Abuse & MBP</u>

Substance abuse is common among MBP abusers, although that does not mean that it is an issue for all of them. It's also important to note that most people with substance use issues are not MBP abusers. This section only covers incidents not covered in the previous section. In this section, I only cover incidents that are not directly linked to Munchausen-type behavior. Why cover those at all in a book about medical abuse? I think it paints a more complete picture. In some medical abusers, substance abuse and medical abuse look like a Venn diagram. They sometimes overlap, as demonstrated in the last section, and they sometimes don't, as demonstrated here.

Shorts

As in previous "shorts" sections, here I only give brief descriptions to illustrate a general pattern.

The Post

When I was a little girl, I had a friend over for the day. My mother decided to take us somewhere in the car. We went down to the garage and piled in the car. Everything seemed normal, but when she tried to turn the normal corner, she misjudged badly and hit the concrete post that had always been there. It was a large pillar that was part of the support system for the garage. It wasn't just a light scrape. We heard and felt it as the metal on the exterior of the car bowed in. She muttered something, got out, and looked at the damage, then continued on her way and drove us to our destination. When my friend's parents heard the story that she was barely sober enough to get out of the garage and still drove us anyway, they were not happy.

Drinking and Lurking

When I was a teenager, my mother developed a creepy habit of drinking and watching me from the shadows where she didn't think I could see her. I would stay up late watching TV, as teenagers tend to do, especially on weekends. She would sit on the landing of the stairs above the TV room where she didn't think I could see her. She would sit for hours watching me as I watched TV. Sometimes, when I got up to go to the bathroom or get a snack I would see her tip-toeing up the stairs, holding her drink, trying to get out of my line of sight in time. Other times, she would think she'd found a shadow that covered her well enough, and she would just sit there, not realizing I could still see her feet and her drink on the step. Sometimes, I would call to her, and she would freeze and not answer. If I asked her about it the next day, she would deny it.

The Zoo

One day, when I was a tween, my mother took me to the zoo. I hadn't been in a long time because I wasn't quite zoo-age anymore. She was very insistent, so eventually, I went along with it, and she drove us there. We were in the reptile hall looking at the creatures through the glass with the rest of the crowd when she drunkenly fell into a man and leaned on him. He reacted indignantly. He and the people with him chastised her about acting like that in a family environment with lots of little kids around. We stayed a while longer, then left for other parts of the zoo. She immediately reversed the story and began gossiping about the drunken man who fell into her at the reptile exhibit.

Bed Time

At a certain point when I was a little girl, my mother developed a habit of reading to me at night after I had gotten into bed. Even though I was already old enough to read, she insisted on doing this, saying that it was educational. She would get a long kid's chapter book and sit on the carpet with her drink in hand, reading to me whether I liked it or not. If I fell asleep before she was done reading, she would wake me up to make me continue listening. This sometimes went on for a very long time. Sometimes, she would drink until she passed out and would just be slumped over on the floor with her drink and her book.

Mouthwash

When I was a little girl, I hated how my mother's breath smelled of alcohol when she got me ready for school and took me there each morning. I told her and asked what on earth that was. She told me it was just mouthwash. There was no mouthwash in our bathroom. I asked her, and she said it was under the sink. I checked under the sink. There was none. A few days later, she made me look under the sink again and look at the mouthwash bottle that was there. It was as if she thought this would change the fact that it had never been there before.

The Interview

When I was approaching kindergarten age, my mother took me for an interview at a prestigious kindergarten that she very much wanted to be in the social circle of. She drove me in for the interview wasted. They picked up on it immediately. They informed her that they weren't dealing with this and that it would be a no. They took pains to clarify to her in front of me that it was because of her behavior and that I should not be made to feel bad for this. As soon as we left, she launched into me, blaming me for having failed the interview.

15. Stealing and MBP

About

About Stealing & MBP

Other MBP cases involving this pattern: The stealing/fraud column in the pattern spotting chart is by far the most populated column of all. At first, this may seem unsurprising because medical abuse usually necessitates fraud to pull it off. Upon closer inspection, however, many abusers are involved in stealing and fraud totally unrelated to the medical abuse. In many cases, medical fraud is part of a much larger pattern of stealing and fraud. Donald Harvey, for example, broke into an apartment, stole from it, and then set it on fire.

You should also see the "Neighbors" section. There are a bunch of stealing incidents in there, but there's no point in repeating them.

Checks

<u>Incident</u>

When I was a little girl, my mother tried to teach me how to alter checks. She had a lot to do on her own, and she wanted to pass off some of the work to me. She would take an old blue ballpoint pen with an ink eraser on the end and erase the original writing, then write in what she wanted.

I was too young to understand that I was being taught something illegal. I asked her why we were doing this. She told me the people who wrote her the checks had written them wrong, and she needed to fix them. I asked if she could just get them to write her a new one, and she said she didn't want to bother them. That would be impolite. I tried to help, but I could never get it right. I would press too hard and rip the paper or too softly and leave a smear of ink. She gave up on me helping and did them all on her own.

In another incident involving checks, the guy at the checkout at the little market in the building pointed to a display he had at the register. People who had been in trouble for writing bad checks were on there. He would not do that the first time, but if it kept on happening, he would put them up. My mother was on there. He explained that he didn't want to, but he felt he had no choice.

Black Coral

Incident

When I was little, we would go to Cozumel every spring. At the time, they had a lot of advertisements for black coral jewelry. My mother got in trouble for stealing from these jewelry shops, then retold the story as if it had been some other lady we never met. After that, she always spoke badly of the black coral shops. She would act very judgmental of other tourists interested in buying it, and of the shops selling it.

BBQ

<u>Incident</u>

One day, when I was a little kid, my parents took me to a barbecue. I was hungry when we showed up because they hadn't fed me, as often happened. My parents stood around and socialized with the other adults while I trailed along with them, waiting to be fed. The others were eating, but we weren't. I asked for food, and they told me we would eat later. I heard this a lot, and it often meant I just wasn't going to get fed at all. I asked other adults with food if I could have some. The homeowner pointed out to my parents that they hadn't even been invited and that even those who had been invited had brought food to contribute instead of showing up expecting to be fed.

He took pity on me, seeing how skinny I was, and went to go see what he could find for me. He was grilling up burgers for himself and a friend, but he would see if he could find an extra hot dog for me or something. While he was busy doing that, my parents stole the two remaining burgers off the grill that he had been working on for himself and his friend. They snarfed them down, giggling conspiratorially with each other. The homeowner came back, discovered what they'd done, and kicked them out.

Hanging Baskets

Incident

My mother had a pattern of stealing things and then making sure that the people she'd stolen from found out. I'm not sure if she was testing them or just enjoyed their discomfort and frustration. For example, in the house we lived in at the end of my high school years, one of our neighbors had a nice, big, expensive hanging basket of flowers. One day, my mother stole it and hung it on the front porch so that it would be obvious from the sidewalk. She had to give it back a bit later. Logically, I think she had a pretty good idea that she would have to when she did it.

Plants

<u>Incident</u>

Shortly after we had first moved into the house when I was in high school, my mother dug a plant out of the next-door neighbor's front yard and planted it in ours, well within view of that neighbor. She told me the neighbor had dug it up and given it to her as a housewarming present.

Later, she called me over to socialize with the neighbor who was working in her yard. She prompted me to mention the plant and the story behind it, which I did, completely unsuspecting. The neighbor then responded that she was wondering what had happened to that plant and that she wanted it back. This may have been an effort to judge how far she could push our new neighbors and gauge their reactions for future reference.

Jewelry Store

<u>Incident</u>

One day, my mother invited me to go shopping for a birthday present for my father's mother. The extended family had pooled money and given it to her so that she could buy a special piece of jewelry from all of them. A strange thing happened as we went from jewelry store to jewelry store downtown. Stores buzzed everyone else in but refused to buzz us in. When we did get into stores without buzzers, they objected, claiming that my mother had stolen the last time she was in there. I had thought this was the initial shopping trip, but it wasn't. She had invited me to go back to the stores she'd already gotten into trouble in, probably in hopes that bringing an innocent kid with her would defuse the situation, confuse them, or make them hesitant to have her arrested.

The Brick

<u>Incident</u>

In another year, when my mother was put in charge of shopping with the pooled extended family money for my father's mother's birthday, she pulled another trick. The area my grandmother lived in had recently had a big redo of a public park nearby. Donors could get their names on a brick on a bridge in the park. The family chose to surprise my grandmother by taking her for a walk through the park so she could see the brick with her name and her deceased husband's name on it. My mother hadn't been counting on the walk. She figured we would just tell my grandmother that the brick was there. I was so excited for my grandmother to be surprised by the brick.

As we went to the park, my mother was acting a bit funny and dragging her feet. The whole family took my grandmother to the big opening of the park, and we walked along looking for the brick. When we couldn't find the brick, we asked about it. No one had ever donated for that brick. She had pocketed the money everyone else in the family had given her.

16. Reversing Parent/Child Relationships

About

<u>About Reversing Parent-Child Relationships & MBP</u>

My mother clearly had a need to infantilize me and delay milestones, as discussed in the "Not Ready For" section directly after this one. How does this square logically with reversing a parent-child relationship and forcing me to parent her in some ways? It doesn't. Abuse isn't logical. Reversing parent and child roles is not unique to MBP. You see this in whole or in part in lots of forms of abuse.

The Fetuses

<u>Incident Tags/Trigger Warnings</u>

fetuses in jars

<u>Incident</u>

Sometimes, my mother would take me to a different museum than the one she "volunteered" at. The museum was huge. It was my favorite museum that I always looked forward to. I wanted to go to other exhibits, but I had to do the fetuses first. That's the way it worked. It was an exhibit showing the stages of fetal development with some real fetuses on display. There were these rows of jars that towered above me. They creeped me out at first, but she taught me not to be afraid of them. Often in the background were voices of other visitors exclaiming over them. Sometimes, it was very emotional people. In some of the jars, the fluid was a bit darker or lighter, cloudier or clearer. There was a bit of a chemical smell. We would sometimes stand there so long my legs would ache. Sometimes, we were waiting until others were out of the way. I would crane my neck up.

The routine was always the same. If I wanted to see the rest of the museum, I would have to listen to her talk about how she had killed me at a certain stage of development and then tell her I forgave her for that. I would try to explain to her it wasn't me, but she would insist and make me forgive her for killing me. She would point out particular stages of development, identify a particular jar, and then tell me that one was me. Reverse parenting this reaction and comforting her was the cost of admission to my favorite museum.

The Surgery

<u>Incident Tags/Trigger Warnings</u>

surgery

<u>Incident</u>

I was in the kitchen. It was in the house out of state we were in when I was three. Although we were in the kitchen and I was hungry, I wasn't getting food at the time. I was down on the floor. We were alone. I didn't feel like anything was physically wrong with me, and I didn't understand why we were going to do this. I wasn't in pain. Her voice was a bit whiney. She was talking about how scared and upset she was over the fact that I was going to have surgery. I tried to talk her out of the surgery, but when that didn't work, I tried to comfort her about it. I was three, and I was managing her emotional reaction to an unnecessary surgery she was forcing me to get.

The Grand Canyon

suicide, heights

Incident

When I was nine, my mother took me on a summer trip to the southwest U.S. We went to view the Grand Canyon one day. She made a big deal of how much she was looking forward to it, but I didn't understand what all the fuss was about. We pulled up to the tourist area in a rental car. We were surrounded by the southwest earth colors and lots of other tourists. At my age, I couldn't figure out why they were so interested in seeing the canyon. It was too hot. I was nine and hadn't gotten my adult sweat glands yet. I was so overheated. It was a dry heat, but still way too much. We walked to the edge to look. In those days, there wasn't as much protection from the edge, although there was some.

All of a sudden, my mother, who had been so excited about this, began going on and on about how much she just wanted to throw herself over the edge and end it all. I tried to calm her and talk her out of it, but she would not be deterred. She didn't make any actual moves, such as trying to go over the barrier or anything like that. She just kept on saying the same things over and over again about jumping and how much she wished she could. She whined and whined. The guide in uniform was mad at her. I didn't realize it was a bid for attention, but he did. So did some of the other tourists around us. I couldn't understand why they were acting hostile towards her, but looking back on it, this was a completely understandable reaction. They could see what she was actually doing. She wasn't going to jump. She wanted a scene.

I did my best to try to handle the situation I thought was going on, unaware that it was all just about the act. I listened to her, responded to her, and told her it was ok. I tried to understand and comfort her and calm her. I tried to talk her out of it, and when she wouldn't budge, I told her I would be ok to take care of myself and that she shouldn't feel guilty if she couldn't go on any longer.

Eventually, she dropped the act. She didn't get the tears out of me that she wanted or the concern out of the crowd that she wanted. We got back in the car and left as the guide continued to scold her.

Venting

<u>Incident Tags/Trigger Warnings</u>

talking about sex

<u>Incident</u>

My mother often vented to me as one adult would to another and shared age-inappropriate information in the process. When I was 9 or 10, she would constantly vent instead of allowing me to do my homework. Every day when I came home from school, I wasn't allowed to spend any alone time or do any homework until I'd listened to hours of her venting about her difficulties. At the same time, she would be angry if my grades reflected this.

Often, this would veer into her telling stories of sex with my father in a little blue beetle she claimed to have owned in college. Other times, it would be other sexual stories or stories of just whatever was on her mind. Other times, she would talk to me about difficulties she was having with my father and ask me to take her side. I wasn't allowed to move on with my day until I'd devoted a solid chunk of time listening sympathetically and giving sympathetic responses.

Acting Company

Incident Tags/Trigger Warnings
sex work, inappropriate conversations with children

Incident

We sat in the "dining room," which was really just the area between the kitchen and living room divided by the furniture arrangement. The window lined with black-painted radiator covers was behind me. My mother sat to my right, and my father to my left. The extra food she controlled was to the right. The table was one of those ones with extra pull-out sections.

I remember the sound of my mother's voice when she was mocking someone. She really overdid the sarcasm and theatrical nature of it. She emoted a lot. My father at first laughed along with her, then got uncomfortable at a certain point and wanted the conversation to change. She was talking about "the cheetah girls acting company." According to her, this was a sex work ring that operated in one of the buildings down the street. I was a little girl and far too young for a conversation like this. I couldn't understand what she was talking about, so she explained the concept to me. I was obligated to laugh and joke along with her.

In retrospect, I think that she had made up this group and that there was nothing going on in the building down the street. Based on other incidents, I think she was doing that thing she always did, where she reversed a story about herself to externalize it. This isn't quite an example of reversing the parent-child relationship like other incidents in this section, but it is an example of her acting as if I was someone she could talk to as one adult would to another, even when I was very young.

So Much Calmer

smashing butterflies

Incident

The butterfly enclosure at the museum was outdoors, covered in screen to keep them from escaping, with pavement underfoot. They let in a limited number of people at once. It was a temporary exhibit. We had to watch where we stepped to keep from accidentally stepping on them. Signs warned of this, and the workers repeated the warning. There were a variety of surfaces for the butterflies to land on, including lots of plants. I remember the sound of the crowd buzzing and oohing and awing carried through the fresh air.

I was a teenager at the time. My mother had brought me, and she was very excited. She had claimed that she had worked the exhibit but had the day off and was bringing me to visit. In reality, I don't believe she had ever even been allowed to work the exhibit. We paid and entered. The people there immediately recognized her and were concerned. My mother had earlier told me a story about a lady freaking out and smashing the butterflies as if she was talking about a third person. She would only later admit the story had been about her. The workers were clearly nervous around her and didn't want her in there. Their body language and voices made it clear. Slowly, they got a bit more comfortable as they realized she was in a different headspace that day.

We did a brief walk around the exhibit and chatted with workers who were keeping a close eye on us. By the end of the walkthrough, when we were getting ready to exit, the workers approached me and tried to get me to volunteer in the exhibit during my summer break. I had no interest and politely declined. They kept pressing the issue. I was just some random teenager who'd walked through the exhibit like so many others. Why were they trying so hard to get me, in particular, to volunteer there? It was because they couldn't get rid of my mother, and she was so much calmer when I was there. They remarked over and over about how much calmer she was and how much it would help to have me there. Babysitting my mother was the last thing I wanted to do with my summer break. After I'd told them no a few times, I told them I would think about it, which they correctly guessed meant no.

17. Not Ready For————-

About

<u>About Developmental Stages & MBP</u>

Forcing delay of developmental stages is a common tactic of MBP abusers. This also fits a pattern of forcing codependence.

Other incidents in this book that involve this pattern: The 'Easter Bunnies' incident in the 'Exposing me to substances' section.

Other MBP cases involving this pattern: Deedee Blanchard's abuse of Gypsy Rose matches this pattern. She lied about her daughter's date of birth and developmental stage.

Shorts

<u>Tags/Trigger Warnings</u>

control, pain, education, coercive control, school embarrassment, mental health\

<u>Incidents</u>

As in other "shorts" sections in this book, here I give a brief list of incidents that illustrate this pattern.

Walking

When I was three, I was not allowed to walk yet. I had been walking, but then my mother had changed her mind and told me it wasn't allowed. It hurt my knees to crawl even though I was getting too big for it, and it was slow to get around that way. One day, a neighbor saw me walking, and I told her not to tell. My mother dropped it and let me walk shortly after that. I'm not sure if this was a coincidence or if the neighbor had a word with her.

Reading

I always loved stories and picture books, but when I asked my mother to teach me how to read, she told me I wasn't ready and wouldn't understand. I decided to try to figure it out on my own anyway, but she caught on. If she saw me puzzling over the words, she would withhold the books. I stopped because I didn't want them taken away altogether. At least I could still look at the pictures. Once I was sent to school, I learned how to read, but she still insisted on reading to me at home even though I could read for myself. If she caught me reading on my own at home, she would be irritated and ask me why I thought I had permission to do that.

One day, my teacher suggested I was ready for children's chapter books instead of picture books. My mother said no. The teacher gave me one anyway. We had quiet reading time at school, and I could work through it on my own. My mother didn't find out until it was too late, and I'd already passed the milestone by finishing the chapter book on my own. My mother was angry about this. In her mind, it was all about whether or not she was ready for me to do this, and the teacher was out of line.

Dressing

One day, when I was a little kid, my mother laid out a sweatsuit for me to wear to play outside, but then got distracted doing something else. I put it on myself. She was angry that I had dressed myself instead of allowing her to do it. She told me to undress so she could re-dress me. We started going back and forth about it. She told me that I could take it off or not, but that either way, she was going to redo it. She told me that if I didn't take it off, she would hurt me taking it off and hurt me putting it back on. I took it off, and she dressed me again in the exact same outfit, pulling my limbs through the outfit as if I were a doll and couldn't do it myself.

Eating

When I was a little kid, my mother had an odd fixation on separating all my food. If I got a fast food hamburger, she would take it apart and have me eat all the pieces, such as the bread, the pickles, and the meat, separately. If I got a slice of pizza, she would pull the cheese off and scrape the sauce off so that all of the ingredients would be separate. At social occasions, I would sit with a group of kids from the neighborhood, or from school, or at a birthday party and watch them eat the food as it was served. I would go to eat the food as it was served, too, but she would stop me. I would ask if I could eat it like they were, but she would say no and then take it apart.

Testing

One of the major roadblocks my mother had to trying to pass me off as special needs was that school standardized testing could reveal I had knowledge and intelligence she claimed I didn't have. I took my first standardized test in the first grade, and she jumped into action, trying to find a way around this. She convinced me that it was very important to fill in the bubbles very lightly with just the slightest shading. It worked that year. The scanner failed to pick up my answers. They caught on to her, though, and it didn't work in future years.

At one point, my mother tried taking me to a developmental specialist in hopes of convincing them to make a diagnosis. Beforehand, she purposefully looked up questions they would ask and coached me to give wrong answers. She could not let on that she wanted me to give wrong answers. She had to try to convince me that I had been wrong and that the new answers she was feeding me were correct. When they asked me why I was answering certain questions oddly, the truth came out. I'm not sure if they believed me or thought I was embarrassed and covering, but in either case, she didn't face any consequences.

In another incident, she took me for an IQ test and then argued with the specialist when he diagnosed me as having a high IQ. I was a little kid, and the specialist remarked that I knew a lot more than other kids my age. For years afterward, she rolled her eyes and scoffed at his supposed ignorance.

3rd Grade

On my first day of 3rd grade, my mother was having a particularly bad day. She had gotten through the first day of kindergarten, first grade, and second grade, but that day was a bit too much for her for some reason. Maybe she was on something, or maybe she was just doing particularly badly lately. She dropped me off at the classroom, and I left her side to take my seat. She told me to wait, but the school day was starting. It was time for me to get seated and for her to leave. She pitched a fit like a three-year-old. She grabbed onto me and wouldn't let me go. I began dragging myself across the classroom to get to my seat as she clung to me. This caused hilarity among my classmates, and I was humiliated. My mother turned to the teacher and said in a panicky, squeaky voice, "I'm sorry, she just has a really bad problem with separation anxiety." "Who has a really bad problem with separation anxiety?" the teacher asked in a way that was somehow both kind and pointed all at once. My mother repeated herself, missing the teacher's point and lacking all self-awareness. The class's laughter continued as the teacher and my mother went back and forth. Eventually, I made it to my seat and sat down. She was made to leave.

Deodorant

When I began to go through puberty, my mother decided that she wasn't ready for this either. One way of attempting to deny reality was to deny me the ability to use deodorant. In her mind, I wasn't old enough to need it yet. In reality, this was painful for both me and the rest of the class. Eventually, I took some and began to use it in secret. A lot of times, my mother's issue was with the dread leading up to milestones, and she would calm down after I'd passed them. When she caught me with the deodorant, I lied and said I'd been using it for years and thought she knew already. She dropped it after that. The big deal had been crossing the milestone. If she'd thought it had been long past, she would simply let it go. I had only recently bugged her to allow me to use deodorant and gotten a no. Maybe she had not been sober enough to remember this interaction.

Driver's Ed

When I was fifteen, my school allowed me to sign up for driver's education. It was not required, but I knew if I told my mother that and asked permission, it would be a no. I signed up without her permission and then told her that it had been required. She was aggravated with the school for this but never caught on until I'd already gotten my license.

18. Attention, Control and Separation Anxiety

About

About Attention, Control, Separation Anxiety & MBP

My mother sometimes suffered intense fits of separation anxiety that she either couldn't control or refused to control. I believe this separation anxiety was deeply linked to her desire for attention and her desire for control in general.

Attention

I won't repeat every incident in which my mother acted out for attention here because I would be repeating a huge portion of the book. MBP behavior isn't solely focused on attention. As I've shown in other parts of this book, there's a significant component of sadism and sometimes other motivations as well. It is an abuse pattern that I think isn't carried out by people who dislike attention, though. It seems that attention is usually at least part of the motivation.

I'm not sure where my mother's disproportionate need for attention came from originally, but I know that it was something that her adoptive mother exploited early on. She would remark that my mother was the easiest child to control because all you had to do to get her to do whatever you wanted was to withhold attention. She couldn't stand it, and she would do anything to make it stop. As I have described elsewhere in this book, my mother had a variety of serious behavioral problems during her childhood, including hurting and killing animals. This doesn't sound like a child who is easy to control. I'm not sure if my grandmother was in denial about this or if she just didn't care much about it. From what my mother told me when I was a child, her disagreements with her mother often centered around things like who she would date and what classes she would take. It seems possible that my grandmother cared about these things but not about the animals.

Separation Anxiety

In the "Not Ready For—-" section directly preceding this one, I describe an incident in which my mother freaked out on my first day of 3rd grade.

That incident belongs in this section just as much, but I will not repeat it here since you can skip back and read it if you have not already.

This was not the only such incident. There was a nearly identical incident when I was about three years old. Just like the 3rd-grade incident, it involved a milestone. This may also have been connected to the repeated fake stories my mother told about various people's parents drowning. I was going for swimming lessons. My mother was the one who had signed me up and brought me, but when it was time for me to get in the pool, she lost it. I wanted to get in the pool like the other kids, but she clung to me and threw a fit.

<u>Control</u>

I believe my mother's life centers around control in large part. She doesn't control her own urges and behaviors, but she does devote a huge amount of time to controlling those around her. Again, if I were to list all of her controlling behavior here, I would be restating a large portion of the book.

This controlling behavior was a main feature of both her ordinary life and her criminal behavior. In ordinary life, she attempted to assert control in parenting in ways that were not even close to age-appropriate or appropriate at all. In her criminal behavior, she tended to opt for up close and personal control, such as strangling, as opposed to more impersonal attacks. She wanted to control everything, including life and death.

19. Grandiosity, Inferiority, and Slacking

About

<u>About Grandiosity, Inferiority, Slacking & MBP</u>

My mother had a strong tendency to make grandiose claims about herself. These claims were false. In many cases, she claimed to have accomplished things she actually probably would have been able to accomplish had she simply been willing to do the work. In addition to this, she seemed to have a strong preoccupation with people thinking they were better than her. Many times, this was not actually the case, but she was absolutely convinced of it and could not be convinced otherwise. She would sometimes lash out over this. I think this was all connected. She had this pattern of failing to do the work, claiming to have done the work, claiming what she could have earned through the work anyway, and then getting extremely defensive about positions others had earned that she hadn't.

Both grandiosity and slacking are connected to her making the fake museum ID and giving tours instead of doing the actual work to earn the job. The entire faking authority and intelligence section, in general, fits here, but I will not repeat it since it is elsewhere in the book. This is also connected to the "Hurting to be right" section and the "Parking Lot" incident in the "School" section.

This behavior pattern was connected to MBP in several ways. Being a mother of a sick child, especially a seriously or mysteriously ill child, carries its own implications of specialized knowledge and hard work. Just like in these other examples, however, it was something she had fabricated. She wanted credibility, respect, and deference without actually having to do anything. I think she also wanted to feel that she had outsmarted everyone else, including medical professionals.

Shorts

Hostile attribution bias, putting on airs
Incidents

College Report Cards

My mother always made a big deal about how she was a college graduate. She spoke of being in advanced classes only for the smartest of the students. Her parents had saved her college report cards, but they didn't reflect this. They were mostly D's and F's. As it later turned out, she'd never actually graduated. The report cards always had the same type of comments. They stated repeatedly that she'd simply failed to do the work, noting that she was capable but just hadn't bothered. They warned that she would flunk out if this continued, and then, as it turns out, she did.

She had always told me tales of her graduation ceremony, her classes, and her college experiences. They were all made up. Meanwhile, if I got a C in a class, she would convince the entire family to stop speaking to me.

The News Letter

In the "Faking authority and intelligence" section, I describe a fake newsletter she'd sent out naming her as holding all the positions in the group. I won't repeat it here, but it's worth having a look at if you are reading this section. In fact, that entire section connects to this one.

Phrasing

My mother often put on airs when she spoke, but this wasn't consistent, so the speech pattern I grew up learning was very odd. The way I spoke that I picked up at home sometimes made people think I was a military kid who moved around a lot. I just thought it was how people spoke. At the same time, when I was little, I didn't know which words were curses or not because of how much she cursed around me. I couldn't identify the bad word in a sentence like, "What is all this shit?" I also thought that there were two categories of seasoning called "erbs" and "herbs" because she sometimes inconsistently pronounced this in a European way despite the fact that none of us had ever even been to Europe.

One day, we had a family friend over, and this person corrected me for using "can." I didn't understand what she meant. My mother scolded me and told me that I knew better. She supposedly didn't know where I'd picked that up because, according to her, we always used "may" and "can" properly. I thought she'd just gone insane. In my mind, all of a sudden, she was telling me to use the name of a random month instead of "can" in a sentence. I had never heard of this in my life.

My mother often refused to admit that she didn't know what a word meant. For example, one day, I went to school with homework, stating that the definition of the word pachyderm was an umbrella because she had confidently stated this multiple times.

Better Than

My mother would occasionally get it into her head that total strangers thought they were better than her. She would then make a big deal of this.

One day, we were on a road trip, and we passed by one of those big walls that separated a housing subdivision from the highway. I asked my mother what it was. She launched into a tirade about how people had built it to keep us out because they thought that they were so much better than us. In reality, of course, those walls are just there to protect nearby people from accidents, noise, and exhaust.

One day on summer break, we were out of town, and we went to a little tourist attraction. I saw another section with stuff I was interested in and asked if I could go there. My mother said no because the guy working there thought he was better than her. She had heard him say so, she said. In reality, she did not know him. They hadn't had words. We had simply walked past him, and he hadn't said anything bad about her. I don't know if she had hallucinated this, or if she had made it up, or if she knew he hadn't literally said this but believed him to be thinking it.

There was a very similar incident later in town at a movie theater parking lot. We passed a crowd laughing and having fun. She made an assumption that it was about her and that they were making fun of her. She confronted them and yelled at them. They had not been talking about her at all.

This pattern also may connect to her reaction to the movie Cop Land, which I describe in the "Imitating Stories and Banning Stories" section.

I think part of what my mother was experiencing in these incidents is what is known as "hostile attribution bias." I don't think that fully explains this, though. There was more at play here. I think that this was intertwined with a lot of her other behaviors described in this book.

20. Trophies

About

<u>About MBP and Trophies</u>

When people think of criminals keeping trophies, they will probably usually think of stalkers or serial killers. This is also a pattern you will sometimes see with MBP abusers. This should not be surprising because there is a fair amount of overlap between stalking, serial killing, and MBP. Multiple people in the patterns chart practiced multiple of these crimes. I am no psychologist, but my understanding is that for these criminals, the trophies are about somehow being able to relive the crime or hang onto the crime.

Shorts

<u>Incident Tags/Trigger Warnings</u>

physical abuse, medical abuse, stealing

<u>Incidents</u>

This is not a section with separate incidents like some. This section only has shorts because there's no need to elaborate further on these points.

***

My mother often stole things and then claimed people gave them to her. She was more likely to do this with stuff they wanted or stuff that they had some sort of emotional attachment to. You will see examples of this in various other incidents throughout this book. This included plants she dug from other people's gardens and planted in her own and things she stole from other's apartments in the building. A lot of the time, the stuff she did this with had no economic value. She especially seemed to like it if they knew but couldn't do anything about it. Sometimes, she liked telling people they'd given the things away to her and then waiting for that information to get back to the people she'd stolen from to watch the reaction.

***

Once, my mother saw a scene in a TV show in which a character bit on something for the pain while some painful wound was being set. Afterward, the show displayed the teeth marks on the item for dramatic effect. My mother became very enamored with this idea the way she sometimes did with medical stuff. She decided that she needed to do something painful to me while I bit on a pencil. She wouldn't stop until I left teeth marks. She kept the pencil for years afterward and talked about how much she liked it, not realizing or not caring how creepy it was.

***

At the end of the shorts section in the Traditional MBP section, I have a blurb about being dragged to an amusement park while badly injured. While there, my mother bought me a little Hawaiian Punch drink that came in a plastic bottle shaped to look like one of the characters from the advertisements. She kept this for several years afterward and always treated it like a special nostalgic souvenir. This did not happen with any other items from any other amusement park trips or trips to other attractions, just specifically this one, the one where I was very badly injured and suffering.

***

My mother loved to collect photos of me after medical procedures or supposed "accidents." She had photos of me after surgery, photos of me injured, bruised, cut, and bandaged.

***

My mother liked to save things from medical procedures I'd had. Sometimes, I would question why we still had them. She would say we might need them again. I would insist we wouldn't. She would just insist that I never knew and we might again.

21. Gremlin Mode

About

<u>About Gremlin Mode</u>

I have chosen the term "gremlin mode" as an easy to understand and remember way of describing this particular personality trait or cluster of behaviors my mother had. I don't mean the same thing as "goblin mode," a term that is sometimes used in social media to describe a greedy or hedonistic mode. I mean something more like a tendency towards destruction and damage for destruction and damage's sake. Do you remember the old Twilight Zone episode with the gremlin on the wing of the plain, or the Simpsons' parody of this in a Halloween episode, or the Gremlins movie franchise? That's the basic idea. It's destructo-mode, for lack of a better term. It's the general tendency to do and enjoy doing pointless, destructive crap. This stuff isn't nearly as serious as the abuse in this book, and on its own, it's not really worth writing about. I'm including it because I think it helps paint a fuller picture of her behavior in general, which could be helpful for those studying MBP.

Shorts

<u>Incident Tags/Trigger Warnings</u>

sabotage, property damage, manipulation

<u>Incidents</u>

When I was young, I liked to crochet. It was a thing a babysitter had taught me. My mother would sometimes creep into my room and then pull the work I'd done back apart. She claimed that it had fallen apart on its own. If you know how to crochet, you know that this is implausible. She was claiming some sort of spontaneous self-destruction of yarn work left alone on its own. I don't know if she was incapable of knowing that it was a silly lie or if she just didn't care. She was disappointed when I stopped crocheting. She bugged me repeatedly, trying to get me to pick it up again. I told her there was no point because I knew she would just undo it again. She was bummed out when her ability to undo my work was taken away.

***

When I was little, my mother would sometimes creep into my room at night just to tie my hair into knots and tangles while I slept. Sometimes, I would wake up to her doing it. Other times, I would be trying to sleep as she would come up and start doing it, not realizing that I was not asleep yet. The behavior seemed to start after she saw a children's cartoon in which little creatures did this.

***

When I was little, I very much liked slinkies, and my mother very much liked bending up slinkies until they didn't work anymore. I usually didn't have a working salvageable one because of this. She was especially likely to do this after she'd just gotten me a nice new one I was excited about. What, then, was the point of having bought it? I think that was the point.

***

My mother seemed to very much enjoy sabotaging my father's briefcase, especially before an important work meeting. He got one of those briefcases with the combination locks built in, but she figured out the combination and pretended she hadn't. He found out the hard way, came home, and yelled about it a bit.

***

My mother liked keying cars and tried to teach me to do the same. I didn't understand what the point was. She acted like it was lots of fun. She would do it to cars near ours in the building garage and also to our own. When she was confronted, she pointed to the key marks in our own, claiming that she would not possibly have done it to her own car, too.

***

My mother liked to make us late for stuff, especially if anyone else in the family was anxious about being late for something. She seemed to enjoy the anxiety.

***

My mother sometimes enjoyed throwing out important things or sentimental things. She seemed to especially like it if she could trick someone else into throwing out something that meant something to them. She would put it in the trash that person was meant to take out later.

***

My mother sometimes seemed to enjoy ruining something for everyone else in the building. Sometimes, this involved throwing something gross into the building pool or leaving something gross in the hall.

***

When we moved to a house when I was in high school, we had one of those little TV satellites on our roof. It connected to a panel under our back deck that fed into the house. My mother liked to crawl under the deck and mess with the panel. She took the time to figure out everyone's favorite channel to target those specifically. It was gross under there and did not seem worth the effort, but in her mind, the payoff was worth it, apparently.

22. Manufacturing Scandal

About

<u>About Manufacturing Scandal & MBP</u>

Generally, all entries under the crime framing section will also apply to this section, but I've separated those entries into their own section because they seem particularly significant both in terms of how far an abuser is willing to go and in terms of the potential damage to victims. That does not mean that the entries under this section are not significant to the victims involved. I have included this section in addition to the crime framing section because it's important to see that there is a spectrum to this behavior and that it doesn't always involve crime framing.

You will also notice a certain amount of overlap between this section and the section on sexually inappropriate behavior, as well as the sections on non-medical sick stories and emotional sadism. A lot of sections in this book overlap with each other. The point of creating sections is to point out patterns in the behavior, but many incidents could fit into more than one section.

What drives a person to act like this? I don't know, but I can point out some things that my mother would have gotten out of this behavior:
- Attention
- Sympathy
- A story to tell
- Connection (if things had gone as planned).
- A sense of being "the good one" who is put upon, long-suffering, and worthy of sympathy as contrasted with "the bad one" (once again, if these had gone as planned).

A lot of the time, I think that my mother was trying to take things she didn't like about herself and place them outside of herself. She was a sick pervert who acted inappropriately, caused scandal, stole things, broke things, and ruined things for others. A lot of her behavior seemed to emphasize placing this image on others and casting herself as the victim.

The Window

Exhibitionism

Incident

When I was a little girl, before I started going through puberty, my mother took me out to the park outside our building one day. She pointed up at the building and claimed to be able to see a woman in one of the big floor-to-ceiling windows standing there completely naked. I couldn't see anything like that at all, and I asked what she was talking about. She insisted the woman was just standing still there waiting to be seen flashing everyone. She sometimes pointed to things I couldn't see, so I just let it go after a while.

A few days later, we were in the park again. We ran into some building workers. My mother started chatting with them and brought up the subject of the woman in the window. They agreed they had seen it, and they were not happy about it. She stepped back from me, pointed at me, and made a face indicating it had been me. They reacted as one would to an obvious lie. They agreed that it had been our apartment, but the person in the window had obviously already gone through puberty. There was only one person in our apartment who fit the description of a female who had already been through puberty. She continued going back and forth with them about it and insisting as if she could simply get them to ignore the fact that the person in the window had not been an emaciated child but a grown woman with breasts and hips and adult stature.

Note: This is very similar to another incident in a restaurant in which she claimed to be able to see a man flashing everyone from a window across the street despite the fact that no one else could see this.

The Skirt

<u>Incident</u>

One day, when I was in middle school, my mother took me to the uniform store before the school year, as she did every year. We showed up with a list provided by the school of what people in my grade were to wear and looked at what the store had in stock.

We ran into another mother and daughter from my school shopping for the school year. This girl was a few years older than me and was already in junior high. She and her mother had an argument at the counter about skirt length. Her mother wanted a longer skirt, and she wanted a shorter one. Her mother sternly told her to take the shorter one back and bring the longer one the mother had already told her they were getting.

The middle school girls wore jumpers, and the junior high girls wore skirts with the same pattern. We, of course, were still getting the jumper, which only came in one length. For some reason, the store offered the skirt in two lengths, which probably started a lot of arguments like that.

The worker behind the counter turned to us to ring up our purchase while the other mom was still waiting for her daughter to bring a different skirt. My mother suddenly shouted the exact thing at me that the other mom had said to her daughter about how she had already told me no and I was to go get the proper length skirt. She shot the other mom a look of commiseration. It was absurd. We obviously were buying a one-size jumper instead of a skirt. It was also obvious this had come out of nowhere as she was the one who brought the purchase to the counter, not me. I stared at her in confusion.

The other mother looked creeped out and explained to her something along the lines that she knew this wasn't real and that my mother didn't need to do that. This went back and forth a bit, and the worker also called her on it. We checked out and left. My mother never acknowledged the odd situation.

Cement

<u>Incident Tags/Trigger Warnings</u>

Sadism

<u>Incident</u>

When I was three, and we were living out of state in a house in the suburbs, the neighborhood started to do some work. Various spots were getting repaved and getting sidewalks. We would occasionally see wet concrete marked off with the typical little plastic tape. One day, a neighbor told a group, including my mother, a funny story about how her son had played in fresh, wet cement and ruined it. Later, when we got home, my mother told me that I had to be careful not to get in wet cement because it would freeze on me, and I would be stuck that way forever. I told her that wasn't what had happened in the story with the other kid, but eventually, she convinced me. I was so young and impressionable, and she was so insistent. After that, I resolved to keep my distance if I ever saw wet cement.

A few days later, we ran into some people from the neighborhood by another patch of wet cement. At the time, I thought this was a coincidence, but in retrospect, I know it was not. My mother suddenly shoved me hard from behind, flinging me face-first into the wet cement. I was terrified because of the lie she'd told me and started crying. I asked why she'd done that, and she insisted she hadn't. She played her little role in front of the other moms, and then she took me home and washed me off. I think this was a two-birds-with-one-stone thing for her. She wanted the attention and the story like the other mom had, but she also wanted to scare me and upset me.

23. Faking Authority/Intelligence

About

<u>About Faking Authority and Intelligence & MBP</u>

This section has a certain amount of overlap with the "Hurting to be Right" section. It also has a certain amount of overlap with MBP behavior in general:

- Faking authority or intelligence gives one a fake sense of importance, just like being the caretaker of a sick person who is not actually sick does.

- People like this could seek out actual sick people and actually help them. They could also just earn education, experience, and credentials to get actual authority and intelligence. In both cases, they go for the quick fix. They don't want to do the actual work, and they don't care how that affects others.

- Just like with MBP, people who fake authority and intelligence treat reality as a negotiation. Reality is not a negotiation. If someone is trying to negotiate reality with you, disengage and make a note of it. There is no good reason why reality should be up for negotiation. This is not logical.

- Other MBP cases involving this pattern: Hope Ybarra (fake Ph.D.), Christopher Duntsch (faked specialties)

I will also note that faking authority and intelligence was also a huge part of my father's behavior, but those incidents are listed under the "His Cons" section. This section here only deals with my mother's behavior.

Getting Past Security

Tags/Trigger Warnings

Conflict, Breaking and Entering, Catfishing
Incidents

My mother had a fixation on the local natural history museum. It was with all parts of the museum, but especially the Native American halls. At a certain point, she officially volunteered there, but her behavioral issues escalated, and workers struggled with how to deal with her. She entered areas she wasn't allowed in, gave tours she wasn't authorized to do or educated to do, and got into conflicts with workers and visitors. At a certain point, the official volunteering relationship broke down, but she continued to show up, claiming to work there.

I don't know how the relationship between my mother and the museum started. Maybe she volunteered and seemed ok at first, or maybe she started faking right away, and they offered her small volunteer jobs in an effort to contain the situation and redirect her. There's probably a lot about what happened between my mother and the museum I don't know and will never know. These are the glimpses I do have.

The museum had a life-size replica of a Navajo earth lodge that visitors could enter. Actual employees would often give programs there. They used to leave it open for visitors to explore when there was no program going on, but they had to put a stop to that due to my mother. She would enter, claim to be the person giving the program, and trick enough guests to get an actual audience.

One day, we showed up for my mother to give a program. I was dragged along since my mother supposedly didn't have other care available for me that day. Was it actually that my mother couldn't find other care for me that day, or was it that she knew they would be reluctant to physically remove her in front of her little kid? I don't know.

We found it locked and after looking around my mother couldn't find a key. I didn't understand why she was just waiting around instead of going to get someone. I was young enough that I still thought she worked there. Eventually, the actual workers showed up and unlocked it so that they could usher people in and give the program.

They thought they had solved the situation by locking it, but this was not the case. As they stood in the center of the lodge and gave the program, my mother also stood and began to talk over them as if she was also giving a program. This went on and on. They informed guests to ignore her, but there wasn't much they could do.

My mother began to tell a nonsense story about folk beliefs that she was just making up as she went along. She told a story of gods in the sky, but then the story began to get explicit and inappropriate for children, which was a problem because there were several families with young children there. The crowd giggled nervously, unsure of how to react. The actual workers were exasperated.

***

At one point, my mother was actually allowed in the workers' office area. This was a large area behind a keypad-locked door that consisted of a very large bank of cubicles and a few office rooms surrounding the cubicles. She would sometimes bring me along. In the beginning, she would bring me in to meet other volunteers and workers and sometimes leave me sitting in an office room while she went to go do something else.

As the relationship between her and the museum began to deteriorate, her access to this area was questioned and then restricted. One day, she brought me in for an important meeting and told me I needed to be on my best behavior. It turned out that this was a meeting about her behavior and whether she would be allowed back there anymore. A frustrated worker told his side of the story, and she did her best to look like a sympathetic person. She told me she brought me with her that day for that reason. She thought having a young kid there would make them soften their approach. It probably worked that day, but her access was eventually revoked later.

Sometime later, after her access had been revoked, my mother brought me back to the museum and took me to the keypad. She kept trying different numbers. A few employees who needed to get in asked her to excuse them, punched in a number, trying to avoid her seeing, and then shut the door before she could get in. This worked a few times, but eventually, she caught a glimpse of the numbers and got in again.

***

My mother had a similar set of incidents happen in the museum's employee parking area. This was a small lot separate from the guest parking that was only for workers and official volunteers. We used to park there, but then things changed. One day, we pulled in, and the attendant wouldn't raise the gate. They went back and forth about it. She showed him her volunteer badge that hung from a lanyard around her neck. He smiled and responded that he knew it wasn't real. She'd gotten him the last time, he said, because it was pretty good, but now he knew better. He'd been in trouble for letting her in the last time.

We had a similar incident when we tried to go into the employee entrance. Security showed up, telling her she couldn't enter that way anymore.

Hieroglyphics

<u>Incidents</u>

At one point, my mother joined a group of people who read and discussed Mayan hieroglyphs. Some of them were doing it as a hobby, and others were doing it as something that benefited their work. It was a friendly, welcoming group that did not mind amateurs joining. She took full advantage of this and then attempted to take over. Every meeting was at the house of whichever member was able to host at that time. One day, when I was a teenager, my mother had them over. I was around the house when one of them called me over to join them. I had no interest in the subject because kids that age tend to be like that about anything that their parents find interesting. I also thought my mother might not want me to join in. They kept inviting me, and eventually, I joined the conversation out of politeness.

They took turns allowing one member of the group after another to interpret a hieroglyph and then talk about the significance of it and other themes it was connected to. Others would jump in and give suggestions, and they would discuss.

They gave me one and encouraged me to take a turn. I was surprised by this and told them I knew nothing about the subject. They insisted that it was a matter of common sense and that although previous knowledge helped, I could look at it and point out the symbols I recognized. I hesitantly pointed out people who looked important and animals and nature symbols that looked familiar. Occasionally, they would correct me about something or explain to me why something I pointed out was significant or connected to the rest of it.

They gave a few more people turns, and it was clear that they knew much more about the subject than me. They then gave my mother a turn. She confidently launched into an explanation with an air of authority. The other members began to look at each other. One after another politely interrupted with a correction as she went on a long, winding story she had pulled out of nowhere. It was very similar to the story she made up on the fly when she shouted over the actual docents in the earth lodge at the museum. It was a random mish-mash of make-believe about gods that had nothing to do with any of the actual beliefs of the ancient Mayans. They kindly explained to her that she didn't need to make things up. She just needed to use her common sense and point out familiar things that the rest of them could help her with, like all the rest had done.

A while later, my mother decided on a new con. This group sent out an official newsletter periodically. It contained articles about interesting new finds in related archeology in general, what the group in particular was up to, and plans for the future. Titles such as president, secretary, and treasurer were also listed in the credits of the letter. It was an official-looking publication that they'd obviously put work into.

One day, my mother presented me with an alternative newsletter for the group. It was simply a pamphlet she'd used the word processor on our computer to make. It was one of those little one-page pamphlets folded into three sections with a cover section and five little columns. It contained little blurbs. It listed out the credits as the real one did; only my mother was named as the only person in every single position. She had mailed it out to everyone in the group and even, I think, some people outside the group. The actual group explained to everyone that it wasn't legitimate, not that they really needed to. It was pretty obvious.

Shouting Over

My mother continued to have incidents in which she would crash an exhibit and pretend to be an expert working at the museum throughout the years as the museum added new exhibits. These occasionally ended in shouting matches in which she was removed from the exhibit, though not from the museum entirely, as far as I know.

At one point, the museum added an elaborate new ancient Egypt exhibit that was very popular. It had long wait times for quite a while. It included parts where visitors could walk through passages simulating an actual pyramid, see mummies, and view replicas of ancient technology such as irrigation methods and papyrus-making methods.

One day, when I was still little, she took me there and told me that she was giving a tour and I could tag along. I believed her and was excited. She began to speak over the crowd as if she was giving a tour, and people around naturally responded as if she was, assuming that some random person wouldn't just do that. Soon enough, though, we ran into another tour group. The actual tour leader explained that everything my mother was saying was incorrect and that she wasn't an actual tour guide. At first, people acted with disbelief, and my mother attempted to roll through. Quickly, though, it became apparent that she was, in fact, making things up. She couldn't keep up as the actual tour guide confronted her, corrected her, and quizzed her on facts. The crowd that had been following my mother laughed nervously and dispersed.

Later on, the museum got a temporary showing of a traveling Albert Einstein exhibit. It included things like his actual childhood report cards and various other historical pieces. It was a popular exhibit, and the museum had a worker who was an expert in the subject use props to explain relativity to visitors as they waited in line outside the exhibit.

We had gone as a family to see the exhibit, which my father was also interested in seeing. As we waited in line, my mother began to take issue with all of the attention and air of intellectual authority being on this worker and not her. She began to sigh and roll her eyes and say that his explanations were incorrect. My mother did not have even a basic understanding of math or physics, let alone an expert-level understanding of relativity. At first, the man tried to politely ignore her, but eventually, her behavior escalated to the point she was thrown out of that area of the museum.

Lorenzo

My mother enjoyed making up tall tales, making up sick stories, making up scandals, and claiming that her behavior was actually someone else's. One day, she came home with a story of a strange new volunteer at the museum named Lorenzo. Eventually, it would turn out that this man never existed. He was simply a made-up character that she used to talk about her own behavior at the museum without admitting to any of it. I also cover this in the "Non-Medical Sick Stories" section but for other reasons. She always came home with stories of something inappropriate he'd done at the museum. Sometimes, it was that he had come onto people at the museum who had no interest in him and made them feel uncomfortable. Other times, it was hygiene issues, such as picking his teeth publicly.

One day, she came home and complained about an incident she'd had with Lorenzo. According to her, he had been giving tours without any knowledge of the subjects and had been made to undergo training so that he wouldn't be kicked out entirely. She explained that she was one of the people in charge of training him. She claimed that he had failed to do any studying at all, failed the tests in the morning portion, gone out to lunch, and simply not come back. She claimed that he had left people there waiting to realize he would not come back because he was having issues with authority. This is essentially the same scenario as described in her own report cards. See the "Grandiosity, Inferiority, and Slacking" section.

Jeopardy

296

My mother had a little trick she liked to pull around the house to make herself seem smart. She would memorize old Jeopardy episode questions and then pretend that shows were new instead of reruns. She would be doing something with Jeopardy on in the background and then casually toss out a question as if it was simply part of her body of knowledge. Compared to the rest of the behavior above, it's pretty tame, but it's still part of the larger pattern of behavior.

24. Catfishing

About

<u>About Catfishing & MBP</u>

Catfishing can overlap with many other categories in MBP patterns of behavior. It can be a tool abusers use to create the illusion of people who verify their stories. It can be a method of attention-seeking. It can be a way of hopping from person to person faster than possible in person as one's lies are found out. It can be a method of grifting and conning people out of donations. It can be a method of making victims look like unreliable witnesses.

The internet didn't become a part of personal use in society until part way through my childhood. The childhood of a person suffering such abuse now would probably look somewhat different than mine did. In this section, you'll see examples of pre-internet catfishing, such as phone calls and letters.

My mother did escalate the catfishing (or at least I gained more awareness of it) after I reached adulthood, and the internet was more thoroughly a part of modern life. This may have been because of changes in technology. It may also have been because I was no longer in the house, and she was looking for a new way to channel her behavior. Cases in my adulthood will be a different book.

- Other MBP cases involving this pattern: See the 'Stalker' series in the 'Pretend' podcast listed in the recommended reading appendix of this book.

Incidents

Tags/Trigger Warnings

Catfishing, inappropriate behavior towards children, death, parental death, creepy letters, stealing,

Incidents

The Boy on the Bus

When I was a freshman in high school, I started at a new school. Like most new kids in high school, I was socially anxious and just trying to fit in. Like an unfortunately large number of kids, this was complicated by a dysfunctional situation at home.

I often took the bus home and saw kids in my class who I recognized but didn't know well. When this happened, I would say hi but not presume to sit next to them. Instead, I would keep going and sit alone if I didn't find anyone I knew better. At one point, I did this, and then another kid sat next to the boy I had passed. To my surprise, they began a conversation about me. The boy I had passed said that we talked every night at length on the phone but that I'd acted like I barely knew him on the bus. I had never spoken to him on the phone. I didn't even know his number. This was a high school freshman, and someone had spent hours on the phone with him, posing as me, another high school freshman. At the time, I was baffled, but in retrospect, it seems pretty obvious who that was.

The Dead Dad

One day in the fall of my freshman year of high school, my mother told me I'd gotten a phone call. In those days, we only had a landline. I picked up the receiver, and the person on the other end of the line told me that she was my classmate. We'll call her Janice. That was not her name. I had interacted with Janice a bit at school. She was also new. It seemed plausible that she'd called me, and I never questioned that it was her.

The person on the line started with small talk but quickly pivoted to talking about feeling like an outsider because her dad was dead and the other kids at school had dads. It was kind of an abrupt and unnatural shift in the conversation, but I didn't question it. I couldn't imagine anyone making up something like that. She went on and on about how she missed him, wished she had a dad, and felt different from the other kids in school. She also asked repeatedly if I had anything like that I wanted to open up to her about. This went on for over an hour. I tried to comfort her and struggled for the right things to say. At the end of the conversation, she emphasized that I should not tell anyone about the phone call because it was private, and she didn't want to share this stuff with anyone else.

When I saw her at school later, I mentioned the phone call, but she acted like she didn't know what I was talking about. I figured it was because of what she'd said at the end of the call about not speaking of it again, and I didn't question it. Years later, someone mentioned a restaurant her father owned. I asked what they were talking about since her father was dead. Her father wasn't dead, and she had no idea about the phone call.

Fingerprints

When I was a little girl too young to read, my mother had me help her with a task involving letters. We were sitting at the dining table with papers and the typewriter. She would have me feed paper into the typewriter, and she would type up a letter. She would then have me remove the paper, fold it into an envelope, lick the stamp, lick the envelope, and seal it. All fingerprints on the paper and envelopes were mine. What was she sending, and to whom? I still don't know.

Gifts

My parents always pocketed the gifts relatives would send me and replaced them with other gifts. My mother later reversed this story and accused her relatives of doing that with gifts she would send their children. I don't believe they ever did this. Over the years, I got a variety of presents supposedly from others in the family. They would sometimes be accompanied by a note supposedly from those same relatives explaining the significance of the gift. Often, they would be something age-inappropriate, such as a book well below my reading level. My mother would then laugh at these relatives for not understanding children's developmental stages.

Often, when these presents were not something age-inappropriate, they were a thing to wear, such as a necklace, a pin, or a shirt. I would wear them to see these relatives on purpose. When I mentioned this and thanked them, they were always confused. They didn't recognize these gifts at all. Whenever they asked about a gift that had actually been sent that year, I likewise would have no idea what they were talking about. Worst of all, on the occasions when they would recognize what I was wearing, these things would turn out to be stolen.

My Great Aunt

Whenever we went to visit my father's aunt, she would call me by my initials. Once, I asked her why she called me that, and she said it was because that's how I always signed my letters to her. I had never written her a letter and had no idea what she was talking about.

25. Made Up Tragedy

About

<u>About Made-Up Tragedy & MBP</u>

MBP abusers sometimes make up illnesses about others without actually making them sick, but sometimes follow through a step further and actually make people sick. MBP abusers also sometimes make up tragedies about others.

This begs the obvious question. If making up illnesses about others without following through on making them sick is the tip of the iceberg of a set of behaviors that includes sometimes actually making others sick, is there an analogous corresponding category to making up deaths of actually killing people? We know that some MBP abusers do become serial killers. I don't know of any cases in which a medical abuser claimed a person died in a non-medical tragedy and then followed through, but has anyone been looking for these cases? Would we see them if we weren't looking for them?

Clueless

<u>Incident Tags/Trigger Warnings</u>
Munchausen, MBP, Made Up Tragedy, Death

<u>Incident</u>

One day, some old friends of my parents came into town. I didn't know them, but my mother decided that we were going to take the daughter of the family, who was about my age, out to see a movie while the rest of the adults did stuff together. We took her to a popular mall and let her choose the movie. She chose Clueless, which had recently come out.

Before we met up with her, my mother told me that we were taking her out to make her feel better because her mother had just recently died. She told me an elaborate story of how they were very close, and the girl used to be skinny and beautiful, but then her mother died, and she developed insomnia and put on weight quickly due to eating in the middle of the night. She explained that this was traumatic on a second level because her mother was pretty and thin, and this made her no longer look like her mother. She told me she was self-conscious of it and not to bring it up.

When we met up with the girl, she was not actually large, just not malnourished like I was. We took her out to dinner at the mall before the movie. I told her how sorry I was about her mother. She asked me what I meant, and I explained what my mother had told me.

In fact, her mother was still alive. She was, needless to say, confused and very creeped out. Suddenly, it was clear that she was with an adult stranger who had woven this strange story. This was in the days before it was normal for a child to have a cell phone, so she had no way to contact her parents. She went through the rest of the evening politely and quietly, and I think simply counting down the minutes until she was reunited with adults she would feel safe with.

I think my mother was "borrowing" in this case because the main character in Clueless discusses losing her mother in a freak liposuction accident at the beginning of the movie. My mother had likely read about the movie ahead of time after the girl had chosen it.

The Dead Cousin

<u>Incident Tags/Trigger Warnings</u>
Munchausen, MBP, Made Up Tragedy, Death, AIDS

<u>Incident</u>

It was the late 80's or early 90's when my mother decided that she'd had a cousin who died of AIDS back in the 60's. The world was terrified of AIDS and deeply homophobic. The AIDS quilt had recently been on the news. Not yet having figured my mother out, I bought her story hook, line, and sinker, as they say.

Her story blew up when her aunt and uncle, who had supposedly been this fictional cousin's parents, came to visit. I asked them about their son, curious to know about my relative, who I'd never had a chance to meet. They were confused, but based on their reaction, I think they were already aware she had a tendency to do stuff like this; otherwise, there would have been a bigger reaction. After they left, she doubled down and claimed that they were so homophobic and hateful that they simply chose to stop acknowledging his existence after he came out. Nope. Their reaction wasn't pain, hate, anger, or trauma. Their reaction was confusion, followed by dismissal. There was no cousin by that name. There never had been.

The Drowned Mom

Incident Tags/Trigger Warnings
Munchausen, MBP, Made Up Tragedy, Death, Drowning
Incident

I was in high school when my mother decided that one of our neighbors had drowned. It was one of the moms in the neighborhood, and she told a very sad story about how she had taken her two small boys fishing on vacation when one of the little boys had accidentally dropped his pole in the water. Supposedly, the mom had gone into the water to retrieve the pole, gotten tangled in the weeds, and never came back up. She painted a picture of two little boys sitting in a small row boat as the minutes ticked on.

I had mentioned to someone else in the neighborhood how they had lost their mother. The person I was speaking with was a friend of the supposedly dead woman who had just been speaking with her recently. She was fine. Not only that, but the fishing expedition had never happened. The supposedly dead woman and her friend were understandably creeped out.

The Mugging

<u>Incident Tags/Trigger Warnings</u>
Munchausen, MBP, Made Up Tragedy, Mugging

<u>Incident</u>

One day, my mother decided that one of our old family friends was deeply traumatized by a recent mugging. In fact, he had not been mugged at all. She told a story of how the assailant pushed him down, threatened him, and took his money. She described his trauma symptoms and his difficulty in going about life normally after it happened.

It later turned out that the whole story was completely made up, and he had no idea what I was talking about. It sounded very similar to a series of bad muggings that had been on the news lately, but those hadn't happened to anyone we actually knew. This was one of a series of fictitious muggings that she claimed happened to a variety of older friends of hers.

26. Making Up Illnesses About Others

About

<u>About Making Up Illnesses About Others & MBP</u>

Have you ever met someone who made up random sick stories about others? Sometimes, MBP abusers do this without actually bothering to make people sick. This doesn't mean that they never make people sick. It just means that they didn't bother to that particular time. When you observe behavior like this, it's common to brush it off as just a weirdo being a weirdo. Think twice next time you observe something like this. It's the tip of the iceberg of a much bigger and more dangerous set of behaviors.

Incidents

<u>Incident Tags/Trigger Warnings</u>

Munchausen, MBP, allergies, anaphylaxis, PMS, breasts, alcohol, smoking, acupuncture, back pain

<u>Incidents</u>

Crossing Guard

One day, when my mother came to pick me up from school, she launched into a bizarre story about how she'd just been talking to the crossing guard, who had been going on and on about how bad her PMS was. We could see the crossing guard in the distance out the window, and I think her choosing the crossing guard may just have been based on who was in her line of vision but out of earshot at the time. She wouldn't let the subject drop. I shrugged it off, but she kept repeating herself, apparently not having gotten the reaction she wanted from me the first few times. She went on and on about how tender and swollen the crossing guard's breasts were and how if she even accidentally brushed against something, she'd be in terrible pain. It was bizarre. I'm not sure what kind of reaction she was looking for.

Family Friend

We had a family friend who my mother liked to make things up about. He was the dad of a couple of the kids my age in the apartment complex. This is also one of the people she made up a mugging story about, as mentioned in the 'Made Up Tragedy' section. On one occasion, she decided that he had a genetic condition that made him horribly sick to his stomach if he had even a drop of alcohol. I later saw him drink a cocktail, and he was just fine. When I tried to warn him there was alcohol in it, he had no idea what I was talking about and why I would be worried about him accidentally drinking alcohol.

On another occasion, she decided he'd gotten an acupuncture staple in his ear to help him quit smoking. She claimed that this thing worked like magic. They put it in his ear, and he never had the urge to smoke again, but he had to wear it for the rest of his life because if he ever took it out, he would have irresistible cravings to smoke again, according to her. He never had a staple in his ear, and he had no idea what I was talking about when I asked him about it.

Lifeguard

When I was a little girl, one of the lifeguards at the building pool was a thin young woman. My mother would talk the lifeguards' ears off if they would let her.

I was skinny since I was not being fed properly. My mother would always compare us as physical types even though she was fit since she exercised and kept in shape, whereas I was more emaciated. My mother started insisting that we both had bad backs since that was a thing that happened to skinny young women, according to her. She went on and on about it. The lifeguard took issue with her and called her out for making up a physical ailment about both of us. She insisted that neither of us had bad backs, which was, of course, true. Neither of us had a bad back. A lot of people brushed off my mother's behavior, but she called it out.

Allergies

This one is a repeat of one of the ones in the shorts section of traditional MBP, but it bears repeating here.

My mother would occasionally decide that a random person in her life had terrible allergies. Allergies were kind of a go-to catch-all for her. One year, she made a big to-do about the idea that her sister-in-law was so allergic to cats that her parents would have to lock the cats in the basement so that my aunt wouldn't throw up. In another incident, she claimed that an uncle of hers was so allergic to peanuts that if his wife ate peanut butter ice cream and then kissed him later in the day, he would die. He had no idea what she was talking about when this came up later. In another incident, she claimed that her adoptive father was terribly allergic to metal and could never touch it.

27. Sick Stories About Famous People

About

<u>About Celebrity Stories & MBP</u>

I've never known my mother to stalk a celebrity, although I would not be at all surprised to learn that she had. I know that she has stalked non-celebrities, including myself. There's not much else to say here that I didn't already say in the "about" pages of the last two sections. If you haven't read those, it's worth reading those over if you're going to read this section.

Incidents

Munchausen, MBP, death, drowning, car accidents, cancer

Incidents

The Widower

There was once a celebrity whose wife had recently died of cancer who came to a publicity event in the city where we were living. I believe it was at the museum my mother often pretended to work at. I won't name the specific celebrity. Whenever I saw him on TV, my parents would talk about how weird he was in person. When I asked them about it, they told me a story about how he had reacted badly about them approaching him about his wife, who had recently died. They considered this to be his bad - his social dysfunction - not theirs.

What I have gathered from the retelling of the story over the years boils down to this. He was obligated to continue with certain events despite his loss, as sometimes happens to celebrities. They had approached him and quizzed him about his late wife in an off-putting way. This is not surprising, given my mother's fascination with sickness and death and my father's poor social skills. He reacted as one would expect a person to, and they were ushered away. They never really seemed to have let go of this experience and forever after branded him as a weirdo.

The Drowning

In the 80s and 90s, Michael Jordan was a big deal for anyone who followed basketball. At one point, he did an interview that included a photo shoot of him involving water. My mother spun a whole story around this. She claimed that his father had drowned when he was a little boy and that he was still terrified of water. In reality, his friend had drowned. I guess my mother decided that the father's drowning made a better story. In fact, his father did not die until 1993. Notice the similarity between this and the drowned mom story in the "made-up tragedy" section. My mother seems to have a fixation with drowning parents traumatizing children. This does not match anything in her actual life. Maybe it is symbolic of something in her mind, but if it is, I don't know what.

Fake Sightings

My mother had a big thing for fake celebrity sightings. I'm not sure what it was about. I think she enjoyed the attention of having a story to tell. Sometimes, she also seemed to enjoy antagonizing people by causing a fuss and insisting they were, in fact, a celebrity. She knew it wasn't them. At various different times, she claimed to have seen various basketball players and coaches, Jerry Springer, and Stedman Graham. At one point, she went around telling people in the building and health club that one of the people who lived and worked out there was Stedman Graham. It was pretty obvious that he wouldn't have been living in our building. I think she just liked making him uncomfortable and drawing other people into that experience unwittingly.

28. Non-Medical Sick Stories

About

<u>About Non-Medical Sick Stories & MBP</u>

What is a non-medical sick story? It's a story about something people see as a sickness, even though it's not a physical illness or a diagnosable mental illness. Lots of stuff can fall into this category. I will group them into "isms" and "other." By isms, I mean things like racism, classism, sexism, homophobia, and other prejudices. You will notice in the examples I provide that my mother used these in both directions. She told non-bigoted people false stories of bigotry while telling bigoted people false stories of things such as interracial marriage or adoption, for example. What mattered to her was a reaction from the other person identifying a sickness in the story she told, whether or not there was actually rationally any sickness at all implied in the story. She seemed to get an identical charge or fix out of both.

This is one of the categories in which my mother's behavior was serving multiple purposes at once. For example, she has a desire to tell sick stories, whether medical or not, but she also found it useful to use non-medical sick stories to badmouth whistle-blowers so that others would not listen to them. Nothing quite prevents people from being willing to listen to each other like the categories of hot-button issues in this section. It benefited her to keep people in her life from comparing notes with each other. As a sadist, she also enjoyed the pain and conflict that these false stories created.

I strongly believe that this is one of the sections in this book that represents a larger pattern amongst MBP abusers in general. I believe that more about this will come out as society grows to learn more about MBP and get better at identifying cases.

- Other MBP cases involving this pattern: In "Sickened" by Julie Gregory, she tells of an incident in which her grandmother falsely claimed that an African American man had given her a popcorn ball that was tainted or poisoned.

Examples of "ism" non-medical sick stories I have heard my mother tell:

- Falsely claiming to someone against racism that a person said something racist.

- Falsely claiming to a racist that a person was sexually active with other racial groups.

- Falsely claiming to people that others were LGBTQ+ during times when this was less accepted in society.

Examples of other non-medical sick stories I have heard my mother tell:

- Falsely claiming a conflict happened between two people that did not

- Falsely claiming someone said something nasty or judgmental that they did not.

- Falsely claiming someone was very stupid and telling false stories to illustrate this

- Falsely telling embarrassing stories about others that never happened

Incidents

Incident Tags/Trigger Warnings

Munchausen, MBP, bigotry, prejudice

Incidents

The NoseBleed

We were on a family vacation in a mountainous region. We saw a little trail of blood on a trail in a tourist area that looked like someone had gotten a cut or skinned a knee. My mother had no further knowledge of this than the rest of us. She suddenly claimed it had been an African-American girl with a nosebleed she'd personally seen. This could not possibly have been true. She had happened across it with the rest of us. She went on and on about African Americans getting nosebleeds in mountainous regions.

The Elevator

One day my mother came home from the video rental store with an odd story of an Asian man in the building elevator farting out loud repeatedly during the elevator ride. She then went on to make up an explanation of cultural differences, claiming that this was totally normal behavior in Asia.

Unhappy

My mother sometimes said that she had been very unhappy during the time we lived out of state when I was three to four. When I asked her about it, she said she didn't feel like she fit in. She illustrated this with a story in which she had told a neighbor we were thinking of moving to a different location, and the neighbor responded that we couldn't move there because there were only "blacks and Jews" in that location. I later found out that my mother had reversed this story.

Jump In

When I was a little girl, my mother took me to some type of Native American ceremony. She convinced me that we were meant to jump in and join. We were not. She knew this. She had convinced me that I was being rude if I didn't. By the time I figured it out, everyone else was looking at me, annoyed as she was sitting to the side laughing.

Smells

In the "Random" section of this book, I tell of my mother's smell hallucinations in which she was convinced I smelled terrible. This sometimes seemed to have happened to her along racial lines as well. She once told me a story in which a person commented to a maid cleaning an African American woman's room, "They smell different, don't they?" My mother claimed that this was a moment she realized how entrenched racism was when she overheard this. I later found out she'd reversed the story.

Learning Words

As a child, I often learned bigoted words for the first time in the context of a person confronting me with what I had supposedly said. Sometimes, these would be people I was trying to get close to in hopes they would help rescue me. Other times, it seemed totally random. In every case, the people confronting me claimed that my mother had told them I had said those things.

Misappropriating Group Trauma

My mother would sometimes try to claim other's trauma by falsely claiming to be a member of a group. She would do things such as suddenly claim to be Jewish in a discussion of the holocaust or claim to have Native American ancestry in a discussion of the persecution of Native Americans.

PFLAG

At one point in high school, my mother told me that she was a member of PFLAG. I had never heard of this and had no idea what she was talking about. PFLAG stood for "Parents, family, and friends of lesbians and gays." She explained to me that she wasn't sure which family member she'd joined it for, but since other family members had recently gotten opposite-sex significant others, she'd decided it was for me. I told her that this didn't make any sense since I wasn't questioning my sexuality, but she told me she had friends in the group and she wasn't ready to leave yet. This was phrased as me being selfish and not considering her needs. She'd already backed herself into a corner with statements about me she'd made to other family members who were visiting at the time.

It's worth pointing out here that the DSM removed homosexuality as something considered to be an illness in 1987. This particular incident involving my mother probably reflects that she grew up before that shift. Stigmatization encourages her type of behavior, and destigmatization discourages it. Stigmatizing stuff as an illness that's really not just gives MBP types more material to work with. Motive goes away if no one associates disease with something that's not a disease. Take away the controversy that some try to heap on the LGBTQ+ community, and this stops being a behavior. We can't take away all diseases, but we can at least stop classifying stuff as diseased that isn't.

The Exchange Student

At one point, my mother decided that one of the exchange students at our school had been gay. He'd recently left the school because the exchange was over, and it was time for him to go back home. She spun a story about him staying with a family in town because he couldn't go back home since he'd come out because his homeland was deeply homophobic. He was supposedly cut out of his family and left in limbo, unable to return to school here with the exchange over and unable to return to his family and homeland. His family was very upset, according to her. In fact, he wasn't gay or questioning, his family and culture were not homophobic, and he'd gone home as scheduled with no problems. She later told this exact same story about a different exchange student.

The Security Guard

At one point in my early childhood, my mother told me that a new security guard in our building was deeply racist. She claimed that he'd described some of our neighbors as "ghetto boys" and given them problems. In fact, I later learned, she'd reversed the story. He'd stood up to her for saying things like that. She tried to turn others in the building against him, but the other security guards stood up for him because they knew the truth. Shortly later, he died of a heart attack. I don't think all this caused it, but it could not possibly have helped that he had people coming at him for supposedly saying what she actually had.

The Movie Theater

When I was a little girl, my mother took me to the movies, and we ran into a man we knew from the building. She convinced me that I should call him certain words and phrases by convincing me that they were compliments that he would love. I liked him and wanted to compliment him and make him feel good since he was such a nice guy. I repeated what she had said, hoping to make his day. This caused an uproar in the theater. She had convinced me to use deeply anti-Semitic words and phrases. As a small child, I sat there mystified at the reaction to words my mother had convinced me meant very nice things.

Lorenzo

I also mention this made-up person in the faking authority and intelligence section for other reasons. In that section, I mention the parts of this that are more relevant to that subject.

Lorenzo was a fictional Latin American man she'd made up. She often told stories about his bad behavior at the museum, which were really about her behavior. She would then blame this on Latin American culture and sexism. She claimed he did not get along with women and felt they were beneath him. She claimed he could not stomach having a female boss or teacher. She claimed this caused him to discriminate against her. She was always telling embarrassing stories about him being a stupid womanizer.

The Racist Drug Pusher

At one point, my mother convinced our primary care provider that I had a sexual fetish for African-American men. She used this as a justification for requesting an HIV test for me. He was furious and went on a rant and did the test. This was the first I learned he was a racist since the subject had never come up before. I was stunned at the rant and couldn't figure out what was going on at the time.

This guy was the primary care provider for lots of the family, and my mother was the one who had found him and decided that most of the family would see him. I later found out that he was also supplying her with massive amounts of pain pills that she had no medical need for.

29. Religion

About

<u>About Religion & MBP</u>

- Religion holds power.

- MBP abusers exert power over others through manipulation and deceit.

- Some abusers may resent religion for wielding power they do not.

- Some abuses may lean into religion and use it to exert control over others.

- In some cases, these patterns will be multigenerational.

- Not all MBP abusers experience religious hallucinations or delusions like my mother, but it should not be surprising if MBP abusers have an unhealthy connection to religion or a bitter resentment of religion.

- You will not necessarily see this in all cases.

- Examples of other MBP cases involving this pattern:

- In Sickened by Julie Gregory, she describes her grandmother hallucinating Jesus after going driving looking for him.

- Donald Harvey performed occult rituals.

Preacher

Incident Tags/Trigger Warnings

Religion, paranoia.

Incident

There was frequently a Christian preacher in front of the Chinese restaurant kitty-corner from the building our apartment was in. I could see him from the window, but I wouldn't have noticed him unless my mother had pointed him out. Twenty floors up, I couldn't hear what he was saying, but she claimed to be able to. Cars passed by on the busy 4-lane road between the guy and our building. He would sit on the corner with a microphone. There were tall buildings up and down the street with lots of people. It was a good area for foot traffic. She railed against him with building management as if they could have done anything about it.

Some in our building mentioned that they liked him and that he was a nice guy, but she could never be convinced of that. She would claim he was talking about her but would never say what she thought he was saying, no matter how many times I asked. We would see him out the kitchen window. The windows had screens built in but only opened a few inches because of the stoppers screwed in. She reacted even with the windows closed, claiming to be able to hear him.

This scene played out many times across weeks, months, and years until, eventually, the preacher moved on and found a new spot. Her reaction was always angry and dismissive. She couldn't be persuaded that he was not talking about her.

Rosemary's Baby

Incident Tags/Trigger Warnings
Religion, possession, horror

Incident

We watched a lot of movies and TV. This was different because she spoke negatively of the movie and seemed angry. We spoke of it multiple times. I wasn't allowed to watch it. I asked why. She said she was against "Rosemary's Baby" because it made some people think its premise was real and think that their baby was actually like that. I laughed at how stupid the people were who thought that not realizing she was talking about herself.

Points To Make

Horror movies are not in any way to blame for my mother's illness or for what I went through. The idea that we could prevent violence by preventing violent movies is misguided. I strongly believe that my mother would have held similar paranoid beliefs and that I would still have gone through the same abuse had there been no such movie.

Advice for Third Parties

If you hear someone talking like this, do not brush it off. It suggests that the people, especially children, around them are in danger. If someone suggests they believe this about any children, you need to contact social services and anyone in their life who can step in immediately.

Pixie

<u>Incident Tags/Trigger Warnings</u>

Religion, paranoia

<u>Incident</u>

My mother had 2 well-worn thick books. One was on fairies, and one was on gnomes and trolls. They listed types and had illustrations, along with accompanying folklore. I think one was Good Faeries/Bad Faeries by Brian Froud. One was Gnomes by Wil Huygen. She would spend hours going through them with me. She said that what was in them was real and that this was why she needed to teach me about them. This happened several times over the years.

I remember going over the books with her in the bedroom with windows that faced west. We sat on the edge of the bed with our feet digging into the old brown carpet. Outside was the general hum of the city's air traffic above and car traffic below.

She often called me Pixie even though I would ask her why and tell her that wasn't my name or any nickname I'd agreed to. When I was younger, she would make me get pixie haircuts even though I didn't want them. As I got older and she noticed that this wasn't the norm for other girls in my school, she relented. She liked to appear to fit in.

Sometimes, she would tell me the books were fiction. Sometimes, she would tell me the books were true. Sometimes, she would tell me I was one of them. She had a specific listing picked out in the fairy book, and she would tell me that's the type I was.

<u>Points To Make</u>

It would not be productive or useful to stop recording folklore. These books are in no way to blame for my mother's mental illness or the abuse I went through. My mother would still have been sick, and I would still have been abused had these books never existed. As you will see throughout this book, my mother was very capable of coming up with strange beliefs all on her own. It is likely that these simply helped her articulate ideas that she already had. It would be a loss if people hesitated to record folklore because of this.

<u>Advice for Third Parties</u>

Although at first glance, this seems less threatening than the Rosemary's baby delusion, it is not. There is an old folk belief, still discussed in some new age circles, that a child can be a "changeling," meaning a fae folk replacement of a human child. There are documented cases in which people have killed people because of this belief, just as there are documented cases in which people have accidentally killed people while attempting to perform an exorcism.

I will repeat the advice in the previous incident:

If you hear someone talking like this, do not brush it off. It suggests that the people, especially children, around them are in danger. If someone suggests they believe this about any children, you need to contact social services and anyone in their life who can step in immediately.

What is Death?

Incident Tags/Trigger Warnings

Death

Incident

I was five years old. My father's father had just died. I liked him and was looking forward to seeing him and wanted to know where he was. Everyone was acting differently. My mother took me out by the pool, away from everyone else, to explain things to me. She told me about death and that he had died. She told me it was like you go in the ground and sleep forever and never wake up. I asked her if one could dream in death. She said no. I kept on questioning if one could wake up or dream, but she was emphatic and insistent that this would never happen and that there would never be anything after death. When I wouldn't let it go, she explained that he would rot in the ground and that, eventually, there would be nothing left. This hung over me every time she tried to kill me. Every time over the years I lost consciousness from smothering or strangulation, I thought how unfair it was that this was the last thing I would ever feel. I think that a belief in God or an afterlife didn't afford my mother the power over me that she wanted.

Broken Lambs

Incident Tags/Trigger Warnings

Religion, Death, Lost Faith

Incident

I was eight years old. We were at my mother's parent's house for her father's funeral. She had all these miniature porcelain lambs in a drawer that she was sorting through. She kept on breaking them. They used to mean something to her, but now she said they were stupid. She had gotten them when she was a kid and wanted to be a Sunday school teacher when she grew up.

Later, a relative suggested taking all the grandkids to see 'All Dogs Go To Heaven' to help us understand and cope. She did not want me to see this because she said it would mislead me into believing in heaven, and she didn't want that to happen.

Catholic School Money

Incident Tags/Trigger Warnings
Religion, Catholic school abuse scandal, bribery

Incident

The school had seen signs of severe abuse but hadn't called social services. One day, we changed from our usual schedule. We stayed late so that my mother could meet the principal and give her a check. It wasn't tuition time. It wasn't how people gave tuition or donations. We met the principal late in the evening after everyone had gone home for the day. We had gone out of our way and off schedule. My mother insisted that I be the one to hand the check over. I had never done anything like that before, but she said it was important because the principal would like that. She was visibly amused. She thought it was cute and funny that I would be the one handing over the check. I didn't understand what it was for or why it was funny. She acted like she did when she thought she was being clever - smiling at herself and repeating the thing she thought was clever over and over again. She was very smug about it.

The principal was visibly surprised to see me there, thinking she would be meeting my mother alone. She was visibly uncomfortable when I reached out with the check. She asked why I was handing it to her. I told her it was because my mother told me to. She was visibly ashamed and uncomfortable. She didn't want to take it from me. She wanted to take it from my mother. I couldn't understand why she wasn't taking it. She didn't explain it to me. My mother didn't explain it to me. They just continued in their back and forth. I stood there confused. Eventually, she told my mother that she would take it but that she wouldn't take another one. That would be the final one. Despite that, they continued to take my parents' tuition payments and official channel donations up until I graduated, and they never said a word to the police or social services.

Points To Make

The response from the principal was in no way helpful or ethical. Deciding you won't take money in the future just makes it cheaper for people to keep abusing their kids and leaves them with more money to pay off more people later. If you're scared of reporting to social services, just do it anonymously. She may have been scared of telling the school that the donation she promised wasn't coming through, but if this was the case, then it demonstrates a profound moral bankruptcy of the church if they would have been angry with her even after an explanation. She may never have told the church about the donation and may simply have had her own plans for the money. If that was the case, it speaks for itself. You gain nothing morally by staying quiet but refusing to take future payoffs. It's just cowardly.

<u>Advice for Third Parties</u>

If you know about anything like this, report it. You can do it anonymously. I give you a 100% guarantee that if you have seen signs of abuse, others have too. They cannot know it was you, and if they claim to be able to, they are trying to flush the reporter out by accusing everyone it could have been.

What's going to happen if you don't report it? That fact will come out eventually when the victim grows up. It may even come out sooner than that. Just imagine everyone in your life knowing that about you. What do you believe happens to us after death? Do you want to explain the check at the pearly gates? No amount of money is worth it.

Cahokia Mounds

<u>Incident Tags/Trigger Warnings</u>
Hallucination, Psychosis, Religion
<u>Incident</u>

When I was a little girl, my mother took me on a road trip to the Cahokia Mounds. These are remains of a sophisticated prehistoric civilization in what is today Illinois. There is a visitor center with educational information near the old sites. My mother made a big deal of it. She was very excited. I, like many kids that age didn't understand what all the fuss was about.

She was elated when we got there, and that's when things changed. She kept on asking if I could hear them. I could not. Neither could any of the other tourists there who were visibly uncomfortable with the situation. She went on and on about how wonderful it was. She claimed that she'd always known there was something around there before she'd found out about the site because she could hear them whenever we passed nearby on our road trips to and from her parents' house. I think what happened was that she experienced auditory hallucinations, whether natural or drug-induced, on her way to see her parents, and then later learned of the site and assumed there was a connection. I have placed this in the religion section because, despite her insistence that she was an atheist, this seemed somewhat like a religious experience for her.

Ruins

When I was a little kid, my mother would take me to see ruins on our trips to Mexico every spring break. These were often in the Yucatan, though not always. This was a huge deal for her. She would spend lots of time fascinated over them. Sometimes, she would go up to a room at the top of a pyramid, go inside, and spend a long time there. When she came out, she would suggest I go in. I would go quickly in and out, not seeing what the fuss was. She wanted to know if I could hear them like she could. I could never figure out what she was talking about. She insisted that she was talking with the gods. She never provided any sort of an explanation as to how this squared with her haughty and condescending attitude towards those who believed in religion or her insistence that she was an atheist.

Kachina Dolls

337

Religion

Incident

My mother had two Kachina dolls she kept in a cabinet. Sometimes, she would take them out, move them around, or fuss over them. She told me that they were her friends.

The Man in the Crowd

Religion

Incident

One day, when I was a little girl, my mother told me a story about a mob of people she was in a long time ago. She said they were all trying to get to this one man. He was cornered on the edge of a cliff with nowhere to go; then, suddenly, he had gotten away with ease. They were all dumbfounded. She said, 'We couldn't believe it.'

At the time, I could not understand what she was talking about. I had never read the Bible because she had made a big deal of keeping it away from me and not allowing me to read it. She had even pressured the Catholic school she was sending me to into going along with this. I now realize that she was telling me a story from the Bible as if she had been there. The original is in Luke 4. In the original, the crowd in the synagogue is angered by Jesus's teachings, and they drive him to the edge of a cliff in anger, but he miraculously walks through the crowd and goes on his way. I don't know why she told me this or whether she actually thought that she had been there.

30. Acting Possessed/Dissociated

About

<u>About Acting Possessed or Dissociated & FDIA</u>

Did my mother do this because she was dissociating or because it was a conscious choice to try to scare me? I don't have the answer to that, and I likely never will. She was clearly disturbed but also clearly sadistic. It's even possible that some of the instances were genuine dissociation and that others were attempts to scare me. Although most MBP abusers likely don't display this behavior, I still include it here because it's a critical piece of the story of my childhood and the abuse I lived through.

- Other MBP cases involving this pattern: Another abuser, Beverley Allitt, blamed activity on poltergeists. This included fire setting and poisoning a dog. Interestingly, this same abuser is also one of the ones who, like my mother, left feces in odd places.

2 Different Voices

sexual abuse

Incident

In the sexual abuse section of this book, I describe my mother sexually abusing me in a set of incidents titled 'The Monster.' I am referring to that same series of incidents here. She would sometimes strangle me unconscious with one hand while molesting me with the other. Other times, she would sit on my face without underwear so that I was unable to breathe. I was so young that I believed a monster to be doing it. I now realize who it was because she was the only one in the apartment. I learned that the best way of surviving was to play dead. This caused the monster, whom I later realized was her, to lose interest.

Sometimes, I would later see her pacing back and forth and fretting outside my door. I would only see her, but I would hear two different voices. One was a high-pitched voice panicking about me being dead. The other was a low, gravelly, growly voice that was cavalier about the whole thing and insisted that this was what she had wanted all along. They would argue back and forth. It was confusing for me because I could not see anyone else there. We were alone in the apartment. I now realize both of these voices were coming out of her. Was she genuinely dissociating, or was this another sadistic bid to freak me out? I don't know.

Sometimes, I would call out to her because I did not know what she was talking about, and I did not know that it was her who had just done those things to me. Sometimes, she would scream in reaction to this as if I had scared her. This seems to suggest that it was not a put-on, at least not all of the time.

Legion

When I was a teenager, my mother and I passed each other in the hall one day as usual. I was about to walk out of sight when she turned and called back to me. At first, I didn't understand what she said, and I asked her to repeat herself. She said again, "Aren't you going to ask me who I am?" I thought she was joking. I told her I obviously knew who she was. This went back and forth for a bit until finally, I decided to humor her and ask her who she was so I could be done with the interaction. She said, "I'm Legion." I had never read the Bible at that point in my life, and so I had no idea what she was talking about or making a reference to. I asked her, and she said again, "I'm Legion." This interaction went on for a bit, and I still had absolutely no idea what she was talking about. She insisted that she was Legion because there were many. I brushed this off and didn't think about it again until after I'd moved out of the house and read the Bible. It's a reference to Mark 5 in the Bible, in which Jesus drives demons out of a man. Some refer to this as the story of the Gerasenes demoniac.

At the time this interaction happened, she knew I hadn't read the Bible because she had specifically gone to great lengths to prevent it over the years. Either she was trying to psych me out and was too disorganized to realize that I wouldn't get the reference, or she was just having an actual mental health or drug-induced episode. I'm still not sure what that was about.

Exorcism Show

Incident Tags/Trigger Warnings

Burglary, break-in

Incident

I generally don't write about any incidents past the age of 18 in this book, but this one is worth noting for how it connects with the other incidents in this section. When I was in my twenties, I went out of town to a cousin's wedding. I stayed at a separate hotel from the rest of my family since I wanted to be safe from my parents.

One day, I found that my hotel room had been snooped through, and other relatives later confirmed that this had been my parents. The television was not still on the channel I had been watching before. It had been changed to an exorcism 'reality show.' This required some planning. She needed to know when I would be returning to the room and what would be playing on the channels at that time.

31. Imitating or Banning Stories

About

<u>About Stories & MBP</u>

My mother had a pattern of imitating or banning stories. This included movies, music, plays, urban legends, and books. This included both fiction and works based on true stories as well. I can tell you for certain that this is one of the patterns in this book that applies to other MBP abusers as well. The practice of imitating the stories is sometimes known as "borrowing." The practice of banning us from hearing certain stories or giving certain stories bad reviews in hopes no one else would watch or read them demonstrates how important it is to bring MBP further into the public eye. Abusers like my mother attempt to block those stories because they know public awareness increases their risk of being found out.

If you ever wonder if you're dealing with someone like this, I suggest you make frequent use of free online plagiarism checkers, internet searches, and online databases such as IMDB or Google Books. It's also a good idea to run stories by others in case they recognize the storyline from something they have seen or read.

<u>Tags/Trigger Warnings</u>

Birth, horror movies, death, evil, animal torture, disfigurement, poisoning, murder, physical abuse, murder, suffocation, MBP, racial stereotyping, strangling, manipulation, mental institutions, animal death, drunk driving, borderline, abuse, corruption, urination, hatred

<u>Stories My Mother Banned or Wanted to Ban</u>

As far as I can tell, some of these dealt with medical abuse, but others dealt with manipulation, corruption, fraud, or borderline personality disorder. If I have nothing more to say about the story, I simply provide the title. If there is more to elaborate on, I provide that immediately after the title. In general, you should assume that this section contains a lot of spoilers.

Radio Flyer

The X-Files episode involving a MBP accusation ("The Calusari" season 2 episode 21)

Vanilla Sky

Wicker Park

The Night Listener

The Suffocation Commercial - When I was a kid in the 1980s, there was a commercial on TV that played the sound of a baby making normal baby noises and then being suffocated. It didn't show anything, but you could hear the baby stopping breathing. The commercial then stated something about the parent needing help and offered some kind of helpline. My mother was furious with this commercial and was always very defensive about it. She said they should not do the baby suffocation commercial because it would make people want to do that. When it came on, she would get angry and reverse the blame, claiming that the commercial was, in fact, enticing those parents.

The Sixth Sense - It came out in the fall of 1999, towards the very tail end of my childhood, but I wasn't allowed to see it at first. First, she tried to get me to lose interest by showing me Stir of Echoes instead. We rented it from Blockbuster, a short walk from our house. Later, when I asked about Sixth Sense again, she said she had been hoping that I wouldn't still want to see it after Stir of Echoes since we'd watched that instead. Spoiler alert here for both movies. Notice it was so much more of a priority to avoid us watching movies that talked about MBP than to avoid us watching movies that talked about sexual assault and murder. This is because, by a certain age, everyone knows that murder and sexual assault exist based on general knowledge of society and the news. This is not the case with MBP. There is no hope of preventing discovery by preventing public knowledge of the existence of these other crimes. This is why there is a section of this book on making MBP as well known as other crimes under the "what can you do?" category.

Eventually, when it became clear that I was going to watch the movie on my own anyway, and I was about to graduate high school, she rented it for us to watch together. I think her thought process was that if she couldn't stop me from seeing it, she wanted to be there in the room to attempt to distract me, shift the narrative, or at least view my reaction to see if anything occurred to me at the moment. She had two strange reactions. One was in the moment, and the other was a few days later. First was her reaction during the funeral scene. She got angry, self-righteous, and defensive about the father's reaction to the revelation that his wife had killed their daughter. In the movie, it's pretty obvious that the father is shocked and horrified, having been totally unwitting up until that point. Instead of reacting to the character, it was as if she was reacting to my father. She insisted he had known and that the mother was sick and couldn't help it and that, therefore, the father was at least as responsible.

Her reaction a few days later was even stranger. She borrowed from the movie by quoting the Toni Collette character word for word other than swapping out the names of the children: "I'm so tired,————-. I'm tired in my body. I'm tired in my mind. I'm tired in my heart. I need a little help here." I was unclear what to make of what was happening. I didn't know about borrowing at the time and also didn't know about the Munchausen abuse at the time. I immediately spotted the quote and pointed out to her that she'd taken it from the movie. She was unsatisfied with my response. I told her I didn't know what she meant and asked her to explain. She said that she didn't know what she meant either and was hoping that I could explain it to her.

Dream Lover - Spoilers here. In this movie, a woman with Munchausen-type behavior marries a man, begins to ruin his life, and eventually gets him committed to a mental institution. At the end of the movie, he tells her that she's made a mistake by having him declared insane because now he can kill her and use an insanity defense to get away with it. He then strangles her to death.

She was very angry at the end of the movie because, according to her, "she was sick" and couldn't help it. She had no anger at any of the woman's actions throughout the movie and all the harm she caused, but as soon as it came back at the woman, she was morally indignant.

Mommy Dearest - I was never allowed to watch this movie. She always explained that she was afraid I would think she was like that if I watched it.

Rosemary's Baby - Please see the Rosemary's Baby entry in the Religion section. I would just be repeating myself here.

Cop Land - Every time an advertisement for this movie came on, she got angry. When I questioned her about it, she said it was because the guy on whom the story was based thought that he was so much better than everyone else. A movie celebrating a lone whistleblower really pissed her off.

<u>Stories My Mother Imitated</u>

The Sixth Sense - Please see the write-up in the section directly above. This one falls under both imitating and banning.

Single White Female - Spoilers here. I was not allowed to watch this movie. At a certain point later in life, after I'd seen the movie, it got back to me that my mother had retold the dog scene as if it had been a true story and I had been the one who had done it.

Drunk Santa - My parents once took me to a sketch comedy show that had a sketch about a drunken man dressed as Santa crashing a car into a fire hydrant, swearing and throwing up. I later heard this story retold as if I had done it.

Snoopy - There is an urban legend many have heard about a man walking a dog in the park who sees an attractive woman practicing yoga. He decides to go talk to her, but as he's nervously trying to decide what to say, his dog pees on her head like a fire hydrant as she's standing on her head. I believe that's pretty much the whole story. I had never heard this before, and one day, my parents told me the story as if it happened to my father's brother. They had a photo of him with a dog, and they told me the dog's name was Snoopy and that this was the dog in the story. Later, it turned out that this had never happened and that this wasn't even the dog's name.

The Lord of the Rings - This was during my early childhood, long before the movies came out. Back then, you would have to read the book to get the story. It may have been a bit above my mother's reading level because my father read it and told her about it, and she explained that she hadn't read it because it was only for really smart people. Incidentally, describing my father as a really smart person is hilarious. He had been known to write angry letters to authors, accusing them of trying to make him feel stupid by using big words he didn't know. That's another story. My mother had only a very basic and sometimes inaccurate idea of the trilogy. Part of this was her belief that there was a monster in the book who named himself Precious because of how much he valued himself. To everyone else, he was a monster, but to himself, he was Precious. She used to call me this sarcastically, telling me that I was like the monster.

What About Bob? - This movie came out when I was a kid. It was about a patient who took over a psychiatrist's life. My mother loved it. For years afterward, she would pull this routine in which she would take little steps and say something like, "See what I'm doing? What am I doing? I'm taking baby steps." Baby steps was a line from the movie that my mother had, for some reason, fixated on.

Stories My Mother Fixated On

Harvey - She explained that she loved the movie because, like the character, she also saw stuff others didn't see or think was real.

Mr. Bill - This was the Saturday Night Live sketch with the little doll that always gets torn apart and mutilated. My parents would call me this. They thought it was very amusing.

The Producers - My parents showed me the original version when I was a little girl, maybe seven or so. They laughed about how the secretary was like me.

Blazing Saddles - My parents also showed me this around the same age and also joked that I was like the showgirl in it.

Alien 3 - Spoiler here. At the end of the movie, Ripley kills herself in order to kill what is believed to be the final alien in existence, which is about to burst out of her. She throws herself off a platform down to the molten metal below. As she's falling through the air, it bursts out of her, and she clutches it to her so that it won't escape. She looks at peace. She has won. Much as described above in my mother's reaction to the Sixth Sense funeral scene, my mother's interpretation of this scene was based on her own mental workings and not at all on what was actually happening in the movie. She believed that Ripley was clutching the alien because although it was a monster, she was its mother, and she loved it. She falsely interpreted a strong bond between the two of them. To her, that was a special emotional scene that was reminiscent of us as a mother and daughter, and I was supposed to react like her. She would not let it drop when I would not reciprocate her sentimentality about that scene.

The Bad Seed - Spoilers here. Whenever I would ask my mother what her favorite movie was, she would tell me it was The Bad Seed. She loved it. It was about a little girl who was just born bad, and nothing anyone could do would change it. At the end of the movie, the little girl gets away with everything she's done, including murder. She's walking along enjoying her day when she gets struck by lightning and killed. Whenever I asked my mother to explain why it was her favorite, she told me it was because the little girl reminded her of herself. She told me she was very frightened as a child that she would be struck by lighting like that, but she loved it.

The Masks Episode of the Twilight Zone (season 5, episode 25) - Spoilers here. This episode tells the story of a family of greedy potential heirs waiting for the man they want to inherit money from to die. It's Mardi Gras, and he insists on them wearing special masks he has provided. They must keep them on all night. They are all bad people, and he is punishing them. At the end of the night, they find that their faces have transformed under the masks to look as ugly on the outside as they are on the inside. They have a number of sins. One of them, in particular, has been torturing and killing animals. She got defensive about this.

Arsenic and Old Lace - Spoilers here. This was a close second for my mother's favorite movie, right behind The Bad Seed, when I was a kid. In this movie, two seemingly kind, innocent old ladies keep on poisoning people with arsenic. In the end, the main character (their nephew) finds out that he was adopted. He is overjoyed because he hates his family. She enjoyed this scene, but she also very much enjoyed the poisoning scenes.

Carmen - When I was a little girl, my mother told me that my "real mother" was like Carmen from the Opera of the same name. She would get me to fasten a long blanket around my waist and get me to twirl around with it as Carmen did with her skirt in the video we would watch of it. It mostly involved just twirling and flipping my 'skirt.' In reality, this was a blanket with frilly edges and a button that allowed me to fasten it around my waist. It was big on me because I was still small. We 'danced' barefoot on the dark brown carpet. She would play Carmen and tell me that was my ancestry - my real mother's ancestry even though a DNA test now shows she's biologically my mother. She would attempt to copy the dancing and then have me copy her. It wasn't really dancing, just skirt flipping and twirling. It went on for a really long time, and I would get dizzy. We would practice this several times.

32. Bathroom Paranoia

About

<u>About Bathroom Paranoia & MBP</u>

As I pointed out earlier, some of these categories are likely to occur a lot amongst people who commit MBP abuse, whereas others are likely very specific to my own family's dysfunction. This is an example of the latter. I have never heard of this in any other cases. It likely reflects specific trauma in my mother's past and/or some specific fixation in her own individual mental illness. I still include such categories because they help paint a more complete picture of my family's dysfunction and because, in some cases, I may guess incorrectly about what is and is not a pattern common amongst people who commit such abuse.

Paranoia of Me

<u>Incident Tags/Trigger Warnings</u>

Sexual Paranoia

<u>Incidents</u>

When I was a little girl, my mother would sometimes attempt to prevent me from going to the bathroom at relative's houses or at the museum because she believed I was going in there to masturbate. I think this and the other bathroom paranoia described in this section was probably rooted in some past trauma for her, but I don't know that. It's just a guess. Some days, she would be in this mode, and other days, she wouldn't. It was completely unpredictable. Some days, if I went to the bathroom, it wouldn't raise an eyebrow for her. Other days, she would attempt to stop me and then apologize profusely to everyone else around when she couldn't stop me from using the restroom.

I was too young to understand what she was suggesting, so for me, this just fit into that broad range of inexplicable adult behavior. On her days like this, I would come out of the bathroom and hear her apologizing all over the place and hear other people trying to explain to her that this wasn't what was going on. They were clearly uncomfortable with her reaction and too uncomfortable to explain it to me when I asked them what was going on. I only figured it out later in life upon looking back on the memory and the words that had been spoken.

In one particularly memorable incident, we had just gotten off a multi-hour road trip to visit a relative. My mother, of course, went straight to the bathroom. Afterward, I attempted to, and she pulled this act. The end of a multi-hour road trip is no time to attempt to stop someone from going to the bathroom. I went in despite her efforts. It just never occurred to her that I would just naturally have to go after such a long car ride, even though that had been her experience, too. She apologized profusely to my relative, who tried to explain to her that this was not what was going on. My mother would not believe her no matter what. At the time, I didn't even know what she was suggesting, so I couldn't refute it. She had used the same bathroom. I couldn't figure out what the issue was.

Another particularly memorable incident happened at a volunteer event at the museum. This occurred in the work area behind the key code-locked door that she would later be banned from. See the "Faking Authority and Intelligence" section. There was a long line for the bathroom. Again, I couldn't figure out why it was a big deal for me to go to the bathroom but not anyone else. Again, the other adults tried to calm my mother down and tell her that's not what was happening. I couldn't figure out what they were talking about. I think I was about eight at the time.

There was a similar configuration to both bathrooms in the two incidents above, and that may have been the issue in terms of her remembering something from her past. They were both just past a door to the outside, and both were small half baths. She didn't tend to react like this with regard to all bathrooms. I don't remember her ever having this reaction to other relatives or other kids. I think she may have been conflating me with herself and reliving some type of incident from her past. That is speculation on my part. I don't really know what was going on in her head.

Paranoia of Others

<u>Incident Tags/Trigger Warnings</u>

Paranoia

<u>Incident</u>

My mother claimed that people living above us in the building would wait until she went to the bathroom so that they could go to the bathroom at the same time as her so that they could go to the bathroom on top of her. She first told me a story about how other neighbors at the board meeting were crazy because they thought this was happening to them and how they'd disrupted the board meeting over it. It later turned out that this was her usual trick of reversing stories that she knew made her look bad or unwell. She later angrily complained to me about the upstairs neighbors doing this to her. I told her I had never noticed anything. She said that this was because they only did it to her because it was specifically directed at her.

I tried to explain to her that they had no way of knowing when she was using the bathroom and that this didn't even make sense. In addition to the fact that the neighbors could not possibly know when she was going to the bathroom, she also could not possibly know when they were going to the bathroom. Sound didn't carry that way through the building.

She was convinced no matter what I said. This was a preoccupation for her that went on and on. She would often state that she needed to go to the bathroom but wasn't going to because they were doing it again. If I suggested she use the other bathroom instead, she would tell me this wouldn't work because they would just switch to that bathroom.

33. Malnutrition

About

<u>About Malnutrition & MBP</u>

Malnutrition is a common tactic amongst medical abusers. It serves several purposes at once:

- It serves the purpose of sadism.

- It serves the purpose of development delay and decreasing school performance.

- It makes it easier to pass a victim off as sick.

- It makes it easier to actually get a victim sick because starvation depletes the immune system.

- Sleep deprivation plus malnutrition are commonly used together in cult mind control, along with constantly keeping people on edge.

- Other MBP cases involving this pattern: see Sickened by Julie Gregory.

The Ham

<u>Incident Tags/Trigger Warnings</u>

Food

<u>Incident</u>

When I was a little girl, my mother took me on a trip to see my father's mother out of state. I was skinny, emaciated, and hungry. The first thing my grandmother did was invite us into her kitchen and present a ham someone had gifted her. She spoke of how good it was and offered us some. I enthusiastically took what I was offered and gobbled it down. My grandmother was very surprised and happy. She offered me another slice and then another, which I gobbled down as well.

My mother was unhappy about this. She had given my grandmother a story about me refusing to eat or not being able to eat much. Her story was that I either couldn't or wouldn't eat much and that this was why I was so skinny. My grandmother remarked on how glad she was that I liked it and was willing to eat it, which I was confused by because I didn't know about my mother's lie.

As this went on, my mother grew grumpier and grumpier until she finally cut off the food, claiming that I shouldn't eat too much at once. Apparently, my grandmother had planned this out, having believed my mother and wanting to entice me into eating. My reaction made it clear that my mother's story was inaccurate.

Disney

Incident Tags/Trigger Warnings

Food, MBP, isolation, starvation

Incident

I wrote up this incident at the very beginning of my work on this book when I was still deciding how to handle it. At first, I had the idea that I would attempt to write from my perspective as a child instead of as an adult looking back. I quickly decided against this because it was both too emotionally draining and not the best format for getting across a lot of information. I have chosen to leave this one that I'd already written before I made this switch as is. It is about a family vacation to Disney World with the extended family that my mother was very unhappy about my father's mother surprising us with. My mother had previously told her I was unwell, and she had to scramble to find a way to keep me from the rest of the family and keep me weak until the vacation was over and we went back home.

Childhood Perspective

Will I get to eat today?

Yesterday, I hoped for today. The day before, I hoped for yesterday.

They don't believe me.

They insist I was fed when she said I was.

Maybe tomorrow. Maybe tomorrow I will go to the suppers they are always talking about - coming home as a happy family.

I look at the fireworks in the distance. If I was out there like the other people, things would be different. But I am in here. The happiest place on earth.

Spicy Food

Sadism, Food, Malnutrition

Incident

One of my mother's favorite tricks was to wait until I was extremely hungry and then give me only food that was incredibly spicy so that I would be desperate enough to eat it. Sometimes, this would be a grilled cheese sandwich filled with so many hot pepper flakes that you couldn't see the cheese below them or get them out. Sometimes, this would be a dish covered in a sauce so that I couldn't get any pieces without the spice. The sauce would not be a spicy acquired taste that an adult would like. It would be something even an adult who liked very spicy food could not stomach. I would be the only one with the sauce on my food, and I would not be allowed anyone else's food. She would eat her normal food in front of me and laugh, watching my pain as I desperately ate it.

Steak Dinner

<u>Incident</u>

Every week, on the same night, we had a dinner of steak and potatoes. My parents would each get a potato and a steak. I would get a potato and half a steak. The rest of the steak out of the four steak package would be saved for later.

One week, I sat down to eat and found that I only had a potato. I asked for my steak and was told that there wasn't any for me. I pointed out that there were two left in the package, but they said that they were saving that for later. From then on, the weekly meal was me eating a potato and watching my parents eat steak while the rest of the steak sat on a plate off to the side, out of my reach in case anyone else besides me wanted any more. I was allowed only one potato with butter from then on. I was not allowed to replace the steak with a different food to eat with my potato. There was plenty of other food in the fridge, but it wasn't for me. The one potato was for me.

<u>Points To Make</u>

You'll often notice in hearing about various MBP survivors' experiences that the most restricted food type is protein. This is probably an effort to weaken the child. I believe that was part of what it was in my case. You will also see this pattern in the stories of cult survivors. Protein satisfies hunger longer, so restricting protein can also serve the purpose of sadism if part of the goal is to keep a victim hungry.

Hair and Nails

Malnutrition

Incident

I was hungry most of the time during my early childhood. I had bubbles in my fingernails from vitamin deficiency and measured in the 10th percentile of weight for my age group. My pediatrician would tell my mother this was a problem, but he wouldn't actually call the DCFS. He knew she had the money to feed me, and he could clearly see that I wasn't being fed. I think that this failure to act is why this was the particular doctor I was being taken to. I started to eat things that were not food in an effort to survive and help my hunger pains. I ate my mother's chapstick but was scolded and not allowed access to it again. I began to eat my hair and nails. I had no cuticles to eat. I was so skinny that there were no cuticles on either side of any of my fingers, just a nail on top of a finger.

34. His Cons

About

<u>About My Father's Cons and My Mother's & MBP Abuse</u>

My father is and always has been equally guilty as my mother. This book is mostly about her behavior because it is a book about MBP and the cluster of behaviors that surround it. I have prioritized writing about this because MBP is less well-known and needs more public awareness. My father's forms of immoral behavior, such as the cons outlined in this section and the sexual abuse mentioned in that section, are more well-known to society.

I am including this section so that people can get some insights into the larger patterns of behavior in the family. My father's relatives tolerated my mother's behavior because they knew no one better would possibly ever stay with my father. My parents stayed with each other despite their dislike for each other, and sometimes even hatred of each other, because a nasty divorce would have meant mutually assured destruction. I believe there was also an element of codependence at play. I have observed that my mother has a deep fear of being alone. In addition, my father is not very socially intelligent and likely would have been caught long ago without her help.

I don't believe either of their decisions to let the other live had to do with morality or love. It still seems amazing to me, given who they both are as people, that neither ever killed the other.

What does MBP have to do with his cons? MBP is also a con (a particularly cruel and deadly one).

- Other MBP cases involving this pattern: In Sickened by Julie Gregory, the parents committed arson and insurance fraud together. These parents also committed fraud involving foster kids and caretaking of older state dependents.

It's important to note that not all partners or co-parents of MBP abusers know what is going on. My father did, but there are many cases in which the significant other has no idea what is going on.

The Christmas Party

Firing, holidays

Incident

It was Christmas, and I was a little girl. My father brought the whole family to his office Christmas party. He was in charge of a team at the bank because his mother was wealthy. It wasn't directly nepotism because she wasn't a part of the company, but it had the same effect. Leaders were chosen by the amount of investment money they could get, and he had gotten money from his mother.

The party went normally at first, but then it was awkward when it became clear my father had chosen very different Christmas gifts from the office to the children depending on how much he liked their parents. All the kids of those he liked best got expensive gifts, while all the kids of those he liked least got simple trinkets since he couldn't get away with giving them nothing. A few grumbled about this, but they valued their jobs, so they didn't confront him.

Things dragged on, and I thought we were getting ready to go. My father called everyone to gather around. People excitedly whispered about an announcement about bonuses. They had been late that year, and everyone had been expecting them and budgeting for them because they had always been able to count on them before.

My father announced that the company was firing the entire team. The room erupted. People yelled, and someone called his bosses. His bosses showed up a little later. They were stunned that the team was still there. He had been instructed to fire them months ago, and they were still there. Corporate, believing this had been done, had stopped issuing them paychecks, and he had made up some lie about them being delayed. They had thought they were going to get the back pay plus bonuses. There was more yelling, and we left.

A few months later, my father tried to get back into the office with me in tow. Maybe he thought having a small child with him would prevent a bigger reaction from them. We went up to the floor he told me he still worked on. There were glass doors one needed a key card to get past. His key card didn't work. He knocked on the door, hoping to bluff someone into letting him in. The people behind the glass reacted angrily. They had changed the key card code to keep him out because he needed to stop showing up there. He hadn't worked there in months. We left.

<u>Points To Make</u>

My father wasn't a sadist, although he was just as willing to hurt people as my mother was and did hurt people as much as my mother did. Morally, there is no difference, but I think it's still useful to understand the different motivations. My father didn't care about other people's feelings. He cared if they thought badly of him. He cared if he was considered the bad guy. For him, a few more months of people looking up to him as boss mattered more than what happened to those who went without pay because they placed their trust in him. If this had been my mother, I would have said that she did it to inflict pain. In his case, I believe he did it because he didn't care if he inflicted pain.

Brothers

<u>Incident Tags/Trigger Warnings</u>

Stealing, ID theft, financial loss

<u>Incident</u>

My father had an older brother who he put through a lot over the years. As in other incidents, he didn't get off on being cruel like my mother did. He just didn't care if he was cruel in order to get what he wanted. His older brother traded stocks for a living. My father profited by ruining him financially by exploiting the fact that he never thought his own family would use inside information against him. My uncle knew not to share sensitive information about trade strategies and specific stock picks with others he couldn't trust. He just thought he could trust his brother.

By the time he found out it was too late, he lost everything. My father profited by anticipating his trades. Later, my parents enjoyed framing themselves as the benevolent relatives when they bought one pair of sandals from him when he was selling shoes to make ends meet. My grandmother never believed that her son would do that and could never be convinced as to what had happened. My uncle was framed as the screw-up.

Later, my uncle got another start in life when he started his own courier business. This, of course, required him to have a valid driver's license. My father, who was a notoriously bad driver, got enough traffic infractions that he had trouble renewing his license. Instead, he got a license under his brother's name and began to rack up infractions on that one as well. My uncle only found out after he was forced to stop work when his license was suspended. They had words at the next family gathering. Again, my grandmother tried to smooth things over. This had become a pattern.

The Draft

Incident Tags/Trigger Warnings

Draft dodging, lying

Incident

My father had a virulent hatred of draft dodgers, even to the extreme of complaining about them at the end of 'The Sound of Music.' Still, his story about how he'd avoided the war in Vietnam always changed. Sometimes, he said, it was due to a knee injury. Other times, he claimed that his number was not called up. Other times, he claimed that he got an exemption because he was in the middle of his education.

Faking Credentials and Offices

Incident Tags/Trigger Warnings
fraud, breaking and entering

Incidents

My father, like my mother, had a long history of faking credentials and accomplishments. This ranged from lies about his education to lies about his work history to lies about where he was currently working. My father often claimed to have an undergraduate degree in finance and a law degree. In fact, he had an undergraduate degree in sociology and no education after that. He often pronounced finance with the British emphasis instead of the American emphasis. This did not come naturally to him, but he just thought it made him sound smarter. He did similar things with other random words, such as cafe, but he didn't do it consistently.

The New Company

Shortly after my father was fired due to the Christmas Party incident, he started a new financial advice company. This was on paper. In reality, he had no offices or employees. He also named it by simply switching two of the letters in the name of the old company he worked for, hoping to cause confusion. This led to legal trouble.

The Office Buildings

My father occasionally took me to work with him to show off his new offices. Sometimes, this entailed him attempting to enter a fancy-looking office building and being shooed away by security, who sternly told him he'd been warned before. Other times, he got farther than that before security was called.

On one occasion, he took me up several floors into a nice-looking office building. He spent a bit of time supposedly looking around for his office, claiming that since he worked remotely a lot, he'd forgotten which way it was. He finally picked one office that was away from the crowd and where there was no one around to see us. First, he put away all the personal items, such as photos, into desk drawers. He explained that he shared the office with someone else who had left his stuff up. He opened up a duffle bag and began to pull out various things to decorate the office with. This included a bunch of stuff advertising fake credentials. He also had these little company logos encased in a clear stand to show off the companies he'd done business with in the past. In fact, he hadn't done business with any of them. He'd purchased them from a catalog. At some point, an angry man and a security guard confronted him. He'd been warned before. This was the man who the office actually belonged to. He hurriedly gathered up his stuff, and we left.

The Power Plant

At one point, my father's lies got him a job as a financial advisor for a major power plant project overseas. This eventually ended in a fiasco. He actually had none of the knowledge he needed to do this job well. It took several years of mismanagement before they realized what had happened, what his education actually was, and what his work history actually was. By this time, the damage was done.

PanHandling

Panhandling, cruelty

Incident

My father had a terrible hatred of panhandlers, but he also secretly panhandled. He was very cruel when people came up to us begging to the point it was embarrassing for everyone else with him. This sometimes included screaming at them, cursing at them, or throwing a little trinket or drawing they wanted to sell him down to the ground with force. They would scatter, frightened of his reaction. His favorite book, he proudly proclaimed to me at the bookstore, was Atlas Shrugged by Ayn Rand. He insisted that only smart people got it.

My father was occasionally busted panhandling by those who knew he had money. We lived in a big city. If a person (particularly a clean-cut-looking white guy like my father) positioned themselves well, they could make a lot of money panhandling. People were often unconsciously less motivated to give money to rougher-looking people who looked that way because they actually needed the money. He had cans full of coins separated out by type in his home office. The bank would sometimes refuse to deal with the amount of change he brought in to add to an account or turn into bills.

Sometimes, when I was too young to understand where this money had come from, I would help him roll it so that the bank would be more likely to accept it. When I described this to my schoolmates, some of them figured it out but said that they did not want to tell me because they did not want to make me feel bad.

College Money

Stealing

Incident

When I was growing up, my parents repeatedly told me that they had saved up money so that I would be able to go to college. This was a variation on the truth known as a lie. In fact, my father's mother had given them money for me to go to college, and they had spent it already. My father had retired early and bought a very expensive sports car. My grandmother ended up paying a second time for my full college tuition.

Later, my parents reversed the story and claimed that it was their brother-in-law (my father's sister's husband) who had pocketed money meant for his kids' college. They claimed that my grandmother had given us money twice to make it even since she had given my cousins the money twice. My uncle had never done any such thing, and the rest of the family was pretty surprised when they heard what I thought had happened. Then, the real story came out.

My father never owned up to this. I caught him several times claiming to have paid for my entire college education all on his own, giving his own mother no credit at all.

35. Plants

About

Is this a standard part of the MBP pattern? I don't know. On one hand, poisoning a plant is poisoning a living thing. On the other hand, I've never heard of this in any other case of MBP. It may just be that it's not significant enough to have come up in stories of people's lives being ripped apart and, in some cases, ended. Still, this may be important as part of the pattern when it comes to spotting this behavior. Most people have accidentally killed plants. Most people with several dead plants are just not great at taking care of plants. I'll point out that in every case involving my mother, it was others' plants, not her own, that were poisoned. She doted over her own plants. She had hooks specially installed all over the ceilings of our apartment to hang plants from. She watered them and allowed the water to pour out all over the floor until we got carpet mushrooms. Plants seemed to hold a special significance to her. I have no idea what that was.

Incidents

Orange Trees

At one point, my father's mother planted a line of orange trees on her property. Years later, they started to get sick and die. My grandmother knew that someone had poisoned them. She knew from the symptoms. She believed her next-door neighbor had done it, but when she spoke to the neighbor, she claimed to have seen my mother do it. My grandmother refused to believe that.

Poisoning My Plants

My mother had a thing about never allowing my houseplants to live, although she doted on her own.

In kindergarten, I was very happy that I got to grow a carnation. I was excited to take it home. My mother got angry with the teacher and yelled at her for failing to ask her permission and refused to let me take it home.

I asked for a bonsai tree for a Christmas present one year when we were living in the apartment, not realizing that my mother had killed my previous plants. She got it for me but informed me that it would not live. I couldn't understand what she was talking about and how she thought she knew that. I followed the instructions carefully, and it withered away and died.

One year, for the science fair, I did an experiment comparing identical plants growing with different fertilizers. She later admitted to switching them and their labels around while I was at school so that the experiment would fail. She only admitted this to me after the science fair. I presented my project at the science fair before I was aware of this. The judge awarded me a certain number of points for my work and procedure despite the experiment not having been a success in confirming my hypothesis. My mother pitched a fit in front of everyone and claimed several times that he was only giving me points because he was sexually attracted to me. This was in no way true. I was 12, and he was completely horrified.

When we moved into the house, she made a big deal of letting me choose one herb for the herb garden she was starting. Sure enough, that one died, and all the others around it lived.

It seems she started out not happy with me having plants but later decided she wanted me to get them and then see them die.

Stealing Plants

I have mentioned stealing plants in the Stealing section. I will mention one more plant-stealing incident here. When I was a teenager, we had neighbors down the street whom the family was friends with. The wife and mother of that family had a little memorial Norfolk pine that was to remind her of a dead relative she was very close to. I believe it had been from the relative's house or yard. One day, we got one just like it out on the back deck. My mother said that this neighbor had given it to her. Soon after, we had the neighbors over for dinner on the back deck, and my mother prompted me to mention it, just as she had with the other neighbor's plant that she'd dug out of the yard and replanted in ours. The neighbor at dinner said she'd wondered what had happened to that, and she wanted it back.

Kindergarten Roses

See "Fixations on Teachers" in the "Creepy Towards People at School" section. I would just be repeating myself here.

The Building's Plants

My mother also had a thing about messing with the plants in the building we lived in. She got scolded for this by the building staff repeatedly. She would go over to a new planter and start stroking the leaves and blades of ornamental plants, practically whining about how beautiful they were. I couldn't understand her obsession. When building staff would see her do this, they would tell her to leave the plants alone. Apparently, they had caught her damaging and killing new plants before. At the time, I did not believe them when they said this, but of course now I do.

36. Isolation

About

<u>About Isolation & MBP</u>

To some extent, this section will overlap with other sections such as 'Coercive Control,' 'Defenses When Someone Was On To Her,' and 'Preempting Detection and Acting Normal.' These behaviors overlap and connect a lot in life. Separating them into categories here is my attempt to point out and highlight different aspects of this cluster of behaviors.

Examples of other MBP cases involving this pattern: Deedee Blanchard

Incidents

Incident Tags/Trigger Warnings
Munchausen, MBP, isolation, coercive control, ghosting, manipulation

Incidents

Grandma

When I was a little girl, my father's mother took each of my cousins alone for a week as a bonding experience. She would take them to a nearby amusement park, and they would have fun activities to get to know each other through. Each one got their own week with her. I was always so jealous of that. I was invited but never allowed. My parents knew I would talk about the abuse and ask for help. They couldn't allow that.

Dysfunctional Families

My mother purposefully targeted dysfunctional families with children in need of friends for playdates when I was a little girl. She needed to keep me compartmentalized from functional adults and people whose children did not badly need a playmate. She needed people who either wouldn't spot her behavior as off, wouldn't care her behavior was off, or had some reason they felt they couldn't intervene.

She zeroed in on the kid in the building next door who didn't really get along with other kids in the building and whose parents had kept spending holidays with a relative who had been arrested for statutory rape. She zeroed in on the kid who had switched schools after her parent's failure to handle her mental health issues had necessitated her changing schools because she could not get along with the rest of her class. She zeroed in on kids whose parents were desperate for a playmate.

She needed this desperation. It was control. If someone posed a threat to this control, they were out. We would lose their contact information, and in those days before the internet, there was nothing I could do about it.

As I grew older, I would occasionally be confronted by an angry former friend who believed I had ghosted when all along I believed that they had ghosted. I will probably never know how many people this happened with who I never happened to have run into again.

The Babysitters

Whenever a babysitter got close enough to me that there was a danger I might speak out and ask for help, she was let go and scrubbed from our family completely. There was a particular sitter I had when I was 3 to 4 and living in the house where we had moved out of state for a couple of years. I'll call her Candy. One day, she was just gone, never to return again. I couldn't understand it. I wasn't allowed any further contact with her. I wasn't even allowed to know how to reach her in case I decided to disobey.

When I asked my mother about it years later, she was surprisingly honest. She told me that she'd decided I wouldn't have a nanny as soon as she realized that I might get closer to a nanny than to her. As soon as there was a possibility I might like the nanny better, she was gone.

This pattern repeated itself throughout the years. At first, I would object to a change in sitters, but as soon as I started to become comfortable with the new sitter, she'd be removed from our lives completely so that I couldn't even try to contact her. If this meant my mother being vicious to a sitter and starting a big enough fight to prevent any further contact, that's what was done. If this meant lying about a person's whereabouts, that's what was done.

Relatives

When I was a little girl, part of our extended family moved to the city we were living in. I was looking forward to spending lots of time with them. When they first arrived in town, my parents took them out to see some of the city and brought me with them. I thought this would be the first of many outings. It was the last. I kept on asking when we could see them again. When I wouldn't stop bugging my parents, my mother told me that they didn't want to see us.

About a year later, they moved away again, but I wasn't even aware of it at the time. Years later, as an adult, I found out that they had been there longer than I believed and that they had been hurt by the lack of contact, too.

Kid's Club

When I was a little kid, there was some sort of a kid's club on our street just a few blocks away. It may have been a 'boys and girls club' or something similar. I went there briefly before my mother cut off contact with them. I always wanted to go back and would look at it forlornly when we passed it on the way to school. Other kids in school got to go there. She never provided an explanation. One day, the club was simply cut out of our lives. Being unable to wander alone like a lot of kids still were back then, there was nothing I could do about it.

Girl Scouts

I always wanted to join the Girl Scouts when I was a kid. I saw it on TV, and it looked so cool to me. My father's mother was a big fan of them and talked of them warmly. My friends at school came to school in their Girl Scout uniforms on meeting days and invited me to join. I wanted to so badly, but was never allowed, no matter how I begged. An organization like that was one more place that could call family services.

37. Random

About

<u>About This Section & MBP</u>

These incidents are in this section because I haven't identified patterns these fit. This doesn't mean they don't fit into patterns.

Some of these may be common to MBP abusers, and some may not. This section is mainly to paint a fuller picture of my childhood and the weirdness of it. It is also to share incidents that may be part of a larger pattern amongst such abusers that I'm not yet aware of.

Incidents

Floor Beds

For a certain period of time, when I was a little girl, I wasn't allowed to sleep in my own room if my father was out of town. I was required to sleep on the floor beside my mother's bed. This went on sometimes for weeks at a time.

Kicked Out

My mother had a variety of establishments she'd been kicked out of for bad behavior or stealing. These included The Cracker Barrel, Nordstrom, and a local liquor store.

Hiding Places

My mother had a variety of hiding places for things. Sometimes, she would put things in the frame of a canvas print or hide things up her sleeves.

The Basement

When we lived out of state when I was three to four, my father was the only one allowed in the basement. A few times, I was allowed to look under close supervision. There was an old couch and a table. I wasn't allowed to look around on my own. If I tried to go down and see what I was missing out on, they would stop me. I'm not sure what was going on down there. The times I had a look, it was too sparse to be a man cave or anything like that.

The Mechanic

At one point, my mother developed a fixation on a local mechanic and began taking her car there for made-up reasons, much as she had done in earlier years, taking me to the doctor. They kept on telling her nothing was wrong. She would go and talk their ears off for as long as she could get away with it.

Dreams

When I was a little girl, I had a variety of nightmares, which I would sometimes share with my mother. Her reactions to these were sometimes odd. Once, I dreamed that the neighbor kids and I were playing while the adult neighbors chatted. A lion came by, and we closed the door to keep ourselves safe. One of the neighbors opened the door and allowed the lion to attack us. I couldn't understand why he'd done that. Another time, I dreamed that a strange woman was kidnapping me, and I was attempting to scream for help, but no sound would come out. I saw people I wanted to call out to, but it wasn't working.

My mother insisted that she was both the lion and the kidnapper. I did not believe her at the time, but now I think this is probably accurate. In the first dream, I was attempting to work out why other adults just left the other kids and me exposed to that danger. In the second dream, I was processing the fact that asking for help in real life had repeatedly failed to work. My mother was insightful enough to understand the dreams but not insightful enough to identify the problem, or maybe simply unwilling to identify the problem. She told me that I was being mean and rude to have such dreams and that most people would realize that would hurt her feelings. This was phrased as a problem with me having hurtful dreams, not a problem with her causing trauma.

Ashes

There were four jars of ashes in the cabinet in the main room of the apartment. Two were the cats my parents already had before they had me. They wouldn't tell me who the other two belonged to. I felt a sentimental attachment to the two cats because I had known them, and no sentimental attachment to the other two because no one would tell me who they were. I know they weren't ancestors because they were buried elsewhere. One day, my mother switched the jars so the cats were in the decorative baskets, and the others were stashed behind. My father got very upset with this.

Milk Cartons

My mother was mad about the missing kids on the milk cartons. She wasn't mad they were missing; she was mad they were on the cartons. She specifically made a point of buying the milk without the kids on the milk cartons. For those who are not familiar, there was a point when the milk cartons in the U.S. displayed photos of missing children in order to make their faces more well-known so that someone might spot them.

The WheelChair on the Stairs

One day, my mother announced that they would be shooting a movie at the museum where she volunteered. After this, she would occasionally come home with stories of how the museum had to adjust or how she had helped out.

One story in particular stood out. This was because she had reversed the story as she often did, talking about a third person who was really herself. She wasn't consistent about this. She told one story in which she was very helpful towards a man in a wheelchair and another story in which another person caused a problem for a man in a wheelchair. It was as if she was trying them both out to see which worked better. In story one, the elevator was off-limits because of the movie, so she helped a man in a wheelchair down the stairs. In story two, the elevator wasn't off limits, but some guy who was being a pest claimed it was, thus forcing the man in the wheelchair to accept his help, precariously getting the wheelchair downstairs. She talked a lot about how it must have made the person feel. Notice the similarity to "helping" the woman downstairs when the transformer blew. (See the transportation sabotage section).

Albums

My mother kept cutouts of baby images from advertisements and baby supply packaging. They were up on the walls in the nursery in the house, and then she moved them to albums she kept when we were in the apartment. She had several scrapbooks of these babies. She went through them carefully and warned me to be careful with them and not mess them up. When I asked her about them, she said they were how I was supposed to be, but they weren't how I turned out when I was born.

Years later, she was doing the same thing with magazine cutouts of adults, claiming they were her family members who hadn't spoken to her in years. She wrote fake letters from them to go with them, apologizing to her for falling out of touch and taking the blame. Of course, they never actually showed up to visit. They'd never written those letters or sent photos. The cutouts she'd claimed were photos from them were very obvious as cutouts by type of paper, ink, and poses. She claimed they were beside themselves, apologizing all over the place. She'd made the same claim about others who'd ghosted her before, sometimes making them drunk in the story.

Godliness, Cleanliness, and Reading

It became pretty clear early in my schooling that there were things the rest of the class had learned at home before starting school that I had not learned until I was taught in school. This included the concept of God, prayer, saying grace, hand washing, reading, and the difference between curse words and other words. My parents cared deeply what others thought of them, but it never occurred to them that this would reflect badly on them. Maybe they just never thought it through and realized this would all become obvious.

Barbi

Sometimes, my mother would yell at me that she never even wanted me, but she'd just had to have me to get the things she wanted. One day, she caught me saying the same thing to my Barbi doll. She acted taken aback, as if I was being very mean. I told her it was just the same thing she'd said to me before. She said that it wasn't the same because she had a reason to say it, whereas I was just being mean. She genuinely didn't have the perspective to hear how off it was. To me, it was obvious that if it was ok for her to say to me, it was ok for me to say to an inanimate object that didn't have any actual feelings. In her mind, I was being cruel, but she was not.

Smells and Sounds

My mother experienced both misophonia and smell hallucinations. These were usually focused on people she had bad feelings towards, including me. She would sometimes insist that the family had the loudest chewers in the world.

She would also sometimes become convinced that I or others were experiencing extreme flatulence when no one else could smell anything. This was separate from times when she was clearly purposefully manufacturing fake illnesses. In these cases, she would be genuinely disgusted and then later embarrassed if she realized it had been a hallucination. Eventually, I figured out that I didn't need to take gas medication that I didn't need. As long as she thought I was taking it, she would not smell anything.

Some reading this may start to wonder if all of the fake illnesses were hallucinations on her part. I will tell you for certain this was not the case. She often deliberately made people sick or injured with poisoning, supposed accidents, and exposure to germs.

Matilda

When I was a kid, my mother read me Matilda by Roald Dahl. It's a kid's book about a little girl who develops telekinesis after being treated very cruelly. Her guardians are very mean to her, and her feelings build up into the telekinesis. She told me she was scared I would turn out like that. I think it was an accidental acknowledgment of how badly she treated me. Despite the irrational way in which it manifested, she had developed a fear that her cruel behavior may someday come back at her.

Dead Kids

My parents would sometimes attempt to keep me in line by claiming that I wasn't actually their firstborn kid and that I was just the first one who had survived. They said if I misbehaved, I'd end up like the rest, dead. They would pretend like this was a joke around others. It's entirely possible that I was the firstborn and that this was coercive control. I'm not sure.

38. Defenses When Someone Was On To Her

About

About Defenses & MBP

There is a lot in this section about my mother attempting personality assassination and rumor-mongering against those who detect that something is wrong. Some would take that as a reason to keep their heads down and say nothing. There are three major reasons why this is a bad choice.

1. She still went after people who never told on her and often just as viciously. (This fits the parable of the frog and the scorpion, which I often think of when discussing my parents' behavior).

2. If you don't speak up, you may very well be next.

3. Get caught failing to report and protect others when just saying something could have made a difference, and the world will never let you forget it. Just look at Joe Paterno. Think of any abuse scandal in recent history in which someone failed to report. Do you want to be that person?

You can report anonymously and keep proof of this. Some crime-tip websites now work like this.

- Other MBP cases involving this pattern: Amanda Riley (convicted of wire fraud in relation to faking cancer.)

Incidents

Munchausen, MBP, character assassination

Incidents

The Laundry

When I was a little girl, before we got our own washing machine or lived in a building with one, my mother would take me with her to the laundromat on a regular basis. I always looked forward to it because there was a lady who worked there who was so nice.

One day, my mother set about trying to make me scared of the woman. I was looking forward to the next trip to the laundromat, but my mother insisted it would be very dangerous to go back. She spent days trying to convince me that the lady was actually mean and evil and was planning to kidnap me. In reality, the lady had just warned my mother that she would call the Department of Children and Family Services if she saw my mother continue to act as she did. At first, I didn't believe my mother, but by the time the next washing day rolled around, she had me absolutely terrified of the woman. I knew from TV that kidnappers were very scary people who did bad things. She had convinced me that this woman's pleasant demeanor was only a ruse to trick me so that she could kidnap me. I spent the time at the laundromat, avoiding her and making a fuss if she came near me. She wasn't able to get enough information to direct the DCFS with an address or last name. This poor woman was trying her best, and she only got grief because of it.

Remember, you never owe a child abuser a warning or a heads-up. You are better positioned to protect both yourself and children if you report without suggesting to the abuser that you will.

The Doctor

When I was in grade school, we lived in a building with a few doctor's offices in the small mall on the ground floor. My parents both used to see the same doctor in one of these offices. My mother decided to stop seeing the doctor and switch to one outside of the building. She was endlessly peeved that my father would not switch from this doctor and vented about it. This doctor was on her shit list all of a sudden one day.

I think the doctor was on to her, and she suddenly realized that she was in a bad position living in the building where this doctor worked. It also curtailed her ability to commit medical abuse upon my father, though not upon me, because I did not see this doctor. My father was happy with the doctor, and I think with the degree of protection he knew, continuing to see her provided him. He didn't much care if I or anyone else didn't get that degree of protection, though.

Got Weird

The standard go-to defense when a medical professional was on to her was that he or she "got weird." She would never elaborate on what this meant. The vagueness of the accusation was the point. When she stopped seeing a therapist meant to help us deal with family issues, that was the explanation. It was again the explanation whenever she suddenly pulled me away from a specialist whom things had previously been going well with.

Without the context of my mother's behavior pattern, one might think that one specific doctor had turned out to be a pervert, stalker, or creep. She never overtly said so, but when a woman uses a tone, makes a face, and uses that wording, some are bound to draw that conclusion. I think it was useful to her because it made people uncomfortable about asking follow-up questions.

School Counselor

When I was in high school, my mother suddenly decided one day that she hated the school counselor. This was not the career counselor but the counselor who dealt with kids having psychological issues or life changes.

He couldn't prove anything, but he had caught on to her. This was cause for character assassination. She used the same condescending, peeved, and belittling tone in reference to him as she did in reference to doctors who she'd said "got weird."

Looking back on it, he seems like he was a nice guy who could have helped me. At the time, I believed her story that he was off. I now realize she was just trying to keep me from talking to him, which worked. I generally avoided conversations with him, although he invited me to speak with him multiple times.

Me

Eventually, when I would out her about the abuse as an adult, she would turn this character assassination on me. That's a subject for another book, though. This one is about my childhood.

39. Coercive Control

About

<u>About Coercive Control & MBP</u>

Coercive control is an act or pattern of behavior used to punish or frighten a victim in order to take away the victim's independence. It is often aimed at exploiting or isolating a victim. It can include, among other things, stalking, spying, deprivation of basic needs, and degrading behavior. Manipulation is central to both MBP and coercive control. This is still an area that the legal system in many countries is trying to catch up with and address. Please see the proposed legislation section near the back of this book for more on that.

Examples of other MBP cases involving this pattern:

Sickened by Julie Gregory,

Deedee Blanchard's abuse of Gypsy Rose Blanchard.

This section only contains examples from the first 18 years of my life. It's worth noting that these tactics changed and, in some ways, escalated after I left home, but that is a subject for another book.

Incidents

Munchausen, MBP, physical abuse, coercive control, school, manipulation, sexual abuse, poisoning, monsters, stalking,

Incidents

Solidarity

When I was a little girl, too young to understand adult behavior, my mother came up with a cruel tactic for control. It served two purposes at once for her. First, it helped to prevent her from getting caught. Second, it was amusing for her on a sadistic level.

Many adults follow the general idea that parents should have solidarity with each other and present a united front against misbehavior even if they don't know the whole back story. It's common to see a third party observe another adult trying to control a child's behavior in public and back that other adult up by talking to the child as well. You may see it when a child is fussing in line at the store or when a parent is trying to get a child to put a coat on, for example. Naive adults think that they're helping and that this would never be exploited. Nope. Abusers have this figured out. My mother was no exception.

She loved to give an exasperated or pleading expression to another adult in public to lure that person into backing up something truly sick. It was her little secret. Unsuspecting adults would launch into talks directed at me, completely unaware of the fact that what I was in trouble for not cooperating with was sexual abuse or unnecessary medical procedures.

I was so young that I was being sent the message that they knew what was going on and that all adults were like this. I didn't know enough about the world yet to know otherwise. They walked away feeling good about the role they played while my mother smugly enjoyed the fact that she'd tricked them into scolding me for refusing a sexual act, or for wanting to be fed that day, or for refusing an unnecessary medical procedure.

Curfew

I was three the first time running away seemed like a real possibility. I didn't need to know where I was going. I just needed to get far enough away to get help. I thought of walking out at night while they were asleep.

My parents caught on and came up with a lie to prevent this behavior. They told me that I could not leave after dark because of the curfew. When I asked what a curfew was, they told me it was a monster that lived in the sewer that came out after dark and ate children. At three, that was believable. I knew my life was in danger at home, but outside, I was convinced it was certain death.

School

As a little girl, I was never out of sight, except for during school hours when another adult would have noticed me walking out and stopped me. Even the journey to and from school was not a thing she would trust with anyone else. She needed to reduce the contact other adults had with me as much as possible. Every day, she would get on the city bus with me to the school and ride with me. We would frequently run into faculty and staff from the school who took the same route. They would offer to ride with me so that my mother didn't have to take the round trip. She steadfastly refused. To my embarrassment, she would walk me all the way to the classroom in the school whenever she could get away with it, although she was sometimes stopped by a teacher.

In high school, she had to change her tactics somewhat to avoid attracting attention. Even on days I took the bus home, she would be there in the massive cluster of cars doing carpools, just watching the entrance of the school. I often did not find out about this until later when a classmate would tell me. When I would ask her about it, she would tell me she just happened to be in the area and thought some kids might need a ride. She would sometimes be out there for hours. Sometimes, she would tell me that she wouldn't be available to pick me up that day and that I would need to take the bus home, but then I would find out later she'd been out there watching.

At one point, she manipulated a girl one year below me in high school into keeping tabs on me on the bus. This girl was young and naive. When my mother told her that I had special needs and sometimes got lost, she fell for it hook, line, and sinker. She felt important, doing a special job. Her friends tried to explain to her that she was being used. She didn't believe them at first, but eventually, they got through to her. At that point, she knocked off the behavior with a bit of embarrassment.

Privacy

When I was a little girl, I always wanted a diary. I saw kids on TV with them, and I knew that my classmates were allowed to have them. I would beg my mother for one, but I was never allowed. My mother was paranoid that I would write stuff about her in it. Eventually, when she was tired of me bugging her, she said that she would get me one but that I would be required to give it to her for reading and approval whenever I wrote in it. This really defeated the purpose. Any sort of privacy was a threat to her.

College

When I was in high school and discussing colleges, she kept insisting on a small school in town, and whenever I asked her why, she said, "I'm afraid I might lose you." I insisted that this wouldn't happen, but she'd implied that it had happened before with other people, who had gone off to some place too big for her to find them. She tried to control the situation by making me sick and going to the college counselor appointments in my place. I dragged myself out of bed and went anyway like an animal trying to chew its leg out of a trap. I sat there feeling like I was going to die and telling the counselor that I wanted a big school out of town while she sat as an out-of-place adult in the school counselor's office in the middle of the day, insisting on a small school nearby.

Intelligence

Both of my parents claimed that their fathers had worked in intelligence. Claiming to work in intelligence or to be connected to someone who is in intelligence is a common coercive control technique. For example, see the case of conman Robert Hendy-Freegard. My mother came up with a story that her adoptive father was fired from "the company," i.e., the CIA, and then hired by the FBI. My father also claimed that his own father worked in intelligence but didn't come up with such an elaborate story as my mother.

Stalking

My mother would often follow me around if I was out with friends as a teen. She would dive behind a corner or some other obstruction before I would see her, but my friends would later tell me what had been happening.

Sometimes, she would drop me off at a friend's house and pretend to go home, then go to the mall we had plans to go to and follow us from store to store. She would then show up at the friend's house later to pick me up as if nothing had happened. This played out again and again at schools, amusement parks, malls, and probably places I was never even aware of. I only know of the times my friends spotted her and decided to tell me.

40. Preempting Detection and Acting Normal

About

<u>About Preempting Detection and Acting Normal & MBP</u>

This section overlaps heavily with the coercive control section to the point that I often wasn't sure which section to put an incident in. This is well illustrated by both the 911 incident and the school trips.

My parents often remind me of the parable of the frog and the scorpion. They are scorpions, so to speak. Their behavior patterns will never be exactly like everyone else's. They try to blend in and act normal, but as you will see in this section, there are giveaways to look for.

This is my best advice for dealing with people like my parents. Never give them a heads-up that you don't believe them or even that you might doubt their stories and behaviors. Never assume that what they say is true, even if it involves a verifiable element of truth. Assume they're manipulating, snooping, making things up, and generally being shifty. If you ever decide you need to report them, do so anonymously if you can. Never let them know ahead of time or give them any indication that you might report them. Never leave any indication that you distrust them or may report them anywhere that they might snoop. Also, never leave any valuable property or information unattended around them. Don't let them use your electronic devices or accounts. Don't let them near anything they could use to fake your identity.

Remember, if they have to lie, cheat, and steal to preempt detection and appear normal, they will. They'll go much farther than that if they have to.

911

preventing calls to authorities

Incident

When I was in kindergarten, the teacher taught my class about the 911 emergency number. Many of the children already knew about it, but I did not. I came home excited about the useful things I had learned. My mother was not happy. She immediately took the position that the teacher's behavior was inappropriate and not her place. She wasn't "ready for" me to know that information, she repeated several times. I couldn't understand the problem. The teacher had explained the difference between good reasons to call and bad reasons to call so that we wouldn't tie up the line, so that couldn't have been the concern.

It was a bad day for her. She had been blindsided by the fact that I now knew an emergency number to call. She insisted that I never call and that calling was bad and would be punished.

Points To Make

This is a huge red flag. If the school has taken measures to make sure that inappropriate 911 calls won't happen, then there is no reason to object to such teaching. Do the kids in your life know this information? They should.

Legislation

Let's save teachers and school administrators some trouble. If they're mandated to teach kids this information by a certain age, they will have a measure of protection from a parent or guardian trying to pressure them not to teach this. It will also help protect kids in unsafe situations. You can't bend to the will of the odd set of parents and keep the information from the whole class.

Eye Dropper

Munchausen, manipulation

Incident

Occasionally, my mother would pretend to cry by using a bottle of eye drops she'd palmed. I think she had a variety of motivations for this. Sometimes, she wanted attention or leverage in an argument. Other times, I think she just wanted to blend in with others. She didn't always experience empathy like other people.

Other times, when she didn't have the eye dropper handy, she would just cover enough of her face with her hands in fake crying that no one would be able to see that there were no tears. This was less than subtle. When she did this, she would occasionally peek from between her fingers to try to gauge the reaction she was getting. This was a giveaway both because it revealed her dry eyes and because it revealed the comical facial expression when she thought she was being sneaky.

Often, she would use the eye dropper with my father and the face-covering technique with me. I think she felt that she needed to try to be more convincing with him because he was an adult. I could see the eye dropper when she did this, though, because she would angle it to try to conceal it from him, which sometimes made it obvious from my vantage point if I was off to her side. I remember once calling her on it and revealing it in her hand. My father laughed at her, and she scolded me.

Social Skills

Incident Tags/Trigger Warnings

Manipulation

Incidents

When I was a little girl, my parents used to enjoy bragging about their social skills and how good they were at blending in and making people feel comfortable. They were so advanced in the subject, my father claimed, he'd even taken classes in it.

One of their favorite tricks was faking what is commonly known as a sympathetic yawn. For most people and social animals, this is an automatic reaction, not a choice. They simply are more likely to feel the need to yawn when they've just seen someone else do it. For my parents, this was not the case, so they endeavored to make others feel more comfortable with them and make others think they were the same by faking a sympathetic yawn whenever anyone else yawned. They often did this in reaction to me yawning in front of the TV at night. They would sometimes follow this up with exaggerated stretching and random sleepy noises. It was all kind of unnatural. They were getting across the idea they wanted to, but something about it was just a little off.

My father also believed he was good at coming off as non-creepy and non-threatening by staring at a spot in people's foreheads instead of into their eyes. This was a business meeting technique, according to him.

Photography

Physical abuse, unwilling photography

My parents also liked to blend in through photography. The idea was that no matter what was actually happening at home, people would believe what they saw in a photo album. This is a pretty common idea in society and social media. What's different in abusive and controlling families is just how different the reality is from the photograph. Almost everyone occasionally smiles in a photograph when they don't feel like it, but in most households, that's not disguising violence.

One such incident happened when I was about 3. My mother would occasionally take me for ice cream. I usually preferred chocolate. One day, my mother became enraged that I had chocolate ice cream on my face. This was unusual because, being 3, I tended to get ice cream on my face every time we went for ice cream, and she'd never reacted like this before. She began to lash out and yell angrily, then strike my face.

After I'd healed, she took me for ice cream again. I was careful not to get any on my face after the last time. I was so young that I'd internalized what had happened. I hadn't decided that she was an unstable person having an off day. Instead, I was genuinely angry at the idea of messy ice cream on my face. She objected to how neatly I was eating. I wouldn't change the way I was eating. Exasperated that she couldn't get me to recreate the scene, she took the ice cream and smeared it on my face. I was aggravated by the mess and very unhappy. She acted jolly, as if everything was ok and always had been. She pulled out the camera to take pictures. She wouldn't leave me alone until I smiled for the camera.

I think maybe she wanted a redo to document the scene as it should have played out the first time as if this would somehow make it real, as if this would somehow make her the person she wanted to be. Maybe I'm overanalyzing. Maybe she just wanted a photo to contradict me in case I ever decided to talk.

School Trips

Incident Tags/Trigger Warnings
Coercive control, school, manipulation
Incidents

One of my parents' most relied-on strategies for preempting detection was isolation. This became a major issue when I hit the age of overnight school trips. My parents could make sure that I only slept over with friends of the family until I hit this age. All of a sudden, I had a potential path to escape, and that was cause for panic.

Our school usually sent out the girls' class for overnight field trips around 5th or 6th grade and then for progressively longer trips, culminating in a D.C. trip in 8th grade, which was the highest grade in that school. I was very excited about these trips and was really looking forward to the first one. I was very disappointed when the first one got canceled. At first, they said it was rescheduled, but then it ultimately never happened.

Word went around the class that someone's mom had caused such a fuss that they had canceled the trip because she wasn't ready for her daughter to go. It was a class of about 20, and it was an educational trip that I think involved some sort of homework and class credit. They rearranged the schedule and the curriculum all over this one family.

I attempted to soothe my disappointment with thoughts of the next upcoming trip, but then the same thing happened with that one. I later found out that it was my mother. She had bullied the school into canceling the trips because she had not been willing to send me but had not been willing to be the odd family out either.

How do you avoid a situation like this where a school is so scared of a parent that they will rearrange everything around that one parent? Mandated reporting! They had spent so many years overlooking so much truly scary behavior and pocketing donations from my parents. They hadn't been documenting the behavior that scared them, and it just kept escalating until she had that level of power over them.

PART III. MAKE IT MAKE SENSE

Spotting Cases

First, it's important to note that you should not rule out a case just because a particular warning sign is missing or decide something definitely is such a case based on just one warning sign.

Second, it's important to note that there will certainly be warning signs I haven't thought of. Does behavior look like other examples in the book not mentioned here? Does behavior look suspicious even though it doesn't quite match anything in this book?

This is just a list of basics based on my own experience. You can and should add to this list as it makes sense.

So how are you supposed to decide if a supposed illness is a case you're observing in your own life? You don't have to decide. You just have to say something to those who are in charge of investigating such things if you see enough that your conscience tells you something is wrong.

Here are the basics I've noticed, organized by who is in a position to spot them.

For the insurance industry:

- Are you seeing excessive claims in more than one area? For example, are you seeing disproportionate claims for medical problems, fires, life insurance, car accidents, etc., even though they are seemingly unconnected?

- Does a caretaker or person with custody of a sick child have a history of legal trouble for theft, writing bad checks, or fraud? Consider comparing caretakers with warning signs to a service such as Veridoc's check bouncing database or a similar offering from one of their competitors. Also, consider a service that offers multi-jurisdictional arrest record checks.

- Have they switched doctors an unusual amount?

- Have others in their care died or experienced mysterious illness?

- Does a potential victim get an illness at the last possible opportunity before a vaccine is available? In my childhood, this was chickenpox. My mother had been saving it up, so to speak. You can only get it once, and the complications tend to be worse the older you are when you get it. While all the other parents were exposing their kids young, it was the only disease she tried to avoid me getting sick with. I caught it just after the vaccine became available and before my next school physical. It was her last window of opportunity.

For Everyone:

- Have people who've raised concerns been vilified?

- Do they demonstrate a fascination or preoccupation with death or disease?

- Do they fit any patterns in the pattern chart?

- Do they demonstrate envy of people with dead or sick children?

- Does the child seem unusually skinny despite the fact that the family can afford food?

- Does the child hide, ration, or steal food despite the fact that the family can afford food?

- Are there signs of other types of abuse?

For educators:

- Do they object to stages of development like moving from picture books to chapter books?

- Do they seem to get in the way of stages of development, such as objecting to advanced placement or purposefully teaching the child incorrect information?

- Do they object to teaching kids about emergency numbers, first aid, or child safety?

- Do they seem to be a helicopter parent even though they sometimes seem unconcerned with child safety or even abusive? In other words, does the level of control exerted not match the level of concern for the child's well-being that you would normally see in a helicopter parent?

- Do they attempt to prevent overnight school trips?

- Do they intentionally sabotage testing for class placement or development level by, for example:

  * keeping the child up late the night before?

  * medicating the child more than usual that day?

  * instructing the child to fill in Scantron bubbles very lightly?

  * doing something else to disrupt the testing process?

- Do they make excuses to explain away a result that indicates that the child is intelligent or has an age-appropriate development level? For example, do they claim that the child is parroting things without understanding them, or do they claim that someone who gave a good grade was biased?

- Are there indications that a parent has done the homework turned in and done it incorrectly?

- Is the child kept out of extracurricular activities?

Warning Sign Lists Compiled by others:

https://www.ncbi.nlm.nih.gov/pmc/articles/PMC5915702/

(I think the tables in this are particularly helpful.)

Missing What's Right In Front Of You

In this section, I outline several reasons why intelligent people often miss MBP behavior even when it's happening right under their noses. The most basic reason is a simple lack of public awareness, but it is far from the only reason. In examining other reasons, I believe it's important to understand logical fallacies, confirmation bias, correspondence bias, attribution errors, the Overton Window, the Normalcy bias, cultivation theory, cognitive dissonance, NIMBY, groupthink, and various emotional motivations. It's also important to understand certain common abusers' evasion tactics, such as gaslighting (which serves a dual purpose in MBP), and preemptive narrative inversion.

This is not an exhaustive list of reasons why people miss abuse right under their noses. It's simply a short rundown of common reasons. This list reflects my best attempt at understanding reactions I've observed over the years as a survivor without any training in psychology, psychiatry, sociology, or criminology.

<u>Normalcy Bias</u>

Normalcy bias, also known as normality bias, is the tendency to minimize threats, disbelieve warnings, underestimate the likelihood of disaster, underestimate the potential extent of disaster, or believe that everything will remain normal even when this is not logical. This is a common problem in times of natural disasters, epidemics, or other potentially disastrous situations. It poses a serious problem for disaster responders tasked with helping the public in such times. It can also be a major issue when people are facing extreme, potentially disastrous situations in their personal lives or family lives.

<u>Blind Spots</u>

Everyone has them. Manipulators zero in on them. Enough said.

<u>Overton Window/Window of Discourse</u>

Oxford Languages, part of Oxford University Press, defines the Overton Window as "the spectrum of ideas on public policy and social issues considered acceptable by the general public at a given time." You may also hear people refer to this as the "Window of Discourse." Some definitions of the Overton Window specify that it has to do with political ideas and which ideas are politically acceptable. While abuse sometimes touches on politics and public policy, here, it's more useful to think of the Overton Window in a broader sense than that.

Abusers may not know these terms, but they often know the principles behind them. The giveaway is that they do things like badmouthing people famous for speaking out about the forms of abuse they're trying to hide. Raising awareness in general about a form of abuse increases the threat of detection for every perpetrator of that form of abuse. You'll see examples of this in the section on imitating or banning stories in which my mother often tried to prevent us from viewing movies that mentioned MBP. She often badmouthed people who had famously spoken out about MBP but never explained why or mentioned the term. Her criticisms of them were vehement but vague character attacks.

We have already seen what can happen when the Overton Window shifts on a particular form of abuse. A couple of generations ago, child sexual abuse was much less well-known and much less discussed. It would have been unthinkable to say that there was an epidemic of children being sexually assaulted by clergy or by scout leaders, even though it was true. It was thought of as rare even though it wasn't. Children would sometimes be punished for speaking out against a respected adult. A tipping point happened as more people spoke out. We now know it is not rare. We now have laws such as mandated reporting, and we have childcare workers screened. We now know to be on the lookout for signs of such abuse. MBP abusers do not want this to happen with MBP. It needs to happen with MBP. It will save lives.

Confirmation Bias

Oxford Languages, part of Oxford University Press, defines confirmation bias as "the tendency to interpret new evidence as confirmation of one's existing beliefs or theories." Dictionary.com defines confirmation bias as "bias that results from the tendency to process and analyze information in such a way that it supports one's preexisting ideas and convictions."[1] It's pretty easy to see how this one helps abusers stay hidden. People start with ideas such as:

- "This is someone I can trust."
- "People don't just go around poisoning each other."
- "I would know if someone that off was around me."
- "This person is a dedicated caregiver."
- "This child is sick."

These first impressions then shape their interpretations of everything else they see going forward.

<u>Logical Fallacies</u>

A logical fallacy, put simply, is an error in logic or an argument that can be proven wrong with logic. There are many well-known logical fallacies. Here are just a few examples:

- An argument has not been proven wrong, so it must be right.
- A person in authority must be correct.
- Correlation equals causation.
- If something is true of some members of a group, it must be true of the whole group.
- Part of this story is true, so all of this story must be true.

There are specific logical fallacies that survivors of abuse come up against often. This is likely the most common one:

- The accuser seems off, so the accused must not be guilty.

In fact, it's common for survivors to have PTSD or other trauma-related illnesses. The fact that the accuser seems off is often (though not always) a sign that there is actually something to the accusation. In addition, abusers often go to lengths to preemptively make their victims seem off in case they ever make an accusation.

<u>Correspondence Bias/Attribution Error</u>

Attribution errors are errors in thinking in which people incorrectly attribute causes to events or actions. The fundamental attribution error is the tendency for people to attribute circumstances or situations as the causes of their own behaviors while attributing character flaws and personality traits as the causes of other people's behaviors. For example, a person may seem dismissive or short and think: "I am in a hurry." This same person may experience similar behavior from another on a different occasion and think: "This is a rude person."

Correspondence bias is when a person makes conclusions about another's personality or character traits based on behaviors that are actually completely explainable by the situation at hand.[2] For example, a person may see another person behave angrily when that person has a logical reason to be angry but think: "This is a hot-tempered person." In some cases, trauma symptoms, in combination with the fundamental attribution error or correspondence bias, may cause people to distrust or disbelieve an accuser who is telling the truth.

People may often think of the fundamental attribution error or correspondence bias as logical errors that lead to negative and harmful stereotypes. This is not incorrect, but it's not the only type of mistaken belief they can contribute to. Consider an abuser attempting to avoid detection. Such people are often surrounded by people who believe that they are "such a nice person." Spend time talking to survivors of abuse, and you'll hear this story again and again. It won't always be what you hear, but it will often be what you hear. Abusers are not nice people. They are people who behave nicely at strategic times with some people. It is a part of their strategy to avoid detection and exert control.

<u>Cultivation Theory</u>

This is the theory (developed by George Gerbner) that media cultivates people's perception of reality. For example, people's perception of crime is more tied to what they see in the media than it is to reality. This is not necessarily done knowingly. It may, at times, involve an unwitting feedback loop that is not totally distinguishable from groupthink and in which members of the media are not fully aware of the influence they have.

A classic example in the area of crime is the "satanic panic" of the 1980s. This is an example of people overestimating the level of a certain type of crime. The opposite can also happen, however. People who rarely or never hear about a certain type of crime in the media may tend to underestimate a category of crime and falsely perceive it as rare. This can especially be a problem with covert types of crime in which people don't always know that a crime has occurred. The less people are aware of MBP, the less it is detected.

The less it is detected, the less it is reported, and the less people are aware of it existing.

<u>Preemptive Strategies / Grooming</u>

I have never known anyone who prepared for the possibility that they might someday become the victim of MBP. Abusers, however, tend to prepare in case they are ever caught. You will see examples of this in incident sections such as 'Defenses when someone was on to her,' 'Coercive control,' and 'Preempting detection and acting normal.' Abusers may preemptively encourage others to view victims and victims' allies as overly dramatic, prone to falsehoods, and unreliable. They may invert narratives and bad mouth others who they fear may eventually learn and tell the truth. You may have heard the old phrase often attributed to Winston Churchill: "A lie gets halfway around the world before the truth has a chance to get its pants on." Abusers often use preemptive strategies to give those lies a head start.

People often discuss "grooming" in terms of child sexual abuse. It can apply to various different forms of abuse. This is completely different from false grooming accusations with political overtones directed towards the LGBTIQ+ population in recent history. For a good definition and explanation of actual grooming, see https://www.rainn.org/news/grooming-know-warning-signs[1]. Grooming is not just something that happens to victims, it's also something abusers often direct towards others in the victims' circle.

<u>Toxic Triangulation</u>

Toxic triangulation is a behavior often carried out by narcissists, abusers, and those who fall into the dark tetrad. This behavior involves bringing third parties into relationships in order to remain in control and preserve one's own narrative. For example, consider how friends will often take the side of an abuser at the abuser's prompting to deny abuse.

You can help prevent yourself from being used this way by keeping direct communication lines open, refusing to take sides when you don't know all the facts, fact-checking, and choosing to react in a logical and measured way

---

1.   https://www.rainn.org/news/grooming-know-warning-signs

rather than in a knee-jerk emotional way. Those attempting to use you for toxic triangulation will often shut down direct communication between you and the other party, ask you to choose sides, shun the other person, pressure you not to fact-check, and involve you to an inappropriate degree in their personal business. Not all of these behaviors are always present. This is a generality. In addition, they may do these things indirectly. For example, they may tell you lies that cause you to shut down communication with a third party without ever directly asking you to do that.

Gaslighting

As of the writing of this Merriam-Webster recently declared 'gaslighting' to be its 2022 word of the year. Merriam-Webster defines gaslighting as 1: "psychological manipulation of a person usually over an extended period of time that causes the victim to question the validity of their own thoughts, perception of reality, or memories and typically leads to confusion, loss of confidence and self-esteem, uncertainty of one's emotional or mental stability, and a dependency on the perpetrator" or 2: "the act or practice of grossly misleading someone especially for one's own advantage."[3]

You may observe gaslighting behavior amongst many different kinds of abusers, but for MBP abusers, it serves a dual purpose. For other types of abusers, gaslighting is a means to an end. In the case of MBP abuse in specific creating an illness or the appearance of an illness, including mental illness, is the goal.

Cognitive Dissonance

For a good explanation of cognitive dissonance, see https://www.psychologytoday.com/us/basics/cognitive-dissonance[2]. Essentially, cognitive dissonance is the discomfort people feel when two thoughts or beliefs contradict each other. Can you see how this would apply to MBP? Abusers often rely on others' cognitive dissonance, even if they don't have a name for it. They will encourage you to hold beliefs that will create cognitive dissonance when held alongside the truth of the crimes they are committing. This will encourage you to dismiss warning signs without even realizing it.

---

2.   https://www.psychologytoday.com/us/basics/cognitive-dissonance

NIMBY

NIMBY stands for "not in my backyard." More generally, it can apply to a friend circle, family, neighborhood, workplace, or other place you are invested in seeing a certain way. One example of NIMBY is the tendency for people to believe places such as shelters, halfway houses, and psychiatric hospitals should exist but to still not want them in their own neighborhood. Another example is the tendency for people to deny that something very bad or very dysfunctional could happen in one of their favorite places. People may believe things such as:

- burglaries can happen, but not in this neighborhood.
- abuse can happen, but not in this family.
- shootings can happen, but not in this school.

This makes people feel safe and secure, but it leaves them more vulnerable to these problems because it causes them to miss red flags.

Stereotypes and Emotional Motivations

Many believe there's an entire gender you can trust with children who will always be safe to babysit. This is illogical, but it's a difficult belief to let go of for people who have lived according to it. People don't want to see medical professionals, moms, or a variety of other societal roles that way. They want to believe that only truly caring people are in caring professions. Abusers often link what they want a person to believe to what that person wants to believe. Some common desired beliefs my mother and other abusers often exploit include:

- I'm helpful,
- I'm needed,
- I'm good at reading people,
- I'm important,
- I'm in a safe and good family / neighborhood / community,
- I'm smart.

Imagine you have a friend with a child who is always ill. This person praises you often for each of the traits above. You've invested a lot of time into this person, and this reinforces that you are helpful, needed, and important. If this person turns out to be an FDIA abuser, all 6 of these statements above seem to go out the window all at once. I say "seem to" because, in reality, they have not. It's common for smart people who are generally good at reading others to miss this type of abuse. You are likely still helpful, needed, and important to others who have not been as good at reminding you of that.

Every family, neighborhood, and community has some rotten apples, no matter how many insist otherwise. Abusers, however, are good at creating a false emotional connection tied to what they want you to believe. It's easy to feel like all of your positive beliefs have been taken away when FDIA abuse surfaces. They have not been. The abuser just wants you to feel that. It helps them evade detection.

<u>Anxiety and Logic</u>

You've likely observed generally logical people behave in illogical ways in the face of anxiety or other strong emotions. Anxiety can also cause us to only see the surface meaning of things going on around us. Anxiety causes emotional rather than logical thinking. Abuse allegations, hints indicating abuse, and the possibility of abuse in general cause a lot of anxiety. This is especially true for certain kinds of abuse, such as MBP and sexual abuse.

<u>Groupthink and Bribery</u>

Money (or other types of bribery) can be especially powerful when combined with groupthink or disproportionate respect for authority. Criminals don't need to bribe everyone, just critical people. An example of this from my own childhood is the incident in which my mother bribed the school principal. Abusers know they generally only need to influence those who set the tone for everyone else. Who have you trusted because others did?

<u>The Martha Mitchell Effect</u>

Harvard psychologist Brandan Maher first coined the term 'The Martha Mitchell Effect' in the book "Delusional Beliefs." It describes a misrepresentation of a person's beliefs as delusional. This specifically applies to cases in which those beliefs are actually justified. This may be in the context of the medical field, the general public perception, or both.

Martha Mitchell was a well-known figure in the media at the time that the Watergate break-in occurred. She was married to John Mitchell, who was the U.S. Attorney General at the time. She was also involved in Nixon's presidential campaign and made public appearances as a cabinet wife after his election. She became a key whistleblower concerning the connection between the break-in and the Committee to Re-Elect the President. Although Martha Mitchell was not a victim of classic FDIA, those trying to silence her did drug her, hold her against her will, and purposefully promote the idea that she was mentally ill.

In some cases (such as the case it is named for), the Martha Mitchell effect may be helped along by those attempting to silence a person. In other cases, it may occur without any encouragement because what a person is alleging is simply strange, extreme, unusual, or a type of crime that lacks public awareness.

<u>Silence</u>

Nurse and serial killer Charles Cullen was able to hop from job to job for more than a decade and a half despite the fact that people at several of his workplaces caught on to the fact that something was wrong. Hospitals passed him around instead of blowing the whistle. The hospital infamous killer Donald Harvey worked in also silenced whistleblowers repeatedly. The hospital in the Marybeth Tinning case was also notably silent. This was also an issue in the death of Olivia Gant at her mother's hands. In recent news, as of the writing of this book, hospital workers have spoken out about having been fired for blowing the whistle about serial killer Lucy Letby.

People assume that other people would say something, but that's not always true. This means the groupthink effect can apply when that's not even what the group really thinks.

Types of Medical Abusers

As you have probably noticed in the pattern chart, not everyone who commits medical abuse or poisoning is the same. I have included a primary abuse-type column. I have not included a primary abuser type column, because that's not information I have in a lot of these cases. One can say what was done, but it's sometimes more difficult to guess what was going on with the abuser internally.

I believe that patterns of subtypes of abusers will begin to become clearer as society becomes better educated about this form of abuse and better at documenting this form of abuse. I think these subtypes could be best categorized by personality, motivation, and associated behaviors. What follows is likely not a complete list of abuser types, but simply the abuser types that I have observed in my life experience and research. It's important to note that many will have multiple motivations. This list is categorized by primary motivation.

1. Sadists

This seems to have been my mother's primary motivation, although I would say that she had all of the motivations. She seemed to have little in common with those primarily motivated by attention and sympathy, though she did sometimes do things for attention and sympathy. Those she seemed to have the most in common with were others motivated by sadism, especially Donal Harvey and "Jolly Jane" Toppan. Like both of them, she often blurred the line between medical abuse and sexual abuse and was a sexual sadist. This type seems to be one of the types more likely to kill, though not the only type to kill. This also seems to be one of the types more likely to set fires and display cruelty to animals.

2. Attention/Sympathy/Validation Seekers

Hope Ybarra and Lacey Spears were likely such examples, though I cannot say for sure. This type sometimes fakes authority, intelligence, and credentials, although it is not the only type to do this. My mother and Christopher Duntsch both did this and were likely both primarily sadists.

3. Financial Scammers

Teresa Milbrandt was likely such an example. As you will notice in the chart financial scamming is a very common behavior even for those abuses who are not primarily motivated by money.

Hare Psychopathy Checklist

I hesitate to get into this because I'm not an expert, but I also can't deny that this chapter belongs in a book that is largely about spotting patterns surrounding MBP. Please read this section with the understanding that I'm talking about this stuff as a survivor without any expertise in psychology, psychiatry, or criminology.

<u>What is it?</u>

The Hare Psychopathy checklist was originally created by Dr. Robert Hare. The PCL-R (the current version in use) is a checklist used to diagnose people as psychopathic. PCL stands for psychopathy checklist. The R stands for revised. The original checklist was 22 traits. The revised checklist is 20 traits because 2 were later decided not to be useful in diagnosis.[4] If you are interested in a detailed breakdown of the checklist, you can easily find this information online through a search engine.

<u>What are the criticisms of it?</u>

Some have criticized this tool as unreliable and too easy for the legal system to misuse. It's also worth noting that many have done away with the use of terms such as psychopath and sociopath in favor of terms such as antisocial personality disorder.

<u>Is it still used?</u>

Yes, as of the writing of this in 2023, it is still widely used.

<u>How is it scored?</u>

Scores range from 0 to 40. Anyone scoring above 30 is a psychopath, according to this test. Please note that terms such as psychopath have changed in usage over the years. The point of the test is to measure how much a person does or does not fit the criteria regardless of the term that is currently favored.

The PCL-R is revised and has had two traits removed as they were later determined not to be statistically significant. Note that my parents score the same as each other on the revised version.

This scoring standard with a threshold of 30 is used in the United States and many countries, however, some score it a bit more stringently. For example, some countries consider a revised Hare score of 25 or more to be enough for a diagnosis. The average score for the population in general is between 4 - 8. A sociopath is generally considered someone who scores between 18-29, but some do not make any distinction between psychopathy, sociopathy, and antisocial personality disorder.

<u>Hypothetical Otherwise Morally Flawless Medical Abuser Scoring: **12**</u>

What would a person score if they only committed Munchausen or medical abuse and did nothing else psychopathic? The minimum Hare Psychopathy Checklist for any medical abuser in general is: **12**

This is the score one would get by being a medical abuser and living an otherwise morally flawless life. I strongly doubt that such a person exists.

<u>Average Hare Psychopathy Checklist Scoring on the pattern chart: **30**</u>

What does the average person in the pattern chart in this book score? They score about **30** given what the public knows, however, they would likely score higher if graded by someone who knew every detail of their lives. This score would likely be higher if I had as close a look at their personal lives behind closed doors as I did with my parents.

<u>My parents' Hare Psychopathy Checklist scores: **34**</u>

It is likely that those on the pattern chart score slightly below my parents simply because I do not have an inside look at their home lives which would reveal more.

My parents happen to score the same as each other in general and on specific questions. There would have been a difference in scoring had question 22 relating to substance abuse not been removed. My mother had a serious substance abuse problem. This trait was later determined not to be statistically significant. I will also note that I have not checked the poor probation or parole risk trait for either of them because I'm not aware of either of them ever having been on probation or parole.

<u>Should the Hare Checklist be Used in Medical Abuse Cases?</u>

The short answer is "I don't know." On one hand, not all medical abusers are psychopaths, just as not all criminals of any type are psychopaths. In addition, perhaps psychopath isn't even the most useful term, given changes in terminology over the years.

On the other hand, there are key traits on the checklist that connect directly to Munchausen and medical abuse. These include pathological lying and deception, conning and lack of sincerity, callousness and lack of empathy, parasitic lifestyle, irresponsible behavior as a parent or caregiver, and failure to accept responsibility for one's actions. In other words, there is a particular subset of these checklist traits that are inextricably tied to medical abuse. Not all people with these traits are committing Munchausen abuse, but all people committing Munchausen abuse demonstrate this particular subset of traits on the list.

At this time, I believe more studies are needed on such offenders. This is the case in general and not just in terms of the PCL-R.

<u>How Does This Relate to the Dark Tetrad?</u>

Psychopathy is one of the four traits of the dark tetrad. The other three are narcissism, sadism, and Machiavellianism.[5] Maybe rather than trying to decide if medical abusers tend to be psychopaths, it is better to consider whether they tend to fit the dark tetrad. As noted in the pattern chart, all medical abusers demonstrate a higher-than-normal tolerance for other people's suffering, though not all seem motivated by it. Still, a large percentage of people in the pattern chart fit into the sadism column. In addition, while some medical abusers are better at manipulative Machiavellian behavior than others, all tend to demonstrate an attempt at this to some extent in their attempts to deceive others and fabricate illnesses. Finally, medical abusers also seem to demonstrate traits associated with narcissism, including self-importance, entitlement, need for admiration, need for power, exploitive behavior, and lack of empathy.

PART IV. lEGISLATION

426

Legislation

There are several different categories of laws that can help combat medical abuse. Many of them help combat other forms of abuse and other crimes as well.

Laws Specifically Targeting Medical Abuse

It's still rare to see laws targeting medical abuse in specific. This needs to become more common. As of the writing of this Texas is considering Texas 88 HB 3381 also known as Alyssa's Law. Note, this is different from the emergency alert system laws also sometimes known as Alyssa's Law. This refers to a different Alyssa. If made law this would make it a crime to misrepresent medical history to obtain unnecessary medical treatment for a child, elderly individual, or disabled individual. See https://legiscan.com/TX/bill/HB3381/2023[1].

Coercive Control

The world is still in the process of recognizing and criminalizing coercive control. The more jurisdictions pass such laws the safer we will all be.

Here are some examples you can use as templates:

https://www.theacecc.com/billtracker

Reporting Mandate Loopholes

Mandated reporting needs to cover all schools, not just public schools. It also needs to cover all abusive and illegal activity. Schools cannot be allowed to choose to avoid scandal at the expense of the safety of society at large.

Is it really necessary to mandate people do the right thing? Won't most people do that anyway? No, not always.

"The Omission Bias": The tendency to weigh harm caused by action more than harm caused by inaction.

How many children would still be alive today if not for the omission bias? I know I barely survived the omission bias of many adults around me.

When people are fearful of reporting a mandate can help.

Communication between agencies, departments, and jurisdictions

---

1.   https://legiscan.com/TX/bill/HB3381/2023

In the case of serial killer nurse Charles Cullen, investigators caught a break when a sticky note on an older file indicated that other investigators in another jurisdiction had requested identical information on Cullen earlier. In this case, whether a serial killer was caught or allowed to continue killing came down to how good the adhesive was on the back of a sticky note. People's lives should never depend on the quality of adhesive on a sticky note.

Lack of communication between law enforcement is a major problem in fighting crime in general. This is at least as much the case in fighting medical abuse in particular. More needs to be done to facilitate this communication. This includes funding systems for communication, doing more to encourage a culture of sharing information, creating easily accessible systems for sharing and searching communications across agencies, and actively engaging with law enforcement in creating these systems

Clear DNA backlogs

Clearing DNA backlogs can help in two ways. First, it can help directly in proving cases in which abusers sicken victims using their own bodily substances. Abusers will sometimes use their own feces or other bodily substances to sicken others. Clearing DNA backlogs can help connect abusers to cases, especially in cases in which the abuser is targeting multiple victims outside of their own family.

Clearing DNA backlogs can also help by getting abusers put away for other crimes besides the medical abuse that they have committed. As noted in the pattern chart, and in incidents throughout this book, abusers often commit a range of other crimes from arson to sexual assault to fraud and so on.

Duty to Warn Laws

On the surface, these may not look like they have a lot to do with medical abuse. Duty to warn refers to a medical professional's duty to warn law enforcement if a patient has made an explicit threat of serious physical harm or death to another. People often think of a psychiatric patient speaking of committing a mass shooting, or a person telling a therapist of plans to harm an ex for example. These laws already exist, but many don't realize the threat of serious physical harm that medical abuse poses. In fact, it is the deadliest form of child abuse. Duty to warn laws should be adjusted to clarify what is required of workers if they become aware that their own patients are committing medical abuse against another. Laws to guide people reporting these threats need to be clarified and protections for those reporting need to be strengthened.

<u>Pass the Trash laws</u>

Pass the trash laws come in a variety of forms. Many relate to school workers or childcare workers who have been caught abusing children. In the wake of the Cullen case, some jurisdictions began passing these laws in relation to medical workers abusing patients as well. This needs to be expanded and strongly enforced.

For an example of such legislation see New Jersey's Health Care Professional Responsibility and Reporting Enforcement Act, also known as the Cullen Law.

<u>Special Task Forces in Law Enforcement and Social Services</u>

Law enforcement and social services often struggle with caseloads. These cases often take more time to investigate than the average case. Law enforcement and social services often have special divisions or task forces for particular types of abuse. The false belief that this type of abuse is rare means that this is not usually the case with this type of abuse. This in turn perpetuates that false belief by reducing the number of cases investigated and prosecuted. We need more laws to create and fund these divisions or task forces for this specific type of abuse.

<u>More Education for Family Court Workers and Law Enforcement</u>

Education on medical abuse, along with all other forms of abuse, should be provided to all family court workers and members of law enforcement, as well as social workers, family court judges, and others who interact with such cases. This education should be mandatory.

<u>Centralize Medical Record Retrieval</u>

People should be able to fill in a request for medical records that goes to all providers and informs them of which institutions have their records. There is no way a person who has been through this childhood abuse will be able to track down all their records, or even begin to guess at what institutions they would be at without this. This would not create privacy issues so long as the records were limited to the patient and in cases of a child abuse investigation an investigator. Medical records already contain the identifying information needed to achieve this. This would help survivors and investigators by exposing doctor shopping and facilitating building evidence.

<u>Prevent 3rd Party Appeals Unauthorized by the Subject</u>

See the "older ladies" write-up under the traditional medical abuse section.

We can avoid wasting time and money by ensuring that statutes, regulations, and official procedures prevent third parties from involving themselves in benefits cases against the wishes of the actual potential recipient of those benefits. If a person tells the government that they do not want or need a benefit this should be the end of it. I'm sure this is what was always intended, but many times laws are written without anticipating people like my mother and such behaviors.

<u>Make Emergency Numbers Mandated Lesson Plan Material</u>

See "911" under the preempting detection and acting normal section.

Let's save teachers and school administrators some trouble. If they're mandated to teach kids this information by a certain age they will have a measure of protection from a parent or guardian trying to pressure them not to teach this. It will also help protect kids in unsafe situations. This will cut through the pressure to bend to the will of the odd set of parents and keep the information from the whole class.

<u>Add Medical Abuse to Social Work and Abuse Documenting Forms</u>

Today many social work forms and forms meant to be used to document abuse don't contain a section or even a check box for suspected medical abuse. Many contain physical abuse and sexual abuse but mention nothing of medical abuse. This needs to change. Workers need to be able to document this properly instead of trying to fit it into another section.

<u>Life Insurance Reports</u>

Today consumers in the United States, and some other countries as well, can order their own credit reports and similar such reports for free on an annual basis. There should be a centralized system by which people can request a report detailing any life insurance policy anyone has taken out on them. As it stands, life insurance companies tend to require the consent of the person the policy is for. This is a problem, however, in the case of fraud. People should be able to check to make sure no one has fraudulently taken out a policy on them.

PART V. WHAT CAN YOU DO?

431

What Can You Do?

<u>Make it as well known as other forms of abuse.</u>

You can help make this as well known as other forms of abuse so that potential reporters know to look for it. You can help move the Overton window as to whether or not this is a rare crime so that other victims and whistle-blowers who speak out won't suffer from the Martha Mitchell Effect.

<u>Anonymous Reporting</u>

You can report abuse anonymously through several different channels. Most areas have anonymous crime report hotlines and web forms. In addition, you can report to departments of children and family services and remain anonymous. It is not your job to prove a case. It is simply your job to report reasonable suspicions.

<u>Document/Photo/Video it.</u>

This one is important, but you need to be careful about it. Hospitals have a specific procedure to do this while complying with privacy laws. This tactic can be the difference between life and death for a victim. If you have suspicions that could be addressed this way consult an attorney. If you work in any type of medical setting, the organization you work for will likely have attorneys who can guide you in this.

Share Your Own Story

Has FDIA impacted your life? If so, your life experiences are a vital resource for educating society, law enforcement, and the medical community. Most importantly your life experiences are a vital resource for preventing murders and stopping abuse.

Earlier in this book, you saw the pattern chart and my notes on the pattern chart. As mentioned there, the cases with the most boxes checked were those in which we have first-hand accounts from people who lived with these abusers. This indicates that we don't have the full story on the other cases. Only these first-hand accounts provide us with such complete details that can best help society learn to spot and stop other cases.

Writing such a memoir can be a grueling task emotionally, but it is well worth it. It's worth it for what you will contribute to society, and it's also worth it for how it can help you process what you've been through. You don't need to write a memoir if you prefer a different format. The point is just to get the information out there. You can give interviews instead, do a podcast instead, write a blog instead, or hire someone to assemble the information for you in whatever format you choose. If all you can get out is short bullet points please do it anyway. It doesn't matter what format your information is in. All that matters is that it's out there. Above all else, this is about sharing the information. Do what works for you.

Allow yourself and others to remain anonymous if you wish. I have used pseudonyms for myself and others throughout this book.

Be patient with yourself during this process, observe your reactions, and be open to changing your process as necessary for your own well-being. I chose to change my process part way through this when I realized that part of my process was undoing my grounding. I was detailing my five senses for every incident and this was achieving the opposite of grounding. I chose instead to move these descriptions to a one-time writing in the "Setting" section before the incidents. This allowed me to give just the facts in each incident, making the incidents much more bearable to get through.

Finally, do not attempt this process without support. Have support from a therapist and friends before you start down this road. Writing this book has helped me work through my past in a way perhaps nothing else could have, but it is not a project to attempt in isolation. There will be times when you need to talk it out with someone else.

PART VI. CONCLUSION

Conclusion

This is not the end of my story, but it is the end of this book. This book only covers the first 18 years of my life. There is so much more to MBP than even what is in this book. First, there are likely behavior patterns that I have never experienced in my own particular case. Second, there are behavior patterns that cropped up in my own survival story that didn't happen within the first 18 years.

Yes, I do plan to write a book about what I experienced in terms of MBP abuse after reaching adulthood and leaving home. This book would have become unmanageable if I had included that here too. That book will include a lot more about stalking, traffic accidents, and cat-fishing. It will also include a lot more about what some have termed "Munchausen by internet."

For now, I leave you with this:

- You can report abuse anonymously.
- You can help make this as well known as other forms of abuse.

PART VII. APPENDICES

437

Appendix 1 - Recommended Reading

<u>Recommended Reading/Watching/Listening</u>

The following list contains content that somehow connects to the type of medical abuse described in this book or otherwise helps facilitate an understanding of people like my mother. I am not affiliated with any of these content creators. I have simply found their work useful. Some entries here contain a short note explaining why a specific piece of content is recommended. It's worth noting that I have not reviewed all content on the subject matter. There may be very good works on this subject that are not on this list simply because I have not had time to review them. These resources are listed in no particular order other than being grouped by type.

<u>Studies and Academic Articles</u>

1. Munro HM, Thrusfield MV. 'Battered pets': Munchausen syndrome by proxy (factitious illness by proxy). J Small Anim Pract. 2001 Aug;42(8):385-9. doi: 10.1111/j.1748-5827.2001.tb02486.x. PMID: 11518417. Available at https://pubmed.ncbi.nlm.nih.gov/11518417/[1]

2. Faedda N, Baglioni V, Natalucci G, Ardizzone I, Camuffo M, Cerutti R, Guidetti V. Don't Judge a Book by Its Cover: Factitious Disorder Imposed on Children-Report on 2 Cases. Front Pediatr. 2018 Apr 18;6:110. doi: 10.3389/fped.2018.00110. PMID: 29721488; PMCID: PMC5915702. Available at https://www.ncbi.nlm.nih.gov/pmc/articles/PMC5915702/[2]

3. Bass, C., & Jones, D. (2011). Psychopathology of perpetrators of fabricated or induced illness in children: Case series. *The British Journal of Psychiatry, 199*(2), 113-118. doi:10.1192/bjp.bp.109.074088. Available at https://www.cambridge.org/core/journals/the-british-journal-of-psychiatry/article/psychopathology-of-perpetrators-of-fabricated-or-induced-illness-in-children-case-series/6BA67E14F41D8533288F7F183A057D8C[3]

---

1. https://pubmed.ncbi.nlm.nih.gov/11518417/

2. https://www.ncbi.nlm.nih.gov/pmc/articles/PMC5915702/

3. https://www.cambridge.org/core/journals/the-british-journal-of-psychiatry/article/psychopathology-of-perpetrators-of-fabricated-or-induced-illness-in-children-case-series/6BA67E14F41D8533288F7F183A057D8C

<u>Books</u>

1. The Good Nurse by Charles Graeber

2. I Have to Call Someone Mama by Tammy Eady Walker

3. Sickened by Julie Gregory

<u>Podcasts</u>

1. Scamanda (Lionsgate Sound.)

2. Nobody Should Believe Me (Larj Media.)

3. Pretend (Creative Babble. Specifically, see the Stalker series.)

4. Tortoise Investigates (Tortoise Media. Specifically, see the Sweet Bobby series and the Hoaxed series.)

<u>Documentaries</u>

1. Capturing the Killer Nurse (This demonstrates the danger of inadequate policies and policy enforcement. It was released in 2022 and, as of the writing of this, is available through Netflix.)

Appendix 2 - Setting

I'm going to paint you a picture of the surroundings for these incidents. Many of them take place in the same few locations. Rather than describe these settings over and over again in each incident I will describe them all here and reference this section to tell you where an incident took place. I am including this section mostly because many readers find it useful to be able to picture the place where something described happened. Please feel free to skim this section or skip it altogether if you don't feel the need to visualize the setting. You will not miss anything of substance that is not repeated elsewhere.

<u>The Apartment (ages 0-2 and 4-16)</u>

The building was on a busy road that changed over time as we lived there. We were surrounded by traffic and the bustle of the city.

From when I was 0-2 we lived on the 18th floor of the building. When we moved back from out of state we moved to the identical apartment above on 21. When we moved back we had 2 apartments put together, but one door was blocked by a large loaded-down bookshelf so there was only one way out. The unblocked door was very squeaky and by my parents' bedroom so I couldn't try to get out without getting caught. Squeaky metal hinges painted white always gave me away. I would try to get out without being heard but I never could.

The area we spent the most time in was the TV seating area. This was the main area we called the living room. Sometimes I was allowed on that furniture and sometimes I wasn't. It didn't have to do with anything rational like if I'd been playing outside and gotten dirty. Instead, it seemed to depend on the type of mood my mother was in.

The TV seating was an armchair, loveseat, and sofa arranged in a U pattern in front of the TV. The seating had upholstered arms, but the seats and backs had removable cushions on wood. The arms also ended in bare wood. Before the reupholstery, some of the pieces had a lighter beige chevron pattern. Others were similar colors but striped. They were arranged around a square checkered wooden coffee table.

My mother reupholstered this furniture set when I was in grade school. One of the patterns my mother redid them to was a white, green, brown, and red pattern. The other was in the same colors but with a clashing pattern. Hanging over the couch by the TV was a buffalo skull. This was not of cultural significance to my family. It was simply a part of my mother's fascination with death. She avoided questions by redoing the upholstery to these southwest patterns at the same time as she got it so it seemed to be a part of the decor. (See "Buffalo Skull" In the Hurting Animals and Talking to Animals section).

Behind that furniture was the aquarium. The aquarium in the main room had a little multicolor figurine of a thatched hut and a little froggy figurine. It had a plecostomus and those little zebra fish, some little red and blue fish, and sometimes other fish. There were real plants tucked into the gravel in the back. Occasionally some of the fish would just be gone. When I asked my mother about it she said that the girl fish had disappeared because the boy fish had been bothering her for sex too much.

In front of this all was the TV that was the focus of the area. The TV in the main room was a Sony. It was a modern-looking TV at the time, although it was one of the old square vacuum tube TVs. It had a black frame, a silver button panel, wood or fake wood on the bottom and top, and big black speakers built-in on the sides. There was a black VCR resting on top. The remote matched the silver panel on the TV. It had push buttons and looked modern in the 80's.

We had white and black canvas prints of hieroglyphs on the walls. At least one was of someone drawing a thorned rope through their tongue in a blood sacrifice. Another was of a king on a journey to the underworld. My mother would sometimes hide things behind them tucked into the frame of the canvas.

The apartment was mostly lit with brass-colored lamps with cream-colored ridged lampshades. The walls were white and the floors were mostly dark brown dirty carpet.

The "dining room" wasn't actually a separate area from the "living room." It was just separated by seating. On the wall by the dining table was a big cabinet that had medium brown wood and round white nobs. The lower portion of it had wooden drawers and above were the glass cabinet drawers.

In the center was a little nook that went across the whole length that the glass cabinets went over. The lower portion contained the record player and records. The upper glass portion had a variety of indigenous American artifacts or replicas. Jars of ashes were in some of these. (See "Ashes" in Random.)

On the other side of the wall the cabinet was against was a long skinny kitchen. At one end of the kitchen was the fridge and small pantry. At the other end was a small table. When we were young it was a little kids picnic table. My mother later replaced this with spaghetti chairs and a glass table that barely fit in the place. You. couldn't pull the chairs all the way out and only a kid or petit adult could fit.

My room had white walls and white wooden bookshelves with kitten posters I had put all over the walls and ceiling. It had the same brown carpet as the rest of the apartment. When I was younger there was a snoopy lamp. There was a light wood bed, mirror, and vanity set that my mother always insisted we inherited from her family, but that her family knew nothing about.

The apartment had lots of bookshelves. They contained titles such as "Pawnee Hero Stories and Folk-Tales," "Indians of the Plains," something or other "of the High Plains," "The Hoe and the Horse on the Plains," and "The Pawnee Ghost Dance Hand Game". I also remember a Bible, photo albums full of magazine cutouts, and a biography of Eva Peron that she fawned over.

Apartment Pool

The apartment pool was on the second floor of the building. It was down a long glass corridor that smelled strongly of chlorine. The pool was in a glass area surrounded by sun decks. Inside the glass was that fake grass, which was later replaced with a blue non-slip rubbery surface. The pool had painted lanes for lap swimmers who I often got in the way of when I was younger. There were lounge chairs surrounding the pool, and also outside on the sun deck. The lifeguard on duty sat at a desk between the entrance and the pool to check IDs when people came in. There was a small exercise machine room off to the side in the same structure.

Main Beach by the Apartment

The water was to the East. The pier and lighthouse were to the South. The snack shack was to the West across the sidewalk. It was painted green back in the days before a replacement was rebuilt to the South so no one would have to cross the sidewalk. There was a basketball court just north of the snack shack with an old-fashioned tiered drinking fountain in front of it. To the South was a stretch of grass and the parking lot. There was a large walkway of concrete blocks between the grass and the water on either side of the beach. Some were more weathered than others and some had rebar poking out. This is where we would sometimes find the hieroglyphs carved. They looked like the ones on the prints in our apartment.

The House(2-4)

It was a wooden house surrounded by pine trees. Out front was grass and a curving driveway that ran from our house to the main road, intersecting the sidewalk that ran straight along the block. The attached garage had a white door and stone facade on the portion facing the street. The wood of the house was kind of a dull grey-brown and there was white siding with a dull grey-brown roof and decking. There was a small single shrub right inside the grass where the curved drive intersected with the sidewalk. On some days we would drag out a little green kiddie pool with a turtle face into the driveway.

It had a deck out back where the ice cream incident happened. (See "Chocolate Ice Cream" in the Preempting Detection and Acting Normal section.) It had sassafras trees in the back which would create large leaf piles in the fall. We would sometimes jump in them in the fall. There was ivy on the ground around the trees in the back. The back deck had a metal round BBQ with a black top with silver legs. The kid-size picnic table that later ended up in our apartment kitchen was out back too in the leaves and grass.

Inside it had a big stone facade fireplace with metal mesh hanging down in front. The big stones were lighter than the mortar in between. There was a sectioned glass and metal set of doors that closed over the front. A brass metal surrounded it. Just to the side of the fireplace was a step down from the hard floor to the carpeted area that surrounded the fireplace. I had stuffed animals lying around the area sometimes.

The kid's area inside the house had a little wooden slide set with a ladder and a landing. Those creepy cutouts of the babies from advertisements were on the wall in the bedroom. They were just like the ones she told me I was supposed to be like in the photo album. (See "Albums" in the Random section.) They may have been the same ones.

Nearby there was a park we would go to with a chain link fence around it, and swings and those horses on springs. There were benches and trees in the background. The neighborhood was still going through changes. Occasionally there was cement being poured for sidewalks and driveways. (See "The Cement" in Manufacturing Scandal.) There was a field of tall grass we used to cut through that later had houses built on top of it before we moved. In the spring the trees in the neighborhood would bloom white and pink and it was magical to me. I wasn't used to seeing that where we had lived in the city

House (16-18)

When I was 16 we moved from our apartment to a house a few blocks west. It was an old dilapidated house that my parents fixed up. When they were done with remodeling the house it had creaky wood floors, cream walls, and white trim inside. Most of the family time happened in the kitchen. The kitchen had white cabinets, a coil stove, and marble counters with flecks of blue. The marble was cool to the touch and often specked with stray coffee grounds. There was a window behind the counter seating with doors in front and to the side of it. The window looked out on the neighbor's house mentioned in "Opossums" in the Animals section. The counter seating had thinly padded metal stools with designs in the back that would catch your clothes. It was usually filled with the smell of coffee coming from the coffee machine at the counter. There was a TV in the cabinet up high above so that you could watch from the counter. We often watched at dinner there.

Appendix 3 - notes

[1] "confirmation bias." *Dictionary.com.* 2023. https://www.dictionary.com/browse/confirmation-bias[1] (13 September 2023).

[2] Gilbert, D. T., & Malone, P. S. (1995). The correspondence bias. *Psychological Bulletin, 117*(1), 21–38. https://doi.org/10.1037/0033-2909.117.1.21[2]

[3] "gaslighting." *Merriam-Webster.com.* 2023. https://www.merriam-webster.com/dictionary/gaslighting[3] (13 September 2023).

[4] Hare, R. D., Harpur, T. J., Hakstian, A. R., Forth, A. E., Hart, S. D., & Newman, J. P. (1990). The revised Psychopathy Checklist: Reliability and factor structure. *Psychological Assessment: A Journal of Consulting and Clinical Psychology, 2*(3), 338–341. https://doi.org/10.1037/1040-3590.2.3.338[4]

[5] Međedović, J., & Petrović, B. (2015). The Dark Tetrad: Structural properties and location in the personality space. *Journal of Individual Differences, 36*(4), 228–236. https://doi.org/10.1027/1614-0001/a000179[5]. See also Paulhus, D. L., & Williams, K. M. (2002). The Dark Triad of personality: Narcissism, Machiavellianism and psychopathy. *Journal of Research in Personality, 36*(6), 556–563. https://doi.org/10.1016/S0092-6566(02)00505-6[6]

---

1. https://www.dictionary.com/browse/confirmation-bias

2. https://psycnet.apa.org/doi/10.1037/0033-2909.117.1.21

3. https://www.merriam-webster.com/dictionary/gaslighting

4. https://psycnet.apa.org/doi/10.1037/1040-3590.2.3.338

5. https://psycnet.apa.org/doi/10.1027/1614-0001/a000179

6. https://psycnet.apa.org/doi/10.1016/S0092-6566(02)00505-6

www.ingramcontent.com/pod-product-compliance
Lightning Source LLC
Chambersburg PA
CBHW051458150726
47997CB00001B/21

* 9 7 9 8 2 2 4 9 6 7 4 3 8 *